INVENTING LATINOS

Also by Laura E. Gómez

Manifest Destinies: The Making of the Mexican American Race

INVENTING LATINOS

A NEW STORY OF AMERICAN RACISM

LAURA E. GÓMEZ

THE
NEW
PRESS

NEW YORK
LONDON

Requests for permission to reproduce selections from this book should be made through our website: https://thenewpress.com/contact.

Published in the United States by The New Press, New York, 2020
Distributed by Two Rivers Distribution

ISBN 978-1-59558-917-0 (hc)
ISBN 978-1-62097-178-9 (ebook)
CIP data is available

The New Press publishes books that promote and enrich public discussion and understanding of the issues vital to our democracy and to a more equitable world. These books are made possible by the enthusiasm of our readers; the support of a committed group of donors, large and small; the collaboration of our many partners in the independent media and the not-for-profit sector; booksellers, who often hand-sell New Press books; librarians; and above all by our authors.

www.thenewpress.com

Book design and composition by Bookbright Media
This book was set in Caslon Pro and Fort

Printed in the United States of America

10 9 8 7

For you, Dad.

For always being there for me;

for feeding my body, mind & soul;

for astute editing over four decades & finding the best cover art for books;

*for encouraging me with lists of book titles before a word
was written;*

*for always reminding me that, no matter where we are, we're
under the same moon.*

CONTENTS

INVENTING LATINOS

INTRODUCTION

Congresswoman Alexandria Ocasio-Cortez, age thirty, represents New York's 14th congressional district, including parts of the Bronx and Queens. The district's population, just short of 700,000, is 50 percent Latino, with Whites, Asian Americans, and African Americans each composing 12 to 18 percent. AOC, as she is known, is a member of the Democratic Socialists of America and has captured national attention as the youngest woman ever elected to Congress. She describes her race as reflecting "many different identities. I am the descendant of African slaves. I am the descendant of Indigenous people. I am the descendant of Spanish colonizers. . . . That doesn't mean I'm Black, that doesn't mean I'm Native. But I can tell the story of my ancestors." AOC was born in the Bronx to a Puerto Rican father also born in the Bronx and a mother born in Puerto Rico, who said AOC grew up speaking her mind in family dinner conversations.[1] In another interview, she said: "We are all of these things and something else all at once—we are Boricua," using a Spanish word to describe the island's Indigenous Taíno people that has long been embraced as a countercultural signifier of Puerto Rican solidarity and political awakening.[2]

Congressman Ben Ray Luján, forty-eight, represents New Mexico's 3rd congressional district, spanning northern New Mexico from Santa Fe to the Colorado border, west to Arizona, and east to Texas. The district's 700,000 people are 40 percent Latino, nearly 20 percent Native American, and 36 percent White. Luján was born in the village of Nambé, located in between two of the district's several Pueblo Nations. In the context of New Mexico's racial demography, Luján's ancestors include the Spanish colonizers, Mexican settlers, and Indigenous peoples who until recently vastly outnumbered Anglos, as non-Hispanic Whites are called there. "My grandparents made a place for themselves in New Mexico before it was a state," he told delegates at the 2016 Democratic National Convention, invoking his paternal grandfather, a sheepherder, and his maternal grandfather, who became a union carpenter after returning from World War II with a Bronze Medal. Speaking more obsequiously about race, he said, "I know I might not look like your typical member of Congress—I haven't really gotten the bolo tie look to catch on."[3] The reference was ostensibly to his large, turquoise-and-silver bolo tie, but it hinted at his brown skin, his accent (typical of northern New Mexican Latinos). In New Mexico politics, questions of race are never far from the forefront, as a state GOP press release in December 2019 showed: it criticized New Mexico's three congressional delegates—Luján and two women of color—for their votes in favor of the articles of impeachment, "This is why we must all work hard to change the complexion of our congressional delegation." Luján fired back, "as a Hispanic representative of a majority-minority state, I have a responsibility to speak out forcefully when racism and dog whistles are used to further political attacks against people who look like me."[4]

Despite their different registers, AOC and Luján represent Latinx politicians who came of age when the singularity of Latinos—as distinct from "non-Hispanic Whites" and "non-Hispanic Blacks," to use those ubiquitous, bureaucratic terms—is legible on the national stage.[5] Previous generations of Latinos might have emphasized their national origin, AOC as Puerto Rican and Luján as Mexican American, and may well have adopted an additional identity as White or Black. Charlie Rangel, the longtime New York congressman who was born in 1930, anglicized his Spanish surname (his father was Puerto Rican) and founded the Congressional Black Caucus. Born two years before Rangel, Republican congressman Manuel Luján (no relation to Ben Ray) had a twenty-five-year political career; he spoke Spanish fluently and was born at San Ildefonso Pueblo (as were his parents), yet insisted he was White.

Rangel and the elder Luján came of age when racial identity in America was a dichotomous choice, at least in the public sphere—where one had to choose White or Black. This is not to claim people had less complicated identities in the past or to deny how racism constrained their choices. It is to acknowledge, however, how utterly different things are today. Few would contest the multiplicity of racial identities and racial categories in contemporary America. It is especially the case that Americans have more choices about how to present their difference, however they define it—how they choose to convey (or veil) their identities in particular situations.[6] Certainly, it has always been the case that race was situational, but the possibilities for public recognition of one's identity are, today, much more open than even forty years ago, when I was in high school. Today the United States has moved from a two-category racial hierarchy—Whites over Blacks, or even White over non-White—to a multi-race hierarchy in which Whites continue to be dominant in terms of wealth, political power, and ideology.[7]

Inventing Latinos interrogates the how and why of Latinx identity becoming a distinctive racial identity. To say Latinos have different choices, individually and collectively, is to underline how race reflects two intersecting vectors. On the one hand, one can assert, and so essentially choose, a racial identity; but, on the other, racial identities are given to us by others. We might make a particular choice, but it could be disregarded by anyone—from a stranger to a police officer deciding whether or not you belong in a particular neighborhood to a government clerk filling out race on a death certificate (because she is uncomfortable asking next of kin the question). In other words, one's "choice" is constrained in many ways, just as it is for other identities. But to accurately describe racial identity as situational does not fully capture the social dynamic at the heart of this book, which has as much to do with how racial conventions and racism make some people's race less malleable than others. It is equally the case that not everyone's opinion of your race is equally relevant; the cop's opinion matters more than the stranger's, although the latter might be a gateway to the former. So far, these examples have focused on individual interactions, or what sociologists call the micro level.

This book's concern is mostly with two additional levels, the meso level and the macro level, and with how the three levels interact together. For instance, if we consider an institutional context like schooling, we know there is a particular set of ideas about race and racial classification, though, to be sure, these ideas vary and circulate in different ways. We know that it is routine in the United States for teachers, parents, and school administrators to talk about race in a demographic register (say, the make-up of the school or community) as well as a cultural register. Most often, the latter treats race in coded ways that value a color-blind notion of race—the notion that race is irrelevant to the content of one's character, viewpoints, and the like. The most abstract level, and sometimes the hardest one to pin down, is the macro, relating to social structure that is immune from individual manipulation. When we think of broad-scale social realities that shape race and racial classification, these are probably macro dynamics; examples would be the way neighborhood boundaries in a large city reflect decades of racial patterns, including explicit rules limiting what racial groups could live in particular areas; decisions by generations of city officials about where to build freeways, refuse centers, parks, and wide boulevards; decisions by private-sector actors like banks, grocery stores, and owners of rental housing about doing business in particular neighborhoods, and so on.

Webster's defines the word "invent" as "to originate or create as a product of one's own ingenuity, experimentation, or contrivance"; for example, to invent the internet. While that definition does not apply here, the successive two dictionary definitions do: "to produce or create with the imagination" and "to make up or fabricate (something fictitious or false)." This book explains how and why Latinos became cognizable as a racial group—a racial group that is other and inferior to Whites. The third definition applies, though not because this book contains falsehoods. Instead, think of the Latino category as fabricated and flexible rather than as immutable and fixed. Like all racial categories at their origin, "Latino" is a political and social construction rooted in a particular time and place and cognizable only in relation to other, known racial classifications.[8] Yet to say races are invented is not to say they are insignificant or without effect. Race isn't in our heads because it's "real," race is real because it's in our heads.[9] In other words, what we as interacting humans make up, create, or invent has power in our lives. To put it more bluntly: race isn't real, but racism is.

This book is less about how individual Latinos express their identity and more about where Latinos are, collectively, in the American racial system. Overall, the system of racial classification, rooted in American history, exists to maintain white supremacy. This has been the case even when the power structure dominated by Whites has bowed to pressure to protect the civil rights of African Americans and other people of color, whether during post–Civil War Reconstruction or during what some call "the second Reconstruction," the mid-twentieth-century enactment of the Civil Rights Act and Voting Rights Act. Racialization is how society and the state assign individuals to racial groups and the relative position of groups to each other—and it is an important aspect of this story. Racism requires racial categories and mechanisms for sorting people into them. Some mechanisms, like the U.S. census, are formally conducted by the state and tightly regulated by law. Other mechanisms, such as popular culture, are diffuse in terms of production and consumption, but no less powerful. These two examples reflect the two sides of racial sorting: assignment is when institutions classify people into racial categories, and assertion is when individuals racially define themselves.

In fact, assertion and assignment interact with each other in a dialectic process, in which one shapes the other via repetitive interactions over time. In this way, changes in racial classification never begin on a clean slate but, instead, reflect the complex layers of interaction between assertion and assignment that have accumulated previously. When the racial hierarchy evolves to incorporate new categories, resulting in expanding or contracting groups, assignment and assertion cohere around shared understandings of which groups exist in relative hierarchy to other groups. In essence, these dynamics continually occur, but during periods of particular strain on the racial order, such as the first and second Reconstructions, many factors converge to transform what we might call the common sense of racism. This book's central focus is explaining how the common sense of anti-Latino racism has come to exist today, to be taken for granted as natural in the cosmology of American racism. That includes understanding why "Latinos" as a distinctive racial category came into being at a particular time and putting that moment in the broader context of earlier history and contemporary events.

Race is about power, including the power to decide when and how to classify people into this or that racial category and what those very categories are. We think of race categories as essential and immutable, as reflecting notions of blood, stock, ancestry, and DNA. But they are actually political categories, reflecting the power of one group (Whites) to define other groups as inferior to them, as less than fully human. To be sure, groups contest Whites' power over them, including sometimes advocating for a broadening of the White category to include them.[10] Without races, there can be no logic of racism, defined as when a powerful group designates itself as superior in order to oppress other groups they deem inferior. To speak, then, of our contemporary racial common sense is to invoke historically rooted power struggles. As sociologist Rubén Rumbaut puts it, today's racial dynamics inevitably invoke the past, including "the identities of victors and vanquished, of dominant and subordinate groups, of 'us' and 'them,' with their attendant conceits of superiority and inferiority."[11]

Racial logics, or, different racisms, operate in different and connected ways, but always in ways that protect Whites as the unquestionably dominant racial group.[12] In order to understand and combat racism writ large, we must do two things in coordination. First, we must know the histories of specific racial groups (e.g., Latinos, African Americans, etc.). Then, we must uncover the connections among racial logics to reveal how they support each other in the service of white supremacy. I primarily compare anti-Latino racism with anti-Black racism, which is well understood in the popular imagination as the archetypal form of American racial subordination. I am cognizant of the reality that individuals and communities identify as both Black and Latino (or Latino and Black) and by no means diminish that. Here, however, I also seek to reveal precisely why we see these groups as separate and apart in the American racial hierarchy. To a lesser extent than the African American case, I compare anti–Native American and anti–Asian American racial logics, acknowledging as well that they overlap in important ways with anti-Latino racism.

The United States is a racial state, which is to say our society is built on racial hierarchy, across time from the founding to today, across space in all regions, and across levels of social interaction, from the personal (micro) to the community level (meso) to the level of structures such as the law (macro). In a racial state, though racial categories and racism evolve, racial hierarchy persists such that Whites remain the dominant racial group. Simultaneously, just who is "White" is continually contested and evolving. This, of course, has implications for the other side of the coin: who is "non-White" likewise evolves and revolves around which such groups are closest to Blacks, always at the bottom of the racial hierarchy.

One of the most insidious facets of the American racial order is its persistence over time, even in the face of legal, political, and social counter-movements. The Emancipation Proclamation, issued by President Lincoln in 1863, was a tremendous blow to white supremacy. It was followed by the passage of three constitutional amendments: the Thirteenth Amendment, which later outlawed slavery for good, the Fourteenth Amendment, which compelled equal protection of all persons by the states, and the Fifteenth Amendment, which protected African American men's right to vote. Together with the first civil rights laws enacted by Congress with veto-proof majorities, these changes could have led to a society whose social organization was less centered around race and racial hierarchy. Instead, Southern states developed a legally enforced edifice to keep the newly freed men and women down, from essentially endorsing extra-legal terror in the form of lynching to preventing Black men from exercising the franchise (via violence, literacy tests, poll taxes) to forcing Blacks to labor for Whites (the sharecropping system, vagrancy laws, prison work gangs) to segregating them from Whites as a badge of inferiority.

African Americans resisted continually and mightily, with some voting with their feet to migrate north to escape Southern racism. Of course, none of those mechanisms was unique to the South, and northern and midwestern states proved equally adept at using the law for racial oppression such as segregation from cradle to grave that stamped Blacks with inferiority. By this time, the federal courts repudiated the vigorous enforcement of the Reconstruction Amendments and the nation's first civil rights laws. The U.S. Supreme Court gave its blessing to the post–Civil War regime of white supremacy in 1896 in the now-infamous *Plessy v. Ferguson* case, which allowed racial segregation so long as it was "separate but equal." When the Supreme Court finally reversed that ruling six decades later in *Brown v. Board of Education*, white supremacy again shape-shifted to adapt without disappearing, essentially allowing school districts leeway to continue racial isolation by other means.[13]

There are likewise more mundane examples of the racial state in action that were no less powerful in promoting racism and the racial categories necessary for its operation. By the 1920s, there were more than 6,000 clerks who issued marriage licenses in the United States.[14] Rarely overseen by legislatures or courts, they exercised tremendous power to determine applicants' race and, accordingly, whether they would be allowed to marry. As the marriage license bureau clerk for Los Angeles County in the 1920s, it was Leon Lampton's job to comply with a new state law that barred "negro, mulatto, or mongolian" persons from marrying "white" persons. He sought legal advice about whether Filipinos were "Mongolian" under the law; at first the county attorney told him they were not, but a few years later the state attorney general said they were. Neither could judges agree: over the course of more than a decade, two judges allowed Filipino men to marry White women because they were not "mongolian," two judges classified Filipino men as "mongolian" denying their applications to marry White women, and one judge declined to decide the question because he concluded that the "White" woman a Filipino man sought to marry was, in fact, a "Mexican Indian" woman, and thus that the state's anti-miscegenation law was not implicated at all.[15] In one sense, the matter was settled in 1933, when the state appeals court decided Salvador Roldan, a Filipino man, could marry Marjorie Rogers, a White woman, because he was "Malay" rather than Mongolian. But while he won the battle, he lost the war to white supremacists, who, in the very same year Roldan and Rogers married, amended California's marriage law to include a ban on Filipinos marrying Whites. Ignoring the new law nullifying their marriage as "illegal and void," the Roldans raised three children and remained a couple until his death in 1975.[16]

As the example of Filipinos in California illustrates, how groups are defined is subject to negotiation and contestation.[17] For the purposes of this book, Latinos are people who currently live in the United States—whether or not they are American citizens and/or were born in this country—who are descendants of migrants or who themselves migrated from Latin America, and specifically from the former colonies of Spain in the Western Hemisphere. So defined, Latinos are the product two successive waves of colonization, first by Spain and then by the United States, which has significant implications for how they have experienced racism and racialization in the United States.[18] My conception of Latinos necessarily excludes Spanish immigrants to the U.S. and their descendants, who are European. To define Latinos in this way exposes the inherent limitation of the category as one that is legible in the United States rather than globally. It simply does not make sense to speak of "Latinos" or the "Latino population" in a Latin American country or anywhere else in the world. "Latinos" has purchase in the

American racial and cultural landscape and should not be used to refer to persons outside the boundaries of this country.[19]

Fifty years ago it would have been nonsensical to hear anyone refer to "the Latino population." For one thing, only in 1980 did the federal government begin counting Latinos, and that shift did not immediately trickle down to state and local governments.[20] In 1980, 14.6 million people self-identified as Latino; that number will easily exceed 60 million when the 2020 census results are tabulated.[21] As a proportion of the American population, Latinos have gone from 6.5 to 18.3 percent in the four decades since 1980. Current projections show Latinos will be 30 percent of the nation's population by 2060.[22]

Until recently, Latinos were seen as regional national origin groups, rather than as a nationwide minority population. Historically, Mexican Americans lived in the Southwest, Puerto Ricans lived in the Northeast, and Cubans lived in Florida. With the exception of Georgia and Illinois, these three regions continue to be home to most Latinos. By the close of 2019, ten U.S. states had more than one million Latino residents: Arizona, California, Colorado, Georgia, Florida, Illinois, New Jersey, New Mexico, New York, and Texas. At the same time, today's Latinos live in every state and, between 2000 and 2010, all fifty states and the District of Columbia experienced Latino population growth, including many in the South where the Latino population doubled in the first decade of the new century. Since the Great Recession, the Latino population has grown at a slower pace, but it still has outpaced Whites' and African Americans' growth, especially in the South, where the Latino population grew by 33 percent between 2008 and 2018, and in states like North Dakota and South Dakota, where Latinos increased by 135 percent and 75 percent respectively.[23] It is no coincidence that some of the most draconian anti-immigrant state and local laws are coming out of the South, then, where local police are more likely to partner with ICE to detain unauthorized immigrants.[24]

Mexican Americans are both the oldest and largest Latino national origin group in the United States. Their presence dates to the 1846–1848

U.S.-Mexico War, at the conclusion of which 115,000 Mexican citizens received American citizenship. These persons did not cross the border into the United States, but rather, as they say, "the border crossed them" when the United States claimed half of Mexico's total territory as part of Mexico's surrender. Nearly 70 percent of Latinos are Mexican American.[25] Another 10 percent of Latinos are Puerto Rican, the second oldest national origin group. After Spain's withdrawal from Puerto Rico in 1898 after defeat in the Spanish-American War, the United States declared Puerto Rico its colony. Most Central Americans, whose ancestry is from the countries of El Salvador, Guatemala, Honduras, and Nicaragua, have migrated here since 1990 and together make up another 9 percent of Latinos. Cubans are almost 4 percent of Latinos and most have come to the United States as political refugees fleeing the communist regime Fidel Castro established in 1959. Dominican Latinos make up just under 3 percent of Latinos nationally and live disproportionately in New York and New Jersey, and the vast majority migrated after 1980. That leaves the remaining Latinos combined with ancestry in one of the remaining fourteen countries of Latin America—less than 4 percent of all Latinos.[26]

At almost 20 percent of the nation's population, we might expect to see great Latino political power. But Latinos are young relative to Whites and Blacks, including a disproportionate share under age eighteen, such that they are only 11 percent of those eligible to vote.[27] More than 29 million Latinos voted in the 2018 midterm election, up 4 million from the 2016 presidential election. Only a fraction of the increase was due to naturalization by Latino immigrants (less than half a million); instead, the increase reflected the fact that six times as many Latinos became eligible voters in 2018 because they turned eighteen.[28] The diverse migration histories of Latinos shape their participation as American citizens and voters. For example, under the Jones Act of 1917, Puerto Ricans obtained the right to migrate freely between Puerto Rico and the U.S. mainland. While their political rights are limited on the island because of Puerto Rico's status as a colony, once stateside, they may vote and fully exercise the rights of American citizenship. As political refugees, Cubans had the right to become naturalized citizens within a year of arriving here. Today they exercise an outsized role in national politics; of four Latinos in the Senate, three are Cuban American and one is Mexican American.[29] Eighty percent of Mexican Americans are U.S. citizens, with the states along the U.S.-Mexico border having large Latino electorates. In delegate-rich California and Texas, 30 percent of voters are Latino. In New Mexico, Arizona, Nevada, and Colorado, the proportion of Latino voters ranges from 14 percent (Colorado) to 40 percent (New Mexico). In Florida, Latinos are 20 percent of the electorate and now Latino groups other than Cubans make up the majority. In New York and New Jersey, Latinos are likely to exceed 15 percent of those who vote in the 2020 election.

Demographic and voting trends such as these have received a great deal of media attention over the past decade, when it was announced that, by 2044, the United States is on track to become a "majority-minority" nation—that is, a country in which all people of color combined outnumber Whites. According to a national survey conducted in late 2018, twice as many Latinos and African Americans as Whites think a non-White majority will be "very good" or "somewhat good" for the nation. What is more troubling is that three in ten Whites believe the nation's demographic transformation to a non-White majority will be "somewhat bad" or "very bad" for the nation.[30]

Patrick Crusius, the twenty-one-year-old White man who opened fire with an AK-47 at a Walmart in El Paso, Texas, in August 2019 was inspired by what he called "the Hispanic invasion." He drove ten hours from his home in a Dallas suburb to a city on the Mexican border that is 80 percent Latino, knowing he could stop virtually anywhere in the city to hunt down Latino targets. By the end of the massacre, he had murdered twenty-two people and injured another twenty-four; ten Latinos with American citizenship were among the dead, as were eight with Mexican citizenship. Wikipedia's post on the tragic killings proclaimed it motivated by "Hispanophobia," but former presidential candidate Beto O'Rourke, an El Paso native, was correct to label it what it was: "We have a racism in America that is as old as America itself," he said. Rather than the president seeking to stamp it out, he said, Trump calls people "animals, and predators and killers" and warns of an invasion from the southern border: Crusius repeated "the very words used by the president of the United States to justify this act of terror and hatred and violence and death."[31]

While the El Paso massacre is the most recent fatal attack targeting Latinos, there has been an explosion of anti-Latino racism in recent years, alongside White nationalist attacks on Jews, Muslims, African Americans, and others. Polls of Latinos registered to vote show they are feeling the impact: in one conducted six months before the El Paso massacre, more than half reported that racism against Latinos and against immigrants was a major problem; another poll taken just before the 2018 midterm elections found that nearly half told pollsters their situation had worsened over the past year, up considerably from 30 percent a year earlier.[32] Latinos report an upsurge in discrimination in schools, housing, employment, and the criminal justice system. For example, the Supreme Court overturned a Colorado conviction for sexual assault due to a juror's racist statements about the Latino defendant, including that juror's claim that "nine times out ten, Mexican men were guilty of being aggressive toward women and young girls."[33] There is no doubt Trump's rhetoric has made it more acceptable to target Latinos, but it would be wrong to assume the problem was not serious prior to 2015. This book explains why that is the case.

Conventional wisdom portrays Latinos as an ethnic rather than a racial group. The very fact of our collective unwillingness to name as racism, and instead classify as "Hispanophobia," "xenophobia," or "ethnic prejudice," racist attacks and institutional racism targeting Latinos is itself a reflection of the nature of Latino racialization. For one thing, the tendency to think of Latinos in ethnic terms perpetuates the idea that Latinos are perpetual foreigners rather than bona fide Americans.[34] To speak of the immigrant but never the (native) American is fundamental to the racial logic of Latino subordination. It is assumed foreignness—inherent in questions like, "Where are you from?" followed up by, "No, really, where are you from?" or "Where are your parents from?"—that marks Latinos as racial others who do not belong, even when their grandparents were born in this country, and marks White immigrants as racial insiders despite their actual foreignness.[35]

Yet racism among Latinos does not affect all Latinos in the same way. The ethnic frame reinforces a national origin hierarchy that largely corresponds to White skin privilege. Those with greater Spanish ancestry have higher status than those individuals with more visible Indigenous and/or African ancestry. Despite the fact that the range in phenotype due to Indigenous, African, and Spanish roots exists in all Latin American countries, some regions are seen as more White and more culturally European than others. Among Latinos, for example, people from Argentina, which has a comparatively larger European-origin population, fare better than those from Guatemala, comparatively more Indian, and the Dominican Republic, comparatively more Black. Four out of ten Argentinian Latinos have at least a college degree, compared to three out of ten Dominican Latinos and one out of ten Guatemalan Latinos. Even among Latinos with ancestry from countries close in proximity and similar by many measures, an emphasis on ethnicity fosters the denigration of those perceived as farther from whiteness. A case in point is the Caribbean, where Spanish colonizers obliterated the Indigenous population and imported large numbers of enslaved Africans; while Dominicans look down on Haitians, with whom they share an island, Puerto Ricans look down on Dominicans, and Cubans look down on Puerto Ricans.[36]

Another problem with viewing Latinos from an ethnic rather than a racial frame is that doing so pits them against African Americans in a way that supports white supremacy. For example, it encourages Latinos to see themselves as distant from Blacks by adopting the dominant racial narrative that African Americans "deserve" their place at the bottom of the hierarchy, while, in contrast, putting Latinos into the dominant ethnic narrative in which striving "immigrants" overcome the odds to assimilate. In this way, the refusal to see and name anti-Latino racism *qua* racism serves to enlist Latinos in policing the White-over-Black color line. The reality is that the ethnic and racial frames are anything but mutually exclusive. That they are overlapping is made visible by the extent to which even Black immigrants to the United States seek to distance themselves from African Americans.[37] In order to understand how various racial logics work in tandem with each other, we must first call out anti-Latino racism.

This book arrives on the scene a century after the United States enacted its modern immigration and naturalization laws—laws intended to preserve a White nation that were in effect from 1924 to 1965. In 1917, President Woodrow Wilson signed the Asiatic Barred Zone into law, seeking to exclude all immigrants from Asia. Less than a decade later, President Calvin Coolidge signed the National Origins Act, which put in place country quotas for immigrants based on the 1890 census— the last before the nation's transformation by substantial immigration from southern and eastern European countries. Between 1890 and 1920, Italians, Poles, and Jews from Eastern Europe were 88 percent of all immigrants to the United States. In essence, by excluding Asian immigrants and pegging the new national quotas to the 1890 census, American leaders sought to advantage immigrants from the British Isles and northwestern Europe while disfavoring those coming from southern and eastern Europe. In the early 1950s, Congress lifted the ban on migrants from Asian countries and, in 1965, it ended the quota system favoring immigrants from northwestern European countries.

Also in 1965, Congress enacted limits on migration from the Western Hemisphere, making it all but inevitable that large numbers of Latin American migrants would enter the United States without legal authorization. Today's U.S. population reflects these changes in immigration law as well as fertility trends and labor needs in the United States: half of all immigrants today are from Latin American countries, just over a quarter are from Asian countries, 12 percent are from European countries, and 7 percent are from African countries. As a proportion of the entire U.S. population, there are fewer foreign born persons living in the nation today than there were in 1910, 1920, and 1930.[38] It is not so much the sheer number of immigrants (or those presumed to be immigrants) that frighten some people, but the fact that today's immigrants are racially distinctive. In 2010, Mexicans were the largest number of foreign-born persons in the country at 29 percent, and the next nine nations in terms of their share of the foreign-born each were less than 5 percent.[39] Ultimately, this book will show that racism continues to shape immigration enforcement and perceptions of who is truly American.

Chapter 1 of this book provides an origin story for Latinos as a racially subordinated group. The starting point is America's long history of empire in North and South America.[40] This history connects Latinos to other subordinated racial groups: African Americans brought here as slaves and Native Americans who, when they were not exterminated, were forced into geographic zones often distant from their homelands. Due to U.S. imperialism, Latinos should be treated as *involuntarily* present in this country, which, in turn, has substantial implications for immigration and naturalization policies. To say this is not to say that, besides African Americans and Native Americans, everyone else came to this country under fully "voluntary" conditions. Certainly, that was not true for Jews who fled Europe, other Europeans who migrated to avoid political persecution or even famine, or those who arrived as indentured laborers from Asia and elsewhere. It is, however, to emphasize the fact of American complicity in why Latinos are here today in large numbers. Due to American imperialism in Mexico, Central America, and the Spanish Caribbean, Latino immigrants from those regions should be provided a path to citizenship and full inclusion in American society. Additionally, future immigrants from these regions should receive legal authorization to enter the United States and collective naturalization or asylum.

Latinos' phenotypical and ancestral diversity is a product of Spanish colonialism in Latin America. In the first two centuries of colonization of "the New World" (1400–1600), Spanish soldiers and priests encountered an estimated 80 million Indigenous people, only 10 million of whom survived Spanish contact.[41] They died from Spanish military campaigns, contagion from European diseases, and death from enslavement by Spanish priests. This genocide resulted in an acute labor shortage in the Spanish colonies. In order to extract resources such as gold and silver, produce resources such as sugar and coffee, and build colonial cities replete with gold- and silver-decorated Catholic cathedrals, the Spanish crown turned to African slavery. Between 1551 and 1870, Spanish colonizers imported eleven million African slaves to Mexico, the Caribbean, and the Atlantic coast of South America.[42] Chapter 2 considers the resulting *mestizaje*—the social and sexual mixing of Indigenous peoples, Africans, and Spaniards—and its implications for Latinos today. In short, Spain's colonies, while racist to the core, did not prohibit sexual or marital unions between groups. Mexico's case is illustrative of the result: marriage between Spaniards, Indians, and Blacks resulted in a quarter-million free *Afro-mestizos* in the 1742 census, very likely an under estimate of a growing population.[43]

In chapter 3, I consider how Latinos' claim to at least some European (Spanish) ancestry provided a wedge to claim an in-between racial status, with Whites above them and Blacks below them in the American racial hierarchy. Over the course of the twentieth century especially, Mexican American and Puerto Rican Latinos at times received valuable rights—in part precisely to gain their alliance against Blacks—leading them to promote themselves as "White." This is counter-intuitive, since Latinos are a racially subordinated group, but it can be reconciled by returning to the idea that race and racial classifications are political and social constructs. One result has been that Latinos themselves have strategically claimed whiteness as a shield against discrimination, effectively saying, "We may not be truly White, but we definitely are not Black." World War II was a catalyst for the beginning of the end of this political strategy, because overt and prolific racism against returning

Latino veterans led civil rights organizations to question the efficacy of claiming whiteness as a way to blunt discrimination. Another key inflection point was the rise of the Boricua and Chicano movements of the 1970s—themselves inspired by the Black Power movement—which reframed *mestizaje* as a point of pride, at least for young Latinos and the generations to come.

The Chicano Power and Boricua Power moments gave way, soon enough, to a more moderate stance that focused on electoral politics and Latino "representation" of various sorts. In chapter 4, I turn to the story of how the U.S. census first came around to counting Latinos in 1980. This had seismic reverberations—in terms of how Americans thought of Latinos—for everything from retail politics to popular culture to how television ads for laundry detergent targeted Latinos to enforcement of the Voting Rights Act. The census has always been a primary race-making site for the racial state. The implications for the 2020 census were numerous, including the Trump administration's failed bid to include a citizenship question and its rejection of experts' recommendation to fold the current so-called "Hispanic ethnicity" question into the race question by incorporating a Latino option alongside existing race choices. These issues played out in all three branches of government as the president's political survival was thrown into doubt by the Mueller investigation and then the impeachment trial, and they will no doubt cast a heavy shadow over the 2020 elections. The 1980 count of Latinos also has fundamentally transformed how they think of themselves and other Americans, a question at the heart of this book.

1

WE ARE HERE BECAUSE YOU WERE THERE

Myths and stereotypes reinforce each other. The myth sets out the story, the stereotype fits in the characters. It was said, for instance, that the post-war "influx" of West Indian and Asian immigrants to this country was due to "push-and-pull" factors. Poverty pushed us out of countries, and prosperity pulled us into Britain. Hence the stereotype that we were lazy, feckless people who were on the make. But what wasn't said was that it was colonialism that both impoverished us and enriched Britain. . . . Quite simply we came to Britain (and not to Germany for instance) because we were occupied by Britain. Colonialism and immigration are part of the same continuum—we are here because you were there.

—Ambalavaner Sivanandan, speech on the fiftieth
anniversary of Britain's Institute of Race Relations, 2009 [1]

If, for African Americans, the fundamental racial origin story is one of capture in Africa, forced travel to North America, and brutal enslavement itself protected by law, what is the defining race-making crucible for Latinos? The clear answer is that it begins with American colonialism and empire in Latin America. Whether in order to extend the country to the Pacific (Mexico), to extract resources like coffee, sugar, or bananas (Puerto Rico, Cuba, Guatemala, Honduras, Costa Rica), to connect the Atlantic and Pacific Oceans (Panama, Nicaragua), to achieve America's "manifest destiny" in the hemisphere (all), or to provide access to an exploitable labor force (all), the United States has invaded, annexed, covertly and overtly interfered, and governed its way across Latin America for two centuries. The linkages between America's overt and sometimes covert interventions in Mexico, the Caribbean, and Central America, and the migration of people northward from those regions connects with how Latinos experience racial oppression today. Just as Ambalavaner Sivanandan expressed about Britain, colonialism and migration are likewise on the same continuum for the United States.

Beginning only decades after America's founding, with the takeover of Texas, extending through today with Puerto Rico and Guantánamo Bay, the United States has continuously pursued the exploitation of resources and people in the Western Hemisphere. The result has been the migration of poor people from Mexico, Central America, and the Spanish Caribbean for more than a century as an always available source of cheap labor, often one that has been especially vulnerable because of a prevalence of undocumented or temporary workers. Why tell the story of Latino racialization as it has affected only these regions of Latin America? There are two simple reasons. First, because U.S. military, civilian, and corporate intervention in these parts of Latin America has been especially harsh, causing often violent economic displacement that has in turn produced the flow of migrants to fill America's least desirable jobs.[2] Second, the vast majority of Latinos trace their birth or descent to the countries of Mexico, Central America (Nicaragua, Panama, Honduras, Guatemala, El Salvador), and the Spanish Caribbean (Puerto Rico, Cuba, the Dominican Republic). Consider the four most populous U.S. states: in order of population, they are California, Texas, Florida, and New York. They are home to a combined 120 million people, including 60 percent of all Latinos. Of each state's Latinos, between 96 and 99 percent of them trace their ancestry to one of these nine Latin American countries.[3]

The typical narrative about the American footprint in Latin America focuses on the executive branch's formal, ostensibly well-crafted "foreign policy." A standard story begins with the Monroe Doctrine of 1823 and culminates with the Good Neighbor Policy more than a century later. President James Monroe's warning to England, France, and Spain, Europe's three strongest colonial powers early in the nineteenth century, was to keep out of Latin America. Less than twenty years after the massive expansion of the United States via the Louisiana Purchase, the Monroe Doctrine encapsulated the idea of an American nation ordained to expand to the northwest, west, and southwest across the continent and beyond. Within roughly a century of the Monroe Doctrine, the United States would invade Mexico, taking half its territory; challenge

Spain to war, acquiring Puerto Rico, Guam, the Philippines, and Cuba; and achieve a major geopolitical victory by connecting the Pacific and Atlantic Oceans via the Panama Canal. After all that, Franklin Delano Roosevelt's 1936 promise to be "a good neighbor" to Latin America proved easy to make, even as it would be repeatedly broken over the next century.

The reality of U.S. intervention in the Americas was far more menacing than these two symbolic pronouncements on the world stage. Over the course of three centuries, American presidents and Congress have executed colonial power in Latin America by deploying a variety of strategies and tactics. Some of them the United States learned as a colony itself, adopting techniques inspired by British colonial rule. Like the East Indian Company in South Asia, which eighteenth-century British philosopher Edmund Burke aptly called "a state in the guise of a merchant," American corporations sometimes led the way in Latin America.[4] The United Fruit Company is a major player in this story, especially in Honduras and Guatemala, with its directors and in-country employees rotating from the corporation into positions within the governments of the U.S. and Central American nations alike. Frequently, American military intervention was justified in order to "protect" American corporate interests (Central America, Cuba). At other times, outright war, followed by the seizure of territory and people was the strategy (as in Mexico and Puerto Rico). This region, contiguous to the United States, was deemed fit for settler colonialism—understood as the colonial policy of promoting a region's civilian occupation by Whites from the colonizing society in order to displace the native populations.[5] The former Mexico was divided into regions which eventually became all or parts of ten of the most expansive states in the United States, though only when White settlers outnumbered Indians and Mexicans.[6] In contrast, Puerto Rico and Cuba (along with Guam and the Philippines, all four taken from Spain in 1898), were never viewed as colonies to be settled and made states, as the ongoing controversy, 122 years later, over Puerto Rican statehood shows.[7] Instead, they were seen as sites for U.S. military power on a larger geopolitical chessboard. At the close of the Cold War's first decade, Puerto Rico was home to 142,486 American military personnel.[8] Today, 13,520 members of the U.S. Armed Forces are stationed across 34 military sites in Puerto Rico.[9] And despite the socialist revolution of 1959 and more than five decades of a crippling economic embargo against Cuba, the United States has continuously occupied the Guantanamo Bay military base for 123 years.

Since World War II ended, U.S. imperialism in Latin America has been justified by anti-communism and the Cold War. The Cuban Revolution of 1959 and the Cuban Missile Crisis of 1961 drove American opposition to pro-labor populist governments and support for authoritarian dictators in virtually every Caribbean and Central American nation. Covert, CIA-led operations to depose and install such governments characterized American intervention in Central America from the 1950s until at least the 2000s. The U.S. Southern Command—the military's presence in the Western Hemisphere—is formally based in Miami, but its force (Army, Navy, Special Forces) headquarters is in Puerto Rico; in 1999 Puerto Rico replaced Panama in that role due to the end of formal U.S. control of the Panama Canal. The U.S. Navy presence in Puerto Rico includes 200,000 square miles in waters around Puerto Rico that allow it to do everything from testing submarines to testing water-based warfare. Rather than direct military intervention, American control has shifted since the 1970s to a combination of covert intelligence, U.S. military training of local armies and national police, and "foreign aid" for drug interdiction and military weapons, and a combination of public/private international imperialism via agencies such as the World Bank. These stories follow, starting with Mexico, then Central America (Nicaragua, Panama, Honduras, Guatemala, El Salvador), and then the Spanish Caribbean (Puerto Rico, Cuba, the Dominican Republic). A final section describes a program for reparations for Latinos and future migrants that reflects how colonialism and immigration are part of one continuum.

Mexico

The timing of Monroe's 1823 warning to European colonial powers that the United States would control the Western Hemisphere, as its backyard, was far from accidental. It arrived as Spain's hold on its Latin American colonies was faltering especially in Mexico, which fought a war of independence from 1811 to 1821. Formerly organized as the viceroyalty of New Spain, Mexico's independence movement took its inspiration from the French and American revolutions with the goal of becoming Latin America's first republic. Weakened from the long fight for independence and facing resistance from Indigenous peoples seeking their own sovereignty after the collapse of the Spanish empire, Mexico encouraged American settlement of its northeast region, known today as Texas. By 1830, Mexico's liberal immigration policies had attracted so many Americans to Mexican Texas that they outnumbered Mexicans by a four to one margin. Many of them were Southern slave owners who, in violation of Mexico's abolition of Black slavery in 1829, brought an estimated 2,000 slaves with them to Texas.[10] Rather than comply with abolition, the Americans started an armed revolt against Mexico, planning to declare independence upon their victory. At the Alamo in 1836, the Texans suffered an overwhelming defeat, but a few months later they prevailed, declaring the Texas Republic. The Texans cultivated allies on two fronts: with the small number of elite Mexican landowning ranchers and with the federal government.[11]

The Texans sought Washington's economic and political support, both of which were predicated on winning nation-to-nation recognition. Mississippi senator Robert J. Walker urged recognition of the Texas Republic on the explicitly racist ground that the United States had a duty to support "our kindred race" against "the colored mongrel race, and barbarous tyranny, and superstitions of Mexico."[12] Nothing if not consistent, Walker invoked Mexicans' inferiority again nine years later in support of statehood for Texas: "five-sixths" of Mexicans are "semi-barbarous hordes . . . composed of every poisonous compound of blood and color."[13] In a deliberate move to provoke a war with Mexico, the Americans asserted an outrageously expansive border, claiming both Santa Fe and El Paso along the Rio Grande. Armed with a declaration of war from Congress, President James Polk launched an invasion of Mexico 175 years ago. The timing of the war, five decades after the nation's formation, served to simultaneously cohere American identity and undercut anti-war opposition by Whig congressmen from New England.[14] White Americans' view of Mexicans' racial inferiority played a critical role in uniting the nation behind Manifest Destiny, as a newspaper editorialized: "Mexico was poor, distracted, in anarchy, and almost in ruins [after its prolonged war of independence]—what could she do to stay the hand of our power, to impede the march of our greatness? We are Anglo-Saxon Americans; it was our 'destiny' to possess and to rule this continent—we are bound to it!"[15]

Over the course of the next two years, every branch of the American military participated in the invasion, ultimately resulting in the 1848 Treaty of Guadalupe Hidalgo, in which Mexico was forced to cede half of its territory and 115,000 Mexicans received collective naturalization as American citizens.[16] The seven out of ten Latinos who are Mexican Americans began with this population—the original Mexican Americans—and continue with today's migrants from Mexico. After U.S. soldiers captured Santa Fe, Los Angeles, and northern California's Monterey in 1846, they moved by land and water to seize control of Mexico City.[17] Future U.S. president General Zachary Taylor led the ground forces from Texas into the capital city. The U.S. Navy controlled Veracruz, Mexico's most important Atlantic port, by March 1847, and six months later Mexico had surrendered. Mexico sought to protect the civil rights of its citizens who lived in the ceded territory by inserting into the armistice agreement requirements that the U.S. treat them as equals and that their property, whether privately or communally owned, be protected; both provisions were later violated. For its part, the United

States gained the so-called Mexican Cession but also Mexican people, 14,000 in California, 23,000 in Texas, and 75,000 in what is today New Mexico.[18]

The conviction that Mexicans were racially inferior informed every decision about the incorporation of these original Mexican Americans. The peace treaty promised the Mexicans living in the now-American territory they would receive collective naturalization as American citizens, but the Constitution still required Polk to obtain approval for the treaty. Polk's two-day cabinet meeting about the treaty came first. Secretary of State James Buchanan, who would be elected president within a decade, asked rhetorically: "How should we govern the mongrel race which inhabits [the Mexican lands]? Could we admit them to seats in our Senate or House of Representatives? Are they capable of Self-Government as States of this Confederacy?"[19] The next hurdle was the Senate, which held off ratification after an unprecedented eleven days of secret deliberations.[20] In the end, senators ratified the treaty by a two to one vote, but they did so only after adding an amendment that nearly scuttled the entire deal when the revised treaty was returned to Mexico for ratification. The amendment amounted to a bait-and-switch tactic; rather than provide immediate statehood for the entirety of the Mexican Cession, as agreed and as would have ensured the political and civil rights of the new Mexican American citizens, the Senate gave Congress the power to decide when, if at all, statehood would occur in the newly acquired lands.

Although Texas had been admitted by the Senate as a slave state in 1845, Mexico did not relinquish its control over Texas until its surrender in 1848. For California, statehood came almost immediately in 1850. The discovery of gold in northern California in 1849 caused a fivefold increase in California's White settler population, smoothing the path to statehood. The rest of the vast Mexican Cession entered a colonial status that ensured political limbo for the next sixty-four years. The problem was twofold: two-thirds of the first Mexican Americans lived in what is today New Mexico and the rest of the Mexico Cession was actually controlled by Indian peoples who had successfully resisted both Spanish colonial rule and then incorporation as citizens by Mexico. What followed was the gradual breaking up of what remained of the Mexican Cession into regions that—as White settlers and American corporations in railroads and mining, among other sectors, moved into them—became U.S. states. The final two to become states were Arizona and New Mexico. After repeated conventions to draft state constitutions and intensive lobbying efforts by their non-voting delegates in Congress, Arizona and New Mexico became states in 1912. Despite a larger population of enfranchised men than Colorado, Utah, and other western territories, as long as Mexicans and Indians remained the demographically and politically dominant groups, statehood remained elusive for these regions.[21]

The war with Mexico, fought largely by a volunteer army, left young American men teeming to continue colonial exploits, even as private individuals as historian Jason Colby has noted. They were called "filibusters" or "freebooters" and sought, ostensibly without support from the U.S. government, to foment insurrections in other countries (such as the White Americans who formed the Texas Republic or the short-lived California Republic). Inspired by Manifest Destiny and motivated to extend the boundaries of slavery, young men like William Walker left Tennessee to pan for gold in northern California. By age thirty, he had briefly declared himself "president" of Baja California and Sonora, two Mexican states; he then faced trial for launching an illegal war against a sovereign nation under the Neutrality Act of 1794 but was acquitted by a jury.[22]

Ultimately, private businesses with American addresses played a far more lasting role in Latin America than did private individuals, filibusters or not. This corporate colonialism began in the late nineteenth century with substantial investment in Mexican railroads and mining enterprises.[23] These same railways soon came to play a major role in transporting cheap labor to the southwestern United States during the early decades of the twentieth century, where jobs in agriculture and mining awaited them.[24] Far from merely the "pull" factors of these economic sectors, American corporate colonialism dramatically changed entire sectors of the Mexican economy. It displaced tens of thousands of *campesinos*, rural Mexicans who spoke one of dozens of Indigenous languages native to Mexico. *Campesinos* were forced from their homelands to find work in Mexico's cities, and, when that failed, they migrated north to the United States to find work. As inequality grew in Mexico, the wage gap between neighboring countries became irresistible to both poor Mexicans and American agribusiness and other industries that depended on a cheap, flexible labor force. While the Mexican Revolution (1910–1920) led some middle-class Mexicans to move to the United States, the bulk of those coming north in the past century have been *mestizo* or Indigenous Mexicans taking jobs on the bottom rung of the U.S. labor market.

By 1911, the U.S. Immigration Bureau was already reporting that 50,000 Mexicans crossed the border annually without legal authorization.[25] In a cycle that continues today, White elites and workers demonized Mexican immigrants, directly leading to the formation of the Border Patrol in 1924 (the same year, you will recall, in which the quotas favoring immigrants from northwestern European countries were instituted).[26] Proponents of the Border Patrol—which today is the nation's largest law enforcement agency, with 20,000 officers—claimed it would prevent the "degradation" of America, degradation they said flowed directly from the *campesinos'* "mongrel" character, a result of the mixture of "Spanish peasants," "low-grade Indians," and "negro slave blood."[27] Even with the Border Patrol in place, agribusiness in Texas and California called the shots. By 1950, some 90,000 Mexican Americans and Mexicans worked as farmworkers in California, and 160,000 more were based in Texas, including 60,000 who called Texas home yet who seasonally migrated back and forth to harvest crops in other states.[28]

During the Great Depression, Latino workers became scapegoats, subject to the vagaries of local and state reactions to unemployment.

In the 1930s, as many as two million people, including some American citizens of Mexican descent, were deported so that their jobs could be given to Whites.[29] In Los Angeles, labor unions proclaimed "Employ no Mexican while a white man is unemployed. . . . Get the Mexican back to Mexico regardless by what means."[30] In Texas in 1931, the state legislature mandated a 50 percent reduction in cotton-growing acreage, driving jobless Mexican cotton pickers into cities and towns to look for work. When a prolonged drought drove unemployed Mexican American beet workers to Denver in search of jobs, Colorado's governor ordered the National Guard to the New Mexico border to prevent Mexican American farmworkers from entering the state.[31] If they reached Colorado, Mexican workers were greeted with signs reading: "Warning all Mexicans and all other aliens to leave the state of Colorado at once."[32]

When Latinos stood up for themselves, they were imprisoned or deported. In one incident at a Gallup, New Mexico, coal mine, Latino miners went on strike because they were receiving less pay than White miners for the same work. The strike dragged on for months, resulting in the eviction of three hundred Latinos from company-owned housing, which, in turn, prompted an attack on the sheriff who tried to enforce the evictions. The resulting melee led the sheriff to jail two hundred miners, forty-eight of whom were convicted for the single crime of an accidental homicide and the rest of whom were deported to Mexico.[33] Mexican American and Japanese American farmworkers were seen as a threat to white supremacy, both because they engaged in labor activism and because the alien land laws, which prohibited land ownership by those who were not U.S. citizens, were applied to both groups in the western states.[34] By 1940, the Latino population in Texas and Los Angeles County fell by one-third due to "voluntary" departures to Mexico or government-mandated deportations, with one study showing that 80 percent of those pushed out or deported were, in fact, American citizens or legal immigrants.[35]

The reverse played out during World War II, when the shortage of male workers led the United States to establish a bilateral labor agreement with Mexico. Known as the Bracero Program, it recruited young, single men called *braceros*, slang from the root word in Spanish for "arms," emphasizing the hard labor these men did. Between 1942 and 1947, 220,000 Mexican men earned 30 cents a day as agricultural workers in the United States.[36] Like those *campesinos* who went north decades before, these largely Indigenous and *mestizo* men were forced, due to Mexico's austerity and modernization, to migrate from rural villages to Mexico's cities. Given its own economic struggles, Mexico welcomed their employment in the United States, and American agribusiness welcomed them to fill jobs vacated by enlisted servicemen.

Once they arrived at the U.S. border, braceros underwent invasive and demeaning medical inspection, as shown in an iconic photo. Taken at the El Paso, Texas border station, the photo shows dozens of brown-skinned young men lined up, naked with only a paper towel covering their genitals, while an American doctor inspected them one-by-one. By the 1940s, the racist stereotype of the "dirty Mexican" was already well entrenched in the United States. Historical accounts of the creation of the public health bureau in Los Angeles County in the early twentieth century show that officials perceived Mexicans as inherently dirty and disease-infested and, as a result, did not bother fighting poor sanitation due to poverty in Mexican American neighborhoods.[37] Braceros complained both to Mexican consulates in the Southwest and to the Mexican government when they returned about every aspect of the Bracero Program, from those initial exams to American employers' failure to provide adequate housing to the theft of their mandatory savings by Mexican banks. Only in this century has a "Bracero Justice" social movement sprung up on both sides of the border. In a tale of usurpation, the photograph of naked braceros has been reclaimed as a symbol of pride for braceros who left as *campesinos* barely past adolescence and returned home as young men who had seen the world and often become acculturated as *mestizo* workers.[38]

Long after the war made it necessary, agribusiness successfully lobbied Congress to extend the Bracero Program until 1964.[39] In total, some 4.6 million Mexicans participated in the program over the course of two decades.[40] The reality was that it provided a new, legal way to exploit Mexican workers under coercive labor contracts, as if hiring undocumented workers did not give employers sufficient bargaining power.[41] Perhaps paradoxically, unauthorized Mexican migration surged over the course of the Bracero Program era. According to one scholar, such crossings were a way for migrants to resist repressive work contracts that did not allowed for control over one's labor, the formation of families in the United States, or inclusion in American society.[42]

The result was that, even as the Bracero Program was extended, the federal government's new Immigration and Naturalization Service (INS)—the precursor to today's Immigration and Customs Enforcement (ICE)—stepped up deportations of Mexican migrants who had entered the United States without legal authorization. The INS pejoratively named its 1950s deportation initiative "Operation Wetback," using a derisive reference to Mexicans who cross the border without papers whose bodies are presumably wet from crossing the Rio Grande. So many Mexicans were rounded up in Chicago under Operation Wetback that the INS established a Chicago-to-Mexico airlift just for deportations; in total, 3.7 million people were deported under the program.[43] In fact, Operation Wetback was so extensive in Chicago that Puerto Ricans—who by law may live and work on the mainland as American citizens—routinely were asked to show proof of citizenship because they were mistaken for Mexicans.[44] By the late 1970s, the civil rights movement had prompted the discursive shift away from "wetback" to the seemingly race-neutral "illegal alien." Today, of course, that phrase has morphed into simply "illegal," used as a noun to refer to human beings, usually with a decidedly racist connotation.[45]

By the late 1960s, two major trends characterized Latino migration. First, Mexican workers were entrenched as a disposable labor force, deported when unemployment rose or job needs changed (the 1930s, the 1950s) and readily lured north when demanded by specific employers or economic sectors (i.e., the recruitment of temporary farmworkers under the Bracero Program, 1942–1962). A second trend was launched by the 1965 overhaul of immigration laws, rightly hailed as a civil rights landmark for ending the ban on immigration from Asia in place since 1917. The 1965 law also set aside the country quotas from 1924 that had favored immigrants from northwestern European countries. Moreover, it was in 1965 that the policy of family reunification came to characterize U.S. naturalization preferences. Trump derisively refers to the latter as "chain migration" because it allows immigrants who become American citizens to place their relatives on a waiting list to be allowed entry to the United States as authorized immigrants with a path to citizenship. Mexican immigrants have disproportionately benefited from family reunification, yet the same 1965 law implemented quotas on migration from Western Hemisphere countries, thereby limiting Latin American immigration untethered from family reunification.[46]

It was precisely these built-in constraints on authorized Mexican migration—coupled with employer demand for low-wage workers in the manufacturing and service industries—that produced a dramatic increase in the population of undocumented Mexican immigrants in the United States. Between 1970 and 1990, the number of undocumented Mexican migrants increased six times over, from fewer than 900,000 to 5.4 million people.[47] During this period, President Reagan signed into law the Immigration Regulation and Control Act of 1986, providing a path to citizenship for 2 million undocumented immigrants, increasing border enforcement, but continuing to hold employers harmless for hiring workers without legal authorization to be in the country; not surprisingly, then, the law failed to curtail demand for Mexican workers.[48] The 1994 North American Free Trade Agreement, or NAFTA, which in late 2019 was replaced with the United States-Mexico-Canada Agreement, was supposed to reduce undocumented immigration from Mexico by providing Mexican workers with better jobs in Mexico. Yet, NAFTA is widely believed to have had the opposite effect.[49] In response to increased migration caused by the massive restructuring of the Mexican economy due to NAFTA, President Clinton signed into law the

Illegal Immigrant Reform and Immigrant Responsibility Act.[50] Sociologists Nelson Rodriguez and Cecilia Menjívar have called it "the Latino Exclusion Act," nodding to the Chinese Exclusion Act of 1882, because the law fostered "a new atmosphere of exclusion that had not been felt by Latino immigrants since the federal roundup of over a million Mexicans during Operation Wetback in the 1950s."[51] The number of deportations quadrupled in the space of a decade, with Mexicans the majority and Central Americans a significant number. During the final years of the twentieth century, annual deportations increased fivefold, to 208,000.[52]

In some respects, it is the Clinton era that was the precursor to the early twenty-first-century state and local laws that seek to penalize undocumented persons (and discourage future migrants) by cutting off public benefits and restricting private landlords' and employers' ability to do business with them. Here too the result was not a reduction in unauthorized migration but, instead, a strengthening of the bargaining position of employers hiring undocumented migrants which, understandably, increased the demand for exploitable workers.[53] President Obama expanded the visa program for guest workers under which 361,000 Mexican nationals received visas as temporary agricultural workers in 2010; combined with record-breaking deportations, the Obama administration's immigration policy was nothing short of "schizophrenic" because it was giving such visas to the same kind of migrants it was deporting at record numbers in 2009–2012.[54] Once again during the Obama administration, arrests and prosecutions of immigrants skyrocketed, for example, climbing from 13,249 prosecutions in 1998 to more than 60,000 in 2017, the last year of the Obama presidency. Whereas Obama had in 2015, with the 2016 election looming, instituted a slow-down in deportations by directing that 87 percent of undocumented immigrants were to be low-priority for enforcement, Trump ramped up all aspects of immigration detention and deportation.[55] In the first two years of the Trump administration, compared to the last two of the Obama administration, federal prosecutions of immigration crimes increased 66 percent to 99,479 annually; similarly,

Obama's deportations set a record high, only to be surpassed by Trump's first two years.[56]

And yet, Mexican immigrants keep coming north. Today, 10 percent of Mexico's population lives in the United States. Their remittances back to relatives are Mexico's second-largest source of foreign exchange.[57] These numbers, in turn, explain why Mexico has twice—in 1996 and 2005—enacted laws to allow its citizens living in the United States to become naturalized American citizens and still retain their Mexican passports, own property in Mexico, and vote in Mexican elections from abroad.[58]

Central America and the Panama Canal

America's acquisition of the northern half of Mexico in 1848 unleashed a flood of migration westward to California's newly discovered gold mines. While most traveled over land by wagon, some 200,000 went by sea, crossing from the Atlantic to the Pacific Ocean via Central America, the most narrow isthmus in the hemisphere. Cornelius Vanderbilt, who already controlled steamship routes and railway lines in and around New York, offered transportation between New York and San Francisco, relying on a combination of ocean steamships, river steamboats, and a twelve-mile carriage ride across Central America in what would later be Nicaragua.[59] In 1854 Vanderbilt requested American military intervention when native men attacked his business and the British (who had six years earlier established a presence in Nicaragua) refused to intervene. To justify his decision to send a naval ship to Nicaragua, President Franklin Pierce told his cabinet that the natives were "dangerous" and that they were "composed for the most part of blacks and persons of mixed blood."[60] This was reminiscent of the racist trope around "mongrelization" popularized during the war with Mexico, in which Pierce had been a brigadier general serving in key battles, including Mexico City. Although he was born and bred in New Hampshire, Pierce was an outspoken critic of abolitionists, believing they would destroy the young nation by causing a rupture with the South.[61] A year after ordering trips to aid Vanderbilt, Pierce recognized William Walker's claim as president of Nicaragua (the same Walker who had filibustered in Mexico).[62] Apparently, Pierce had not consulted Vanderbilt, who it seems persuaded Costa Rica to oust Walker within months because he feared Walker would endanger his investments by seeking control of all Central America.[63]

And so began American imperialism in Central America, a toxic mix of corporate greed, filibusters, military might, and racism. The complete United States occupation of Nicaragua was delayed by the Civil War and Reconstruction, and later by the Spanish-American War of 1898. It was left to President William Taft to take up the task in 1911. Taft, who by the time he became president had an extensive resumé as a colonial administrator, sought a sea route connecting the newly acquired island colonies in the Pacific (Philippines, Guam, Hawaii) with those in the Atlantic (Puerto Rico, Cuba). Taft had served briefly as the American governor in Cuba and as the first territorial governor of the Philippines. Like most other American leaders, he went to great lengths to convince people (and perhaps himself) that military intervention by the United States was benign. In a 1907 article for *National Geographic* while he was Secretary of War, Taft wrote that American imperialism reflected the "sense of duty only," what he called "national altruism."[64]

Taft's first action in Nicaragua was to order American troops to remove the nation's anti-American president, replacing him with a Nicaraguan who had formerly been employed by an American mining company. The newly installed pro-American president signed a treaty with the United States providing a naval base, control over the Nicaraguan economy, and an exclusive option to build a canal through Nicaragua.[65] When the American ambassador warned Taft that a rebellion was brewing among Nicaraguans, whom he described as having "a majority of Indian and Negro Indian blood," Taft ordered the Marines to Nicaragua, where they remained for two decades.[66] Only in 1936 did the United States judge the climate calm enough to install its chosen leader, Anastasio

Somoza García, whose family remained in power for more than forty years.[67] Under the Somoza regime, American banking, agricultural, mining, and railway corporations reaped great wealth, while everyday Nicaraguans remained impoverished and illiterate.[68]

Somoza's son, also named Anastasio, headed the Nicaraguan National Guard after graduating from West Point in 1946. The younger Somoza made it a point to send his best officers to receive intensive training at the U.S. School of the Americas, where Latin American military personnel were trained by American officers using state-of-the-art military technology.[69] In total, over the course of six decades, 60,000 Latin American military officers and soldiers trained at the school between its early 1940s founding in the Panama Canal Zone and its rebranding in 2001 as the Western Hemisphere Institute for Security Cooperation. Drawing heavily from government records obtained via requests under the Freedom of Information Act, historian Lindsey Gill concludes that the School of the Americas was "implicated in some of the worst human rights violations in Latin America" and that it played a key role in American imperialism in the region by training repressive states and supplying them with arms and other technologies of violence.[70]

In a country of 3.5 million, the Somoza regime killed or disappeared 50,000 people and wounded another 100,000 in the 1970s—proportionally, this would be equivalent to 5 million American casualties today.[71] By 1979, the tide had turned against Somoza and in favor of the Marxist-revolutionary Sandinista movement. Named for Augusto Sandino, the leader of the anti-American resistance in the 1930s, the Sandinistas were recognized by President Jimmy Carter, who, alongside others in the region, offered to assist the new government. But that was not to be as Carter lost re-election to Ronald Reagan, who had campaigned on the promise to reverse the Sandinista revolution.[72] Reagan ordered 20,000 American troops to Nicaragua between 1985 and 1990; during the same period, he ordered a covert operation to support the anti-Sandinista forces known as the Contras, a Spanish abbreviation for counter-revolutionaries. Over the course of five years, the Reagan administration covertly funneled $400 million to the Contras.[73] Since Congress objected to funding, this money came mostly from the proceeds of cocaine sales orchestrated by the CIA, moving cocaine from Colombia to Panama to Los Angeles at the peak of the crack cocaine epidemic.[74] The U.S.-financed Contras killed 31,000 people and wounded twice that number in the 1980s.[75]

Nicaraguan Latinos are split between anti-communist, pro-Somoza migrants and those who were the victims of Somoza and the National Guard.[76] Compared to other Central Americans who succeeded in their asylum applications at the rate of 2-3 percent in the 1980s, during the same period, 25 percent of Nicaraguans seeking asylum were successful (still far below that of Soviet exiles, who were granted asylum 77 percent of the time).[77] Compared to Latinos from other Central American countries, the first-wave Nicaraguans were received much as the Cuban exiles were in the 1960s, as anti-communist "freedom fighters."[78] In contrast, the approximately 40 percent of Nicaraguan Latinos who came to the United states after 1990, when the Sandinistas were defeated by the Contras were far less favorably treated. In 1995, Cuban American congressional representatives sponsored the Nicaraguan Adjustment and Central American Relief Act, which became law in 1997, providing legal permanent resident status (green cards) for undocumented nationals from Nicaragua, Cuba, the Soviet Union (and, to a much lesser degree, to those from El Salvador and Guatemala) if they had lived in the United States for more than seven years continuously, could show good moral character, and would face extreme hardship from deportation.[79] It is due to the special character of Nicaraguan Latinos as split between anti-communist and pro-socialist migrants that, relative to other Central Americans, has led them to have a much higher rate of naturalization as U.S. citizens, at just over 50 percent.[80]

The story of American colonial exploits is particular to each Latin American country, but the connective tissue is the same: the racialization of native peoples as subhuman; the region's geopolitical strategic value; how military exercises support and reinforce corporate capitalism;

human rights abuses by U.S.-installed dictators; and displacement caused by violence and economic deprivation, leading to migration of an exploitable workforce.[81] The creation of Panama and the Panama Canal Zone puts these themes on vivid display. In addition to having the shortest route to the Pacific, Panama was a strategically important hub for the north-south traffic of people and goods on the new railroads connecting South America with North America.[82]

After failed attempts by English and French companies to build the canal, the United States took up the project, at first sending the Marines to the Atlantic Coast town of Colón in 1898. The Marines failed in their mission to persuade the town, based in Panamá Province, to secede from Gran Colombia (a newly independent nation that then included present-day Colombia, Panama, Venezuela, and Ecuador). Five years later, a new president, Teddy Roosevelt, again sent in the Marines, this time having received the assurance that the Panamanians were ready to secede from Colombia. Unwilling to risk a military defeat against the Americans, Colombia declined to assert sovereignty over Panama, in an example of "gunboat diplomacy." In an agreement similar to the one with Nicaragua, the United States in 1903 signed the Hay-Bunau-Varilla Treaty with the new Panamanian government. It provided the United States a ninety-nine-year lease on "the Panama Canal Zone," over which the Americans would have complete sovereignty, and gave the United States the right of military intervention in Panama proper.[83]

American construction of the canal began the following year, although the project took decades to complete. Racism was a central feature of the project from the beginning. The first American governor of the canal zone protectorate said there was nothing wrong with his American civilian employees calling dark-skinned Panamanians the N-word.[84] When enumerators conducted the census of 1910, they counted 26,000 Panamanians living in the Panama Canal Zone and classified three-quarters of them as "Negro," a vestige of the heavy importation of African slaves to the region under Spanish colonialism.[85] The United States preferred to employ English-speaking Jamaicans and other West Indians in canal construction, and tensions arose due to a racial hierarchy in which the best jobs went to West Indian immigrants, including supervisory roles over Spanish-speaking Panamanians. An anti-Black backlash emerged over time, fueling Panama's exclusion of Black immigrants beginning in 1926.[86] Panamanians in the United States today self-identify as Black at the relatively high rate, compared to other Latinos, of 20 percent.[87]

The canal zone essentially functioned as an unincorporated U.S. territory, where persons, American and non-American, were subject to federal police and federal courts, and where several American military bases were located. Even more than most military base zones, clashes between American military personnel, civilian employees, and the locals were common. In the late 1950s and early 1960s, a series of riots tempered the American zeal for empire, and, in the 1970s, President Carter negotiated an American withdrawal to occur in 1999. As with Nicaragua, Reagan took a very different approach to Panama upon his assumption of the presidency in 1981. He supported the CIA's cultivation of General Manuel Noriega as Panama's ruler in the early 1980s. Noriega had trained at the School of the Americas, led the Panamanian security forces, and styled himself the Maximum Leader of the National Liberation. During the Contra war against the Sandinistas, Noriega provided the planes used to traffic cocaine from Colombia to the United States. The CIA turned on Noriega in the late 1980s, accusing him of fraternizing with Fidel Castro and conspiring with Colombian drug cartels.[88] President George H.W. Bush, who had been Reagan's vice president and CIA director before that, ordered Noriega removed by U.S. armed forces. It took six weeks to do so, during which 6,000 Panamanians were killed.[89] Noriega was removed to the United States, convicted of racketeering and drug crimes in Miami, and sentenced to forty years in prison.[90]

The Americans ran the campaign against Noriega from a Honduran military base. Similarly, the 20,000 Contra fighters used Honduras as their base of operations with approval from their American benefactors.[91] In short, the United States created a regional counterrevolutionary force in Honduras. U.S. military aid to Honduras increased more than twenty-fold between 1978 and 1984 compared to the prior three decades. The Honduran military doubled in size during this period, including the addition of the region's most elaborate air force.[92]

For a nation of fewer than four million people, high numbers of Honduran military personnel trained at the School of the Americas: 1,100 in the seventies and 800 in the eighties.[93] The country's notorious "Battalion 3-16"—named for its service to three military units and sixteen battalions of the Honduran army—emerged in 1979 under the leadership of General Gustavo Álvarez Martínez. Álvarez graduated in 1961 from the Argentine Military College, known for its role in Argentina's "Dirty War," during which 30,000 people were murdered or disappeared by military death squads. The 3-16 functioned as an intelligence unit and a state death squad, brutally torturing and murdering Honduran students, scholars, journalists, and other civilians.[94] The U.S. Armed Forces awarded Álvarez the Legion of Medal in 1983, one of the highest honors possible for foreigners.[95] Even today, members of the now officially disbanded 3-16 continue to wield power in Honduras. In 2005 Hondurans elected a leftist president, Manuel Zelaya, who was ousted four years later with help from former 3-16 members.[96] Eight of ten Honduran Latinos migrated after 1990, when the United States formally ended its alliance with Battalion 3-16.[97]

Today, Honduran Latinos are 1.6 percent of all Latinos, close to one million persons. They are an especially vulnerable part of the Latino community because three-quarters of them are undocumented. Not surprisingly, then, Hondurans' rate of deportation is double that of Guatemalan Latinos and triple that of Salvadoran Latinos.[98] Moreover, the number of Honduran unaccompanied children and family units apprehended at the border has dramatically increased since 2016, nearly doubling for children migrating alone and increasing nine times over for family units.[99] Since then, 188,416 Honduran families (at least two or more related persons) left their homes to cross Mexico in order to reach the United States, an astounding number in a short time period. In 1998, an estimated 60,000 Hondurans received Temporary Protected Status (TPS) due to the devastation wrought by Hurricane Mitch, which caused 7,000 deaths in Honduras. TPS is an immigration status that allows undocumented migrants to live and work in the United States when their home countries have been hit by natural disaster or overcome by civil war. The Trump administration in 2019 ordered an end to TPS for migrants from El Salvador, Haiti, Honduras, Nepal, Nicaragua, and Sudan—which together compose 98 percent of all TPS recipients—but in late 2019 federal courts blocked the order, and the Department of Homeland Security announced it would extend TPS until January 2021.[100]

Different countries in Central America have served different U.S. agendas. Honduras was essentially a military base where the United States was either in control or largely unfettered. Guatemala, which shares a southern border with Honduras and El Salvador and a northern border with Mexico, was ill suited to serving as a base of American military operations in the region at least in part because of its proximity to Mexico.[101] (The longer history between Mexico and the United States—the American invasion, occupation of Mexico City, and Mexican surrender that included signing away half of its territory to the United States—has made Mexicans wary of appearing submissive to the United States, and there are no American military bases in Mexico.) Another factor was the size and diversity of Guatemala's Indigenous population, apart from Indo-*mestizos*. The country is divided into twenty-two regions, some of which closely mirror Indigenous groups, which speak different languages. Twenty-three Maya groups divided into four major language groups live in Guatemala, constituting at least 40 percent of the population. Very likely this is an undercount due to pressures for Indigenous people to acculturate to appear *mestizo*, with some estimating that Indigenous people actually compose 60–80 percent of the population.[102]

Yet, as was the case in Mexico, American corporations were not deterred by Guatemala's large and diverse Indigenous population. The United Fruit Company, founded in 1899 (in the 1970s it merged with another corporation to become United Brands Company and then, in 1984, Chiquita Brands International), by 1910 employed 4,000 workers on thirty banana plantations in Guatemala. The corporation controlled the railroads across Central America, which, in fact, an earlier iteration of United Fruit had built to maintain fluid transportation of its fruit to markets in the United States. United Fruit tried to avoid hiring local, Indigenous laborers. In order to build the railways, it recruited hundreds of newly freed African Americans, most of whom died from malaria and other tropical diseases.[103] The idea that Central America was an "ideal" home for resettlement of the newly freed slaves after the Emancipation Proclamation was widespread in the United States. In 1862, President Lincoln, in a meeting with African American leaders, suggested Central America was "an ideal" place for American Blacks "because of the similarity of climate with your native land."[104]

With its earlier failure with African American workers in mind, United Fruit turned instead to English-speaking Black workers from the West Indies. They soon resented the strict segregation in living, social, and work quarters between White American supervisors and Black laborers, and in 1910, six hundred Black workers sought to unionize. In response, United Fruit adopted a different strategy to stoke racial division among its workers. The company hired fewer West Indian workers than before, placing them in higher-paid, skilled positions, often as supervisors over Spanish- and Indigenous-speaking workers native to Guatemala.[105] United Fruit's White managers derided both classes of workers, routinely using racial slurs including the N-word and the word "spig" (likely a variant of spic).[106] By racially dividing its labor force, United Fruit blocked concerted worker organizing, but it also introduced greater conflict. Already high tensions between Black immigrant and native Guatemalan workers were exacerbated in 1914 when Guatemala began enforcing a new law barring cohabitation between West Indian men and *mestizas* (in the Guatemalan racial typography, they were called *ladinas*, women of Indo-Spanish descent, but the term was often applied with respect to Mayan people who assimilated to *mestizo* customs and dress).[107] Just as Panama and Honduras barred Black immigrants in order to signal both racism and resistance to corporate colonialism, the Guatemalan law reflected the new imposition of American-style racism as well as the centuries-old Spanish colonial racial hierarchy of White-over-Indigenous-and-Black racism.

In the 1920s, in another effort at American gunboat diplomacy, the USS *Niagara* docked off the Guatemalan coast, in a move designed to intimidate the Unionist Party from overthrowing the anti-labor dictator, Manuel Estrada Cabrera.[108] In Guatemala's first election later that year, however, the Unionists prevailed, electing Carlos Herrera president. But before Herrera assumed office, a U.S.-backed military coup ousted Estrada. United Fruit persuaded President Woodrow Wilson to order coup-leader General José Martí Orellana to quell mounting labor unrest. By early 1923, Orellana complied, deporting labor leaders leading the strike against United Fruit, who were Salvadoran and Honduran by nationality.[109]

For the next thirty years, Guatemala was free of American military intervention. Leftist Jacobo Árbenz rose to power in 1944, carrying out significant pro-labor and pro-peasant reforms. For example, a new Agrarian Reform Law—designed to break United Fruit's stranglehold on the nation's best land—allocated forty-two acres to each individual farmer from the unused land on banana plantations. Within two years of the law's implementation, 100,000 Indigenous families had received land and credit to begin cultivation. Indigenous and Ladino workers on banana plantations also formed twenty-five unions during this period.[110] When the corporation had exhausted its in-country tactics to rein in Árbenz, United Fruit campaigned for U.S. government intervention. First it persuaded Secretary of State John Foster Dulles, United Fruit's former attorney, and his brother, CIA Director Allen Dulles and a former member of United Fruit's board of directors, that Guatemala's democratically elected president posed a communist threat.[111] The Dulleses then went to President John D. Eisenhower, who in the first decade of the Cold War, was an easy mark. In 1954, Eisenhower ordered the CIA's overthrow of Árbenz, setting in motion a deadly Guatemalan civil war lasting thirty-five years.[112] Guatemalan police and armed forces, including some officers who had been trained by American military personnel at the School of the Americas, murdered 200,000 civilians and carried out the disappearance of another 45,000 between 1978 and 1983.[113] The Commission for Historical Clarification, a United Nations–supported truth and reconciliation body, concluded that 83 percent of those murdered were Maya; it is no overstatement to call the killings an Indigenous genocide. In her 1983 memoir *I, Rigoberta Menchú: An Indian Woman in Guatemala*, Nobel Peace Prize laureate Rigoberta Menchú Tum chronicles the atrocities of the Guatemalan military and paramilitary forces and the power of Maya survivors.[114]

In 1999, President Clinton apologized for the role played by the United States in the Guatemalan genocide.[115] Despite that unique recognition of American complicity in violence in Central America, the United States has been largely unwilling to accept Guatemalan Latinos' asylum claims. Under the 1980 Refugee Act signed into law by President Carter, the United States moved from a collective asylum law based on country of origin to one based on individual identification of refugees.[116] Under this policy, less than 2 percent of Guatemalans who requested asylum in the United States between 1983 and 1990 received it.[117] This is no surprise, since to grant widespread asylum to Maya migrants would be to acknowledge America's role in the genocide. Given that three-quarters of Guatemalan Latinos now living in the United States migrated after 1990, it is likely that the proportion granted asylum in the subsequent three decades is even lower. In short, Guatemalans, particularly those who are Maya, live in a hyper-violent society given the history of genocide and the ongoing history of sexual violence against women, such that their only option has become migrating without legal authorization to the United States.[118] This is borne out by the fact that only one in four of the 1.5 million Guatemalan Latinos has American citizenship, meaning that three in four live in the shadows, subject to exploitation by employers and everyday violence yet again.[119]

During 2018 and 2019, Trump referred to Guatemalan, Honduran, and Salvadoran migrants seeking entry to the United States as an "emergency" for the United States. He spoke of so-called "caravans" of migrants seeking to force their way into the United States without acknowledging that they traveled in large groups in order to protect themselves on the arduous and frightening journey north, especially so for children traveling alone or families traveling with children. In fiscal years 2018 and 2019, 50,656 Guatemalan children traveling alone were apprehended at the U.S. border, and a stunning 235,634 family units were apprehended.[120] Meanwhile, in the midst of this crisis, U.S. Attorney General Jeff Sessions announced that Central American migrants claiming asylum based on domestic violence or gang violence would be summarily turned away.[121] And in late 2019, Trump announced that for the entirety of 2020, only 1,500 refugees from Guatemala, Honduras, and El Salvador combined would be accepted.[122] The "emergency" is of Trump's making, exacerbating a humanitarian crisis fueled by a century of American imperialism in Central America.

The American pattern of imperialism was different in El Salvador, where a small number of wealthy families controlled coffee and sugar plantations after independence from Spain.[123] When the U.S. depression affected global markets in 1932, Indigenous peasants and labor unionists protested, and the government of Maximiliano Hernández Martínez massacred 30,000 mostly Indigenous *campesinos*.[124] The episode was a powerful lesson to Indigenous peoples, some of whom responded by feigning assimilation, speaking Spanish, migrating from rural to urban areas, and passing as *mestizos*.[125] In the three national censuses following the massacre, Indigenous persons were not even counted, suggesting just how strong the pressure was to assimilate.[126]

The first direct U.S. intervention in El Salvador occurred when the Eisenhower and Kennedy administrations, fearing another Cuba in the region, covertly supported an anti-communist coup that came to power in 1961.[127] Under the guise of foreign aid programs such as the Alliance for Progress (1961–1969), the United States built up El

Salvador's security state and promoted "economic integration" that favored American-based multinational corporations.[128] Fidel Sánchez Hernández came to power in 1972 in elections widely acknowledged as fraudulent. His repressive government generated widespread protest by students, labor groups, and a new radical wing of the Catholic Church known as "liberation theology" that preached social justice for poor people.[129] The Farabundo Martí National Liberation Front, named after one of the leaders of the 1932 rebellion so brutally crushed, was gaining momentum, prompting anti-communist hysteria in Washington.[130] The United States responded by providing $6 billion to El Salvador between 1981 and 1992 in a combination of economic aid, covert aid, and military aid.[131] In only three years in the late 1980s, El Salvador's armed forces ballooned from 15,000 to 52,000 troops, thousands of whom the U.S. military trained at the School of the Americas.[132] It was these military forces, organized into brutal death squads, that in the 1980s murdered 75,000 mostly Indigenous Salvadorans.[133] Among the martyrs of the resistance in those years was San Salvador's Archbishop Oscar Romero, assassinated in 1980, whose weekly radio sermons condemned state violence and admonished the United States to end its support for the regime.[134]

The civil war led one in six Salvadorans to flee the country, mostly to the United States.[135] Despite the government's offensive against its political opponents, less than 3 percent of Salvadoran Latinos who have sought asylum in the United States have received it.[136] Indeed, in the 1990s, Salvadoran immigrants freeing the violent civil war were portrayed as "economic migrants," much as Guatemalan and Honduran migrants seeking asylum are today.[137] Today there are as many Salvadoran Latinos as Cubans, and more than 2.3 million and 4 percent of all Latinos migrate from El Salvador. Compared to Guatemalans and Hondurans, the number of Salvadoran children traveling alone and families migrating is much smaller, judging by Border Patrol apprehension numbers.[138] Two-thirds of Salvadoran Latinos now living in the United States arrived after 1990; 30 percent of them are U.S. citizens but most remain undocumented.[139]

The Spanish Caribbean: Puerto Rico, Cuba, and the Dominican Republic

For Americans, the Spanish-American War of 1898 is most famous for Teddy Roosevelt's Rough Riders, the all-volunteer infantry that landed on Cuban shores to fight Spain as it sought to keep power over its last New World colonies. Ironically, Spain's defeat meant American colonial control over Puerto Rico, Guam, and the Philippines, while only Cuba gained independence. America's empire building in 1898 had much in common with the invasion of Mexico five decades earlier, including the prominence of Senator Albert J. Beveridge. As chairman of the Senate's committee on territories in 1902, Beveridge took pride in blocking statehood for New Mexico because its Mexican American majority spoke predominantly Spanish and had no intention of assimilating.[140] In 1898, while campaigning for the Senate, he emphasized a platform of Manifest Destiny: "We are a conquering race, and we must obey our blood and occupy new markets, and, if necessary, new lands. . . . [The result will be] the disappearance of debased civilizations and decaying races before the higher civilization of the nobler and more virile types of men."[141]

As a newly elected senator from Indiana, one of Beveridge's first official acts was to visit the Philippines, where he preached, "No self-government for peoples who have not yet learned the alphabet of liberty."[142] This quote exemplifies the notion of "tutelary colonialism" prominent in the Philippines and Puerto Rico, the idea that the natives of these new American colonies were unfit to govern themselves, thus making it necessary for the United States to rule their countries until such time as warranted.[143] In political cartoons of the day, the people of Cuba, Puerto Rico, and the Philippines "were often pictured as dark-skinned, childlike, effeminate, poor, and primitive peoples . . . standard themes from the old white racist" playbook.[144] On the surface, the objective of American colonial rule in the Philippines and Puerto Rico was the same: to "liberate" island peoples under the thumb of Spain's long colonial rule. In fact, however, the two islands' responses to American invasion could not have differed more. In the Philippines, 400,000 Filipino men, women, and children were slaughtered in the American conquest, compared to a mere 4,000 American deaths.[145] In contrast, there were few natives killed in Puerto Rico. There, a small elite controlled the island, and they fully believed Puerto Rico would be quickly incorporated as a U.S. state.[146] Prior to the outbreak of war in 1898, these elites had been negotiating with Spain for a political status that was in between independent nation and colony. Rather than force independence from Spain, as Cuba did, Puerto Rican elites favored incorporation as a distant province.[147]

The United States organized Puerto Rico and the Philippines as protectorates, quite unlike the New Mexico Territory formed forty-eight years previously. In New Mexico, the majority Mexican population controlled the territorial legislature (with the important caveat that Congress retained veto). In Puerto Rico the Americans did not create a similar representative body. Whereas the New Mexico state constitution of 1912 specified that no one was to face discrimination for speaking only Spanish or only English, the U.S. colonial governor insisted that all Puerto Rican schools provide instruction only in English. Nearly two decades after the American occupation, the U.S. governor finally allowed school instruction in Spanish, but only for the first four grades of primary school. Puerto Ricans' anger at this mandate persisted until 1948, when given the chance to decide the matter for themselves, they elected to have public K–12 school instruction exclusively in the Spanish language.[148]

Since the Foraker Act of 1917, Puerto Ricans have had the right to travel back and forth, much as if Puerto Rico were a state, with its citizens going to visit another state of the union.[149] On the other hand, if they remain on the island, they lack essential rights and privileges, including the right to vote in federal elections or to have voting representatives in Congress, even after 122 years as an American possession. Unlike the Mexican Cession and Hawaii, for example, Puerto Rico never was envisioned as a settler colony where White colonists would eventually outnumber the native, pre-colonial population. Instead, Puerto Rico, despite being so much closer to the mainland U.S. than Hawaii, remains a colony. Legal scholar Ediberto Román concludes that this is so because its "nonwhite, non-European peoples were inherently foreign—and thus inferior—and could not therefore constitute a populace prepared for . . . statehood."[150] The difference between Hawaii and Puerto Rico was twofold. Puerto Rico's people not only differed from Protestant, European stock, but they were read as Black by many Americans. Second, Puerto Rico had not been subject to corporate colonialism as had Hawaii prior to American rule. Today Puerto Rico (like Guam) remains in political limbo, neither a U.S. state or a nation independent of U.S. imperialism.[151]

In his book *Boricua Power*, José Ramón Sánchez contends that the United States treated Puerto Rico as a pool of cheap labor from the moment of its occupation in 1898. To be sure, there is ample evidence for this, but one exception was the rise of Puerto Rican cigar makers in New York City in the 1920s. By 1925, highly skilled cigar making was the largest occupational category of Puerto Ricans in the city, and also one of the best paying due to an all-unionized workforce. But by 1930, the sun had set on Puerto Rican cigar makers as they lost their jobs to mechanization. This left many in New York's 40,000-strong Puerto Rican community unemployed and increasingly channeled into low-wage, unskilled jobs.[152] Puerto Rican migration to the mainland boomed in the late 1940s, as low-wage jobs previously taken by Jews and Italian Americans became available, when those working-class groups began attending public universities in large numbers. Puerto Rico partnered with the New York Employment Service to "train" Puerto Rican women on the island in house cleaning, home nursing, cooking, and child care so that they could go to New York for jobs.[153] In the decade of the 1950s, "more Puerto Ricans moved to the U.S. mainland than did immigrants from any other country."[154]

Puerto Rico's proximity to the continental United States and the fact that its people faced no immigration hurdles fed the exploitation of

Puerto Rican workers on both the island and the mainland. The great Puerto Rican migration of World War II is illustrative of both dynamics.[155] Between 1940 and 1950, the mainland Puerto Rican population tripled to 225,000, and then, between 1950 and 1960, more than tripled again to 892,000 (these are conservative estimates from the census, which likely undercounted Puerto Rican migrants new to the mainland). But this migration did not happen on its own. One rationale of the Americans dictated that the island's agricultural, rural population was backward and needed "improvement." But another, evident over time, was that Puerto Rico's large class of subsistence farmers was pushed off the land, into cities, while the island's rich agricultural tradition became increasingly dominated by corporate farming. In 1940, 45 percent of the island's workers were employed in the agricultural sector, but, by 1970, that proportion had declined to 10 percent.

Two different work programs facilitated this transformation, along with the migration of Puerto Ricans to the U.S. mainland. *Operación Manos a la Obra*—translated literally as "Put Your Hands to Work" but more commonly known in English as Operation Bootstrap—started in 1947 with the goal of funneling workers from the island into manufacturing jobs in the northeast and midwest. A year later, Puerto Rico started the Farm Labor Program, which over decades placed nearly half a million Puerto Ricans in temporary agricultural jobs on the mainland.[156] As with Mexican *braceros* (which was a model for the Puerto Rican farmworker program), these programs functioned as state-run labor contractors, screening candidates, arranging their transportation by plane (which they were obligated to pay for out of their future earnings), and even inspecting employer housing for workers.[157] In this way, these programs functioned as a way to streamline the exploitation of an ever-available, but easily fired, non-unionized workforce from the colonies.

Puerto Rican farmworkers had migrated away from the island as early as 1900, just two years after the American occupation, when five thousand of them became contract laborers on Hawaiian sugar plantations.[158] In 1960, after the Farm Labor Program had been operating for twelve years, Puerto Rican workers earned an hourly wage of 80 cents to $1.[159] The program likely appealed to workers because of the massive displacement of subsistence farmers that produced poverty and malnutrition insecurity in large families, but it may also have attracted those who wanted to migrate to the mainland permanently or at least for longer than a migrant farmworker's tenure. Since Puerto Ricans were free to remain on the mainland without restrictions on citizenship, the Farm Labor Program was an important vehicle for the post-war Puerto Rican settlement; between 1963 and 1987, the largest number of workers went to New Jersey and Connecticut, which large numbers of Puerto Ricans still call home.[160] Operation Bootstrap likewise provided the transition to life on the mainland. Its stated goal was to convert Puerto Ricans from subsistence family farmers (where there were, the rationale went, incentives for large families) to urban, industrialized workers. The plan did, in fact, lead people to migrate from rural towns to urban areas of Puerto Rico, but once they arrived to the island's cities, there was an extreme shortage of jobs, creating urban poverty and migration to the mainland, often via the Farm Labor Program or Operation Bootstrap's manufacturing jobs program, whether in factories on the island or, more commonly, on the mainland.

"Operation Bootstrap was never equipped to create the number of jobs necessary to gainfully employ the mass of Puerto Rican workers (largely coming from agriculture) without significant reductions in the population or the labor force," according to Edna Acosta-Belén and Carlos E. Santiago.[161] Instead, Operation Bootstrap operated as corporate welfare of three types. First, the program provided incentives to mainland corporations to move to the island, at the expense of Puerto Rican workers and taxpayers. These included tax breaks for relocating a factory and a minimum wage deliberately set below the mainland's; even today, the island is still recovering from these features of the post-war economy. The second form of corporate welfare was providing a low-wage, exploitable workforce to mainland employers (likely disrupting

unionized workforces), which was facilitated by government middle-
men whose role was to find and screen workers. Finally, in some cases,
mainland factories received experienced workers who had been trained
in factory jobs on the island, and, thus, who arrived at mainland manufacturing jobs acclimated to wage labor (unlike when they first left the
family farm).

Operation Bootstrap, like the agricultural workers program, laid
the foundation for the massive migration of workers to New York City,
Camden, New Jersey, and Chicago, among other cities. A new arm of
the government, formed in 1947, facilitated workers' transition to the
mainland: the Puerto Rican Bureau of Employment and Migration (later named the Migrant Division of the Department of Labor).[162] It was a
boon to corporations to have a government agency coordinating employment, social services, and acculturation.[163] Indeed, mainland employers depended on the labor department to screen candidates for health
and literacy, with two-thirds of them weeded out.[164] It is possible those
rejected from Operation Bootstrap were funneled to the Farm Labor
Program which had less demanding standards. In the end, programs
like these and others could not protect Latino workers from the vicissitudes of low-wage, insecure employment in the United States, whether
being laid off, subjected to discrimination based on race, national origin,
or language, or downgraded to low-wage manufacturing or service jobs
when the manufacturing jobs for which they had been recruited slipped
away in the 1970s.[165]

Of all Latinos, Puerto Ricans sit in arguably the most ambiguous
position, a direct result of 122 years of colonial status. Puerto Rico provides the base of operations for extensive American military pursuits
including the Southern Command headquarters, is home to corporations that exploit human capital and natural resources, and serves as a
magnet for well-off Americans to play tourist in an "exotic" island close
to home. Since the U.S. occupation began, American colonial governors
have been preoccupied with making Puerto Ricans more enterprising,
even when that turned out to mean, in the context of Operation Boot-

strap and the Farm Labor Program, exploitation as workers in mainland jobs deemed "good for them."[166] The result has been what Puerto Rican sociologist Jorge Duany calls "the Puerto Rican diaspora as a transnational colonial migration" filled with ambiguity: "I define Puerto Rico as a nation, an imagined community with its own territory, history, language, and culture. At the same time, the island lacks a sovereign state, an independent government that represents the population . . . "[167] Perhaps no time since the early years of the American occupation have put into such sharp relief Puerto Rico's colonial subjecthood than recent years, when Hurricane Maria's devastation showed the utter disregard of the federal government and when, because it is not a sovereign (either as a nation or a U.S. state), Congress refused to allow a bankruptcy filing and instead mandated that a U.S.-imposed body decide the island's economic future.[168]

Cuba is only ninety miles from the Florida coast, much closer than Puerto Rico, and was a natural object of colonial desire early in United States history. As early as 1854, Southern expansionists petitioned President Pierce to purchase Cuba from Spain and declare war in the event Spain refused.[169] Spain demurred, and the military option was deferred, at least in part because Pierce feared "another Haiti"—a Black-led rebellion.[170] Americans viewed Cuba in military and economic terms: its sugar industry added value, and Guantanamo Bay became the country's first overseas military base.[171] By 1860, Bostonian Elisha Atkins controlled much of Cuba's sugar production, influencing the course of American intervention to come. Letters to his wife written two years before the Spanish-American War blamed labor unrest on his plantations on "a few negroes supposed to have come from Haiti or Santo Domingo."[172]

In contrast to Puerto Rican elites' warm reception, Cubans had been in a sustained war for independence from Spain when the United States intervened to support them. The strategy had included the abolition of slavery, and, as a result, many of the independence fighters were only a generation or two removed from Africa. In 1899, Atkins, the sugar plantation tycoon, predicted that the "United States withdrawal [from Cuba] would allow 'unscrupulous politicians and ignorant black Cubans' to take control," and, he implied, seize his sugar empire.[173] Washington did not need much persuading: the first colonial governor, General Leonard Wood, actively opposed allowing Blacks to vote; Cubans rebuffed him and in their constitution of 1901 established universal male suffrage without regard to color. The formal American occupation of Cuba was intended to be short-lived, given the strong opposition from the multiracial independence movement. In one of his final acts as governor, General Wood opened Cuba's "public lands" to American investors; the United Fruit Company acquired vast tracts of land in northeastern Cuba.[174] In the 1902 addendum to Cuba's constitution, known as the Platt Amendment, the U. S. retained the power to invade Cuba when it deemed U.S. economic interests threatened.[175]

The U.S. Navy invaded twice early in the twentieth century. In 1903, the United States established a military base at Guantanamo Bay. The base, shortened to GTMO by the Americans, was a strategic post during World War II, when 7,200 American military personnel were posted there (along with another 13,000 Cuban and Jamaican civilian employees).[176] Later the United States cultivated Cuban president Fulgencio Batista, who closely aligned himself with American corporations. With Fidel Castro's communist revolution in 1959, Eisenhower instituted a "temporary" trade embargo that remains in place six decades later. There is little doubt that it pushed Castro toward alliances with the Soviet Union and, later, the People's Republic of China. Cuban opposition to GTMO has only grown since the attacks of September 11, 2001, when President George W. Bush began imprisoning war-on-terror suspects there.[177] Since 2002, 779 men have been imprisoned by the United States at GTMO in order to maximize CIA and military flexibility. As of late 2019, 40 men remained detained.

Dominicans are a growing portion of the Latino population, now at more than 2 million or 3.5 percent of all Latinos. For both Dominicans and Cubans, fully one-eighth of their worldwide population lives in the United States. [178] Not surprisingly, given their ability to freely migrate between the island and the mainland, unlike all other Latino migrants, many more Puerto Ricans live on the mainland (5.6 million) than on Puerto Rico itself (3.7 million).[179] Latinos from each of these three island countries date primarily to the mid-twentieth century, although there were smaller numbers of Puerto Rican and Cuban migrants in the United States before then.[180]

Whereas for Cubans, the United States has welcomed those fleeing the socialist regime, in the Dominican Republic, the United States collaborated closely with the government to limit migration. For three decades (1930–1961), the United States backed the Dominican Republic's repressive, right-wing dictator Rafael Trujillo, such that it was in neither country's interest to allow migration as a form of protesting with one's feet. During that three-decade period, fewer than 20,000 Dominicans came to the United States.[181] Indeed, the first wave of Dominican migrants came when Trujillo was assassinated in 1961. They were affiliated with his regime as members of the ruling class; more than 84,000 migrated in the 1960s.[182] Since the 1970s, Dominican migration has been primarily economic, with, for example, around 300,000 authorized migrants per decade in the 1990s and 2000s, with others entering without authorization via Puerto Rico or otherwise.[183]

As early as 1841, well before ventures into nearby Cuba and Puerto Rico, U.S. presidents considered annexing the Dominican Republic.[184] The Dominican Republic of course shares the island of Hispaniola with Haiti, along with a long history of animosity. The two countries were subject to different colonial powers, with different languages and colonial structures. After Haitian independence, Haiti occupied the Dominican Republic for two decades, from 1822 to 1844.[185] Multiple presidents sent envoys to assess the Dominican Republic's racial fitness, including Navy Commander David Dixon Porter in the late 1840s. He emphasized Dominicans' racial superiority to Haitians: "One was white, Spanish and Catholic; the other was black, French, and irreligious. One was 'civilized' because it courted the United States and Americans; the other was 'barbaric' because it jealously defended its political and economic sovereignty."[186] The most serious nineteenth-century American attempt to colonize the Dominican Republic was in 1869 by President Ulysses S. Grant. The Senate rejected his plan to collectively naturalize Dominican citizens, as it had Mexicans living in the Mexican Cession. As with Lincoln's earlier idea to relocate Blacks to Central America, Grant envisioned African American settlement of Santo Domingo. Missouri Senator Carl Schurz spoke for many when, arguing against Grant's plan, he railed against Santo Domingo's "Latin race mixed with Indian and African blood . . . [who have] neither language nor traditions nor habits nor political institutions nor morals in common with us."[187]

In the end, the United States invaded both Haiti and the Dominican Republic, in 1915 and 1916, respectively. U.S. Marines occupied the Dominican Republic for eight years, but they stayed twice as long, until 1934, in Haiti.[188] An enduring perception of racial superiority over Haiti in the Dominican Republic has been propagated for centuries, including by the Trujillo regime in the nation's myths and museums.[189] According to both elite and popular views, Dominicans have far less African ancestry than Haitians, as well as Spanish and Indigenous ancestry not possessed by Haitians. In this racist narrative, it is commonplace for dark-skinned Dominicans to refer to themselves and those with their complexion as *Indio* (Indian in Spanish), although more as an anti-African designation than one of Indigenous ancestry.[190] When Trujillo objected to the U.S. Marines' departure from Haiti, he justified it by claiming impoverished Haitians would invade the Dominican Republic. In 1937, Trujillo ordered the army to kill 15,000 Haitian peasants who had set up makeshift camps along the Dominican border.[191] Trujillo appealed to American racism to justify the massacre, saying he did it to "preserve our racial superiority over them."[192] President Roosevelt turned a blind eye to the brutality.

Colonialism and Immigration as Part of the Same Continuum

Nearly a century ago, Franklin D. Roosevelt (FDR) sought to placate growing anti-American sentiment across Latin America by proclaiming his Good Neighbor Policy. In point of fact, 1933 did not make the United States a welcome neighbor so much as it marked a new modality of colonialism. Instead of warships and Marines, U.S. domination took the form of American military training for death squads and paramilitary national police with the consent of dictators covertly installed (and sometimes later removed) by the CIA, all with the purpose of fighting communism. Since the end of the Cold War, the United States has shifted its justification for interference in Latin America to the war on drugs. Since the 1970s, and especially over the past three decades, the United States government has spent more than $1 trillion in Latin America on drug interdiction and the war on drugs in general (the largest expenditures have been in Colombia and Mexico).[193] On an annual basis, Latin America now receives more U.S. aid to combat drugs than the region received "in any given year during the Cold War to combat communism."[194]

Today and for the past several decades, America has reaped what it sowed. We should not be surprised that the results have been the migration north of people escaping poverty and state violence. Thus, it should also surprise no one that where Latinos fit in the American racial hierarchy has been overdetermined by at least 125 years of Latino migrants as an easily available, expendable low-wage workforce for American factories, farms, and other corporations. The history of American empire in the Western Hemisphere is powerful evidence that we ought to think of migrants from Latin American countries as the byproduct of colonialism. In his study of Central America, sociologist William Robinson has coined the phrase "trans-national economic colonialism" to describe the movement of capital and people between the United States and its poorer neighbors to the south.[195]

In the case of the five Central American nations where the United States has been the most recently active in supporting brutal military dictatorships, it is especially compelling to treat migrants from these countries as rightfully in the United States, such as by collective grant of refugee status. Indeed, the United Nations in 1981 declared that all Salvadorans who left their country should be considered "bona fide

refugees" and in 1984 the UN argued that Central Americans fleeing their countries were refugees under its definition: "persons who
have fled their country because their lives, safety, or liberty have been
threatened by a generalized violence, foreign aggression, internal conflicts, massive violations of human rights, or other circumstances that
have seriously disturbed public order."[196] The United States defines
refugees much more narrowly, emphasizing that each individual must
make a claim of individualized threat to their life if they remain in
their country. Instead of allowing migrants who make a credible claim
of asylum, in 2019 the Departments of Justice and Homeland Security
stepped up pressure on Mexico, El Salvador, Guatemala, and Honduras to prevent refugees from reaching the U.S.-Mexico border.[197] For
Latino immigrants more generally, the concept of an "open border"
makes sense as reparations for direct and indirect American imperialism in the region.

Unlike the British, Americans rarely think of themselves as colonizers. Following World War II, a weakened Britain seeking to maintain control over its forty-seven colonial territories enacted the British
Nationality Act. Among other rights, it allowed for "an unqualified
right to enter and remain in the United Kingdom."[198] The purpose of the
law was to maintain close ties with its White settler colonies (Australia,
Canada, New Zealand), but its effect was to open the door to people of
color from the West Indies and its colonies and former colonies in South
Asia, Hong Kong, and Africa. Between 1948 and 1962, 500,000 people
of color migrated from the colonies to Britain proper. Another million
people of color migrated over the next decade. Though they made up
only 2.4 percent of the population in England, their visible presence
was enough to prompt a change in policy that restricted immigration
from the British Commonwealth. In 1981, the British Nationality Act
changed the law to, effectively a "Whites-only" policy by limiting legal
immigration to persons who possessed at least one Britain-born parent
or grandparent.[199]

For most of its history, the United States has sought to have it both ways, implementing border restrictions but allowing immigrants from Latin America to enter without authorization in order to fulfill critical roles in the labor market. More severe border restrictions and tighter immigration policies have counter-intuitively resulted in a steady stream of migrants from former colonies or *de facto* colonies in Latin America. It is these migrants who, for more than a century, have settled in the United States, becoming Latinos. Today especially, the 20 percent of Latinos who were not born in the United States live precarious lives, vulnerable to exploitation at work in mostly low-wage, low-skill jobs and fearing ICE raids that could result in deportation and separation from their American-citizen spouses, partners, or children. Significantly, it is not only the 11.5 million undocumented Latinos who live in fear, since Latino families and communities rarely live, marry, work, and worship in only-"legal" or only-"illegal" spaces.

America is at a fork in the road, ready to choose the later U.K. or earlier U.K. model: will we choose the politics of fear, with its accompanying brutality at the border, or the politics of accountability, with its accompanying inclusion of migrants? Modeling a policy on the period of British openness to migration from its colonies and former colonies, the United States should embrace entry, a legal right to work, and a path to American citizenship for Latino immigrants currently in the country without legal authorization. Such a policy would acknowledge American colonialism as well as constitute a form of reparations for historic wrongs: two centuries of economic and military exploitation in Mexico, the Spanish Caribbean, and Central America and the harms of ongoing U.S. intervention. By targeting undocumented migrants already residing here, the proposal would benefit those most vulnerable to exploitation by employers who prey on them. Moreover, future migrants would likewise receive the benefit of the right to live and work in the United States under certain conditions. For example, if someone desiring to migrate could show proof of hardship linked to U.S. government actions in their country—including economic displacement caused by NAFTA, which disproportionately negatively impacted Indigenous Mexicans, or U.S.

training of police and death squads in Honduras, Guatemala, and El Salvador—they would be allowed the opportunity to live and work in this country. Undocumented migrants already residing in the United States would not have to offer such proof to receive benefits.

Other scholars have proposed granting class-wide immigration and/or naturalization to Latin American migrants, although none has done so on such an expansive level. An analysis of the 2014 migration "surge" from Guatemala, Honduras, and El Salvador argued that the United States has a moral obligation to allow entry to migrants from those countries because it selfishly pursued its own interests in the region, contributing to devastating conditions that caused the migration.[200] Taking a broader view, however, brings into sharp relief the patterns of American empire across time and across space—with Mexico, the Caribbean, and Central America as distinct regions where the footprint of U.S. imperialism looms large. In the past, U.S. immigration policy has not generally been designed to redress the wrongs of its colonial exploits, but there are examples of country-specific and category-specific immigration policies. For instance, international law recognizes the rights of refugees, those who leave their country because they fear "persecution, conflict, generalized violence, or other circumstances that have seriously disturbed public order."[201] However, this interpretation under U.S. law has been narrowed since the late 1970s, and increasingly so under the Trump administration.[202]

During the Cold War, the United States earmarked refugees from anti-communist countries for streamlined admission to the country and special resettlement benefits without the need to prove individual persecution or fear of persecution, including those fleeing Cuba, South Vietnam, Nicaragua, and the Soviet Union. At other times, Congress has passed laws providing class-wide refugee status to the abandoned children of U.S. service members in Southeast Asia. More recently, certain categories of Afghani and Iraqi nationals who assisted the military as interpreters have been granted entry as refugees.[203] The advantage of this type of class-based remedy is its efficiency, helping more people more quickly at a time when immigration courts face a backlog of 869,000 cases.[204] A group approach would also raise consciousness about America's role in the existence of Latinos as a racially oppressed group by challenging the notion that Latinos came as voluntary immigrants. And because the lives of Latino immigrants are intertwined with those of native-born Latinos, these reparations would positively affect large numbers of all Latinos.

2

IDEALIZED MESTIZAJE AND ANTI-BLACK AND ANTI-INDIAN RACISM

In other Latin American nations, indigenous communities exist in the here and now, and American Indians are physically present, confronting and challenging indigenist myths. In the Dominican Republic, the "Indians" exist only [in museums] in one-dimensional photographs and three-dimensional glass-cased dioramas and cannot challenge the indigenist myth making of Dominicans. Also, the photographs solve a practical museological problem: how to display a heterogeneous and nearly extinct people as a homogenous and living community. The Museo del Hombre Dominicano thus reifies the mythical Dominican *Indio*.

> —*Ginetta E.B. Candelario,* Black behind the Ears:
> Dominican Racial Identity from Museums
> to Beauty Shops[1]

In the last chapter, we saw how American imperialism resulted in the exporting of white supremacy to Mexico, Central America, and the Spanish Caribbean. Despite the different forms American colonialism took in those places, the result was uniformly the displacement of peasants and workers in those countries, such that migration to the United States was preordained. Once here, most first- and second-generation Latinos (that is, immigrants and the children of immigrants from Latin America) have toiled in the lowest-paying, least-skilled jobs in the agriculture, construction, service, and manufacturing sectors. Those who are here without legal authorization, in the past and today, remain especially vulnerable to exploitation, whether in the formal or informal economy. We now turn to examining racism toward and racialization of Latinos, but we must do so by seeking to understand the legacy of four layers of white supremacy, some of them overlapping in time: under Spanish colonial rule in Latin America; after independence from Spain; under American colonial rule in Latin America (in its various forms as described previously); and in terms of racialization in the United States.

Somos Dominicanos, Somos Indios[2]

Museums are more than repositories of culture to be consumed as leisure on weekends. They play a role in constructing national myths of peoplehood, and some of their most important audiences are children on field trips, who are there to internalize those very myths and reproduce them over a lifetime. Sociologist Ginetta Candelario situates contemporary racial attitudes among Dominican Latinos and those in the Dominican Republic as powerfully molded by state institutions like the Museo del Hombre Dominicano in Santo Domingo as well as via everyday social interactions in places like beauty shops.[3]

Within a quarter-century of Christopher Columbus's "discovery" of the Dominican Republic in 1492, Spanish soldiers and priests decimated the island's Indigenous people, the Taíno, by terrorizing them or forcing them into hard labor. In that genocide, 390,000 Taíno died, with only 9,000 surviving beyond the 1520s.[4] Santo Domingo, the capital then and now, was home to one of the most influential Spanish colonial apologists—Father Bartolomé de Las Casas, known to the Spaniards as "the Protector of the Indians." Las Casas believed Indians, unlike Africans, possessed souls and thus were capable of baptism. His principles were adopted by King Carlos of Spain in 1542 (revised in 1552) to govern the treatment of Indigenous peoples in Spain's New World colonies as Las Leyes de las Indias (Laws of the Indies).[5] The idea that Indians had souls was the justification for ending the most brutal forms of labor exploitation but also led to the widespread importation of African slaves to Spain's colonies.

The Dominican Republic is an apt place to begin our discussion of anti-Black and anti-Indian racism because in 1501 it was the first port where African slaves arrived in the Americas; it was also the location of the first slave revolt in the Americas in 1522.[6] Between 1503 and 1801, when slavery was abolished, the Spanish imported tens of thousands of African slaves into the Dominican Republic. They toiled initially in gold mines and, later, on sugar plantations and cattle ranches, with some sent on to enslavement in European colonies elsewhere in North, Central, and South America.[7]

Racial ideology in the Dominican Republic has been anchored by the notion that Dominicans are racially superior to their Haitian neighbors. The two countries share the island of Hispaniola in the Greater Antilles, located eighty miles west of Puerto Rico and the region's second largest island after Cuba. They likewise share more than five hundred years of a deeply intertwined history, including as colonies of different European powers and of the United States. In 1804 French-colonized Haiti became the first Black republic after a decade-long slave revolt, yet the world's only two republics at the time, the United States and France, refused to recognize the young republic. France finally did so after extracting a huge indemnification payment in order to compensate those French who "lost" their investment in slaves—a payment that accounts for Haiti's extreme poverty to this day. Despite having a population one-third the size of the Dominican Republic's, Haiti controlled the Dominican Republic for two decades (1822–1844) under the banner of "Unified Haiti."[8]

It was nearing the end of this period that American presidents first coveted the Dominican Republic as a colony, before Texas statehood and the Mexican Cession and half a century prior to the Spanish-American War. Going back as far as the Haitian revolution, and fueled by resentment over the Haitian occupation, Dominicans cultivated an anti-Haitian national identity that was rooted in the racist idea that Dominicans are "*los blancos de la tierra*" (the Whites of the island). When emissaries of the U.S. government visited the island in the early 1840s, Dominicans' obsession with distinguishing themselves from Haitians grew even stronger. For example, a representative of the American secretary of state was persuaded by the Dominicans that *mulatos*' presence in the Dominican Republic stemmed entirely from Black Haitian men raping "Indio" women during the Haitian occupation.[9]

With the U.S.-Mexico War, the Civil War, and the Spanish-American War, American military and other resources were stretched too far to pursue designs on the Dominican Republic until seventy-five years later. In 1915 and 1916 the Americans returned with force to the island of Hispaniola: the U.S. Marines occupied Haiti and the Dominican Republic. They trained a young Rafael Trujillo Molina, who at age thirty, when the Marines withdrew, became commander of the Dominican army.[10] Trujillo claimed power over the Dominican Republic in 1930 and ruled until his assassination in 1961. He went down in history as one of Latin America's most brutal dictators, ruthlessly pursuing power in his own country and in Haiti. The U.S. Marines stayed in Haiti for two decades, but Trujillo wanted them to remain longer, having warned the Americans he would take matters into his own hands when American forces withdrew. In 1937, Trujillo ordered the massacre of 17,000 Haitian children, men, and women who lived in a makeshift community along the Dominican Republic's northwestern border with Haiti.[11]

Having terrified his Haitian neighbors, Trujillo set out to drive out all Haitians from the Dominican Republic. One tool was a national identification card, which became mandatory in 1947 as a way to distinguish Dominicans from Haitian migrants.[12] Trujillo, who was light-skinned and Spanish in appearance, promoted the idea of Dominican peoplehood as "Indios." He first funded the Museo del Hombre in the early 1930s as a nation-building project, even though the museum's doors did not open until 1970.[13] Candelario traces the museum's purpose as a vehicle to promote Dominican national identity as a contrast to Haiti's identity as a Black nation.

A crucial aspect of this script is favoring the term "Indio" to describe one's self culturally and racially. Unlike the straightforward Spanish translation as Indian, in the Dominican context, to say one is *indio* is to effectively say "I am not Black." Indio thus refers, more generally, to racially mixed, which is to say, *mestizo* as Indigenous/Spanish ancestry or *mulato* as African/Spanish ancestry. Combining skin color and other physical features such as the texture and color of hair, which Candelario posits is "at the root of race," Indios in the Dominican Republic span the spectrum from White to Black, with the "overarching tendency . . . to 'blacken the white category' and 'whiten the black category'" in service of an expansive middle.[14] At the White end of the range are terms like *rubio*, *blanco*, *pelirrojo* and *blanco jipato*, and, at the Black end, terms like *moreno*, *mulato*, *prieto*, *negro*, *cenizo* and *cocolo*. There are even more terms for the three *mestizo* categories: "White-mulatto range" as *blanco jojoto*, *indio lavado*, *indio claro*, *trigueño claro*, and *trigueño*; "mulatto" as *pinto*, *pinto jovero*, *jabao and indio canelo*; and "mulatto-black range" as *trigueño oscuro* and *indio quemao*.[15] Candelario analyzes the centrality of "*indio*" terminology in the three categories of *mestizo/mulato* groupings as "a rejection of, and replacement for, black categories," and she concludes that the embrace of "*indio*" identity is a simultaneous "disavowal of Dominican affinities with both Haiti [as Black] and Spain [as White]."[16] In this way, Dominicans who identify as "*indio*" are choosing something in-between Black and White at the poles.

For the museum, the problem was "how to display a heterogeneous and nearly extinct people as a homogenous and living community . . . [how to portray] the mythical Dominican *Indio*."[17] As in Cuba and Puerto Rico (and unlike in Mexico, Central America, and South America), scholars of the Dominican Republic agree that any Indigenous ancestors who survived Spanish colonization were long ago socially and ancestrally assimilated into the larger, mostly African-descended population.[18] Without a "real" Indigenous population, given Spanish genocide, and given the massive African slavery on the island for three hundred years, the museum chose to feature black and white photographs of mid-twentieth-century Indigenous people in the Venezuelan jungle—people with very dark skin and jet-black, straight hair.[19] On the one hand, this photographic display only works because no one in the Dominican Republic has Indigenous features or phenotype. On the other hand, it requires an erasure of Dominicans' African history, which, in contrast, can be seen phenotypically in the population. Candelario points to ample archeological evidence of early African life, findings resulting from research funded by the museum itself, but such evidence

is deliberately excluded from the museum.[20] Instead, the original museum opened without any exhibits connected to the nation's African history. Only in the early 1980s did the museum make space for the African
presence in Dominican peoplehood, and only then in what Candelario
terms "a limited account of slavery," occupying about one-third of one
of three floors of exhibition space.[21] Without providing details, Candelario notes that even this limited exhibit of the African presence in
Dominican history came about only because of increasing consciousness
and political activism of Afro-Dominicans, who, like Blacks worldwide,
were influenced by the pan-African independence movements and Third
World movements generally.[22]

In response to these demands, the museum added a visual representation of the nation's "ethno-racial trilogy" at its entrance in the form
of three statues of men in Dominican history: in the center is De Las
Casas, the Spanish priest, dressed in a cassock and holding a cross in his
right hand, and slightly behind to either side of him, showing their relative inferiority, are partially clothed representatives of the African and
Indigenous strands of Dominican peoplehood.[23] To the viewer's right,
a Taíno leader named only Enriquillo stands, wearing a loincloth and
holding an upright spear in his right hand, a symbol of his resistance to
the Spaniards in the early decades of the sixteenth century (although
he later acquiesced to Spanish rule). On the other side stands Sebas-
tián Lemba, shirtless to display his muscular arms raised up in clenched
fists. Lemba was an escaped African slave who for two decades com-
manded an army of four hundred former slaves from a thriving maroon
settlement where he lived until his death in 1547. It is fascinating that,
while the nation's Spanish colonizers are honored (albeit in the form of
a priest—no less one known as "the Protector of the Indians"—rather
than a *conquistador*), so too are Indigenous and African men who vio-
lently resisted Spanish oppression. Women are as invisible in the museum exhibits as they are in its name (translated as the Museum of the
Dominican Man). This is all the more ironic given the promotion of
idealized racial mixture, expressed as Indio and its variants, which itself
results from women's biological reproduction.[24]

On the ground, Afro-Dominicans continue to challenge the dominant racial ideology. For example, they protested a convention of Latin American census officials in Santiago, Chile, in early 2010, demanding the Dominican national census include a question about race. Such a question was last included on the 1960 census; it was likely removed by the Trujillo regime bent on denying the centrality of blackness in the nation. Despite calls to do so, Francisco Cáceres Ureña, the director of the Dominican census, who describes himself as Afro-Dominican, rejected the inclusion of a race question on the 2010 census. He offered three reasons: first, "we are black," explaining that Afro-Dominicans are not a minority population; second, he pointed to anti-Haitian discrimination as a reason that, despite accepting that they are Black, few Dominicans would identify as such in the census context; and that would mean, finally, that the census results would thus produce a false portrait of the nation as White.[25]

Double Colonization and the Racial Positioning of Latinos

The Dominican case reveals, in the context of a single national example, dynamics that characterize post-colonial Latin American nations more generally. While the particular stories vary, the emphasis on *mestizaje*—the racial mixture across Spanish, Indigenous, and African ancestors—is typical. For example, research on Puerto Ricans' racial identity suggests they too downplay their African roots, instead choosing to play up their Spanish and Indigenous ancestry.[26] A similar dynamic played out in territorial New Mexico (1850–1912), where Latinos ignored substantial Indigenous ancestry in favor of accentuating more distant Spanish ancestry.[27] In promoting *mestizaje* as national ideology, Latin American countries likewise promote anti-Indigenous and anti-Black racism. In short, in every colony founded upon Indigenous dispossession and the transatlantic slave trade (including the United States), rulers must wipe away these histories from the memories and, if possible, the bodies of those to be included in the nation. What is perhaps less clear-cut is that

American imperialism, layered on top of Spain's colonialism, has also laid the foundation for these dynamics. Both the Spanish and American colonial regimes imposed a system of status inequality anchored by white supremacy, yet they differed in important ways.

Spanish colonizers encountered an estimated 80 million Indigenous people across Latin America between 1492 and 1600; after their genocide, forced labor, and importation of diseases such as smallpox, only 10 million survived. Many Indigenous communities resisted the Spanish Crown, resulting in a shortage of labor for the colonial enterprises of extracting resources such as gold and silver, producing commodities such as sugar and coffee, building colonial cities, and serving the sexual, domestic, and other desires of those Spanish sent to administer and exploit the colonies. As in the Dominican Republic, the Spanish Crown turned to the importation of African slaves over three centuries, forcing at least 11 million Africans into their colonies in the Americas.[28]

Spanish colonizers had to manage these racial lines closely, making true in secular and religious law what was not so on the ground. The dilemma for the Spanish racial order was the social-sexual interaction among those three groups—colonizers, natives, and slaves. New Spain (later Mexico) was exemplary: the 1646 census showed equal numbers of Blacks and Spaniards (the latter were, in reality, *criollos*, those of Spanish descent born in the colonies), along with ten times as many Indigenous peoples and Indo-*mestizos*.[29] Consider that, after 250 years of Spanish rule, Mexico's population included more than 250,000 free Afro-*mestizos*, or racially mixed persons with African, Indigenous, and Spanish descent.[30] In order to manage such racial mixture yet still maintain white supremacy, the Spanish colonies were characterized by an elaborate *régimen de castas* (caste regime) that catalogued the various ancestry combinations of Indian, Black, and Spanish people, according to phenotypical characteristics, including skin color, hair texture, and facial structure. In Spanish colonial society, these visible differences in a population that was rapidly mixing became indices of social status and racial superiority/inferiority.[31] The multiplication of racial types made it impossible to maintain racial apartheid. Instead, the Catholic Church acquiesced to inter-racial, inter-caste marriage and baptism.

Over time, and across Latin America, these practices facilitated *blanqueamiento* (literally, whitening or bleaching), by which lighter skin, wealth via land ownership or inheritance, and other attributes of social mobility "whitened" otherwise disadvantaged *mestizos* and *mulatos*.[32] At the individual level, this system of whitening incentivized mating "up" in terms of color and other phenotypical markers of Indigenous and, especially, Black ancestry. As legal scholar Tanya Katerí Hernández concludes: "At the individual level *blanqueamiento* revolves around the desire for a white appearance and the ambition of having children who are lighter in appearance through the vehicle of interracial intimacy."[33] Whitening required legal flexibility. *Mestizaje* operated as a way of controlling access to whiteness. In this way, the Spanish colonial system of white supremacy operated differently than did Anglo-American white supremacy, which legally banned race mixture as "miscegenation" and ensured children of White slave masters born to their enslaved mothers would inherit her legal status as slave and as Black.[34] Spain's system worked in part because its colonies operated under a comparatively liberal law of manumission—the law governing how slaves gain their freedom.[35]

Yet it is *blanqueamiento* at the level of state policy that interests me most. While Spanish colonizers set in play these racial maneuvers, post-colonial or anti-colonial Latin American states continued to rely on them. Once they achieved independence from Spain, most Latin American countries enshrined formal equality for citizens without regard to race. In terms of dealing day to day, however, with a racially diverse population of *mestizos, mulatos*, Whites, Blacks, and Indigenous people (some of the last group remained geographically isolated and entirely independent of these proto-nations), formal equality did not mean much. Most newly independent Latin American nations institutionalized *blanqueamiento* as government policy.[36] For example, as we have seen, the Atlantic rim countries of Mexico, Guatemala, Honduras,

Nicaragua, Cuba, and Panama implemented immigration bans on Black and/or Chinese immigrants in response to labor tensions with West Indian workers at American-owned corporations.[37] Latin American nations also worked mightily to recruit European immigrants in order to whiten the nation: Chile provided homesteads to European immigrants and Cuba recruited one million Spaniards the same way.[38]

Even with company like that, Argentina was an outlier. More blatantly than any other Latin American nation, it made recruiting European immigrants a strategy for "racial improvement," attracting one million European immigrants in the last two decades of the 1800s. At the same time, Argentina worked to disappear what it perceived as inferior Asian and Black communities in the nation, for example by lumping them together under a category labeled "other races" rather than specifying them in national censuses between 1895 and 1912. Meanwhile, in those same censuses, it listed separately especially desirable European national origin groups as "races," including "German," "Anglo-Saxon," "Slavic," and "Scandinavian." The 1912 census noted favorably that, for these four racial categories, men outnumbered women two to one, making it likely that these men would pair up with native Argentine women to produce whiter children and thus a whiter nation.[39]

At the same time, there were important differences across Spain's colonies. Consider California del Norte, which became the U.S. state of California in 1850. It had a large and diverse Indigenous population of 300,000 prior to the heights of Spanish colonization from 1769 to 1823.[40] By 1830, after Mexican independence from Spain, due largely to disease, that number was reduced to 150,000. Yet in the first quarter-century of American rule, 1850–1875, after what historian Benjamin Madley rightly calls "an American genocide," the population of Indians in the state of California was decimated, reduced to only 30,000 people.[41] Thus, under American rule, genocide served as a policy to make the region White and thereby enhance its fit with the rest of the United States. In Spanish colonial Guatemala, as in Spanish and Mexican California, the economics of labor did not justify the cost of importing African slaves, so the Spanish forced Maya and other Indigenous people to work.[42] A middle group between Indians and Spaniards emerged, called *ladinos* (instead of *mestizos*), who were not subject to labor in tribute to the Spanish Crown. Precisely to avoid exploitation at hard labor, "many Maya left their communities and adopted Spanish language and dress, in the process blurring the line between Indian and *ladino*."[43]

At the same time, the racially heterogeneous populations of Latin America were difficult for states to manage precisely because of the unwieldy nature of *mestizaje*. For example, the first census of Spanish colonial Los Ángeles (present day Los Angeles, California) in 1781 listed a dozen settler families with male heads of household described as four Indians, two Blacks, two Spaniards, and four *mestizo* or *mulato* combinations of the first three; their female partners were described as Indians, *mulatas*, or *mestizas* (none were Spanish, given that few Spanish women made the trip to the colonies).[44] The sixteenth-century Spanish colonial settlements in what is present-day New Mexico included twice as many Indians and *mestizos* as Spaniards in 1540 and in 1598, leading one scholar to conclude that the "Spaniards" who were their descendants in seventeenth-century New Mexico "were biologically a motley group."[45] Indeed, the incentives to move to the northern frontier of New Spain, as settlers among Indians hostile to Spain's (and later Mexico's) rule, were greatest precisely for those racially mixed persons who, by virtue of taking the risk to move to the frontier, could reinvent and whiten themselves and their descendants.[46] Yet the ratio of Blacks, Indians, and racially mixed persons to those who were White, even allowing for liberal claims of whiteness, made it increasingly difficult for Spain to maintain colonial rule. In 1810 and 1812, Spain enacted laws to provide more privileges and rights to *mestizos* and Indians, including formally abolishing the racial castes, establishing formal equality regardless of racial status, and lifting occupational restrictions. At the time, Mexico's population of six million people was 80 percent Indigenous or Indo-Spanish *mestizo*, and Spain's concessions were too late to stave off independence there and across Latin America.[47]

Mestizaje would prove less useful to the English colonial project. A quarter-century after independence from Spain, Mexico lost half its territory to the United States, and with American imperialism in Latin America came a new kind of white supremacy. It was founded upon English and American approaches to Indigenous people and African slaves. Vastly outnumbered by Indians, the English colonizers of the Atlantic coast had no hope of taking Indian people by force and instead turned to diplomacy, trade, and mating.[48] As the ratio of European settlers to Indians grew, colonial strategies for managing Indians became more diverse, including military campaigns, incentives for assimilation, legal machinations to steal Indian land, treaties to push Indians westward, and genocide. In 1619, only a decade after Jamestown's founding, a shipload of human cargo arrived carrying Africans who had been kidnapped and then brutally transported to a distant land to labor and serve. Twenty-five years later, more slaves lived in New York City than any other North American city, north or south. Ten of the first sixteen American presidents owned slaves, evidence of African slaves' fundamental role in creating the American nation from the ground up.

It was these two distinct components of Anglo-American white supremacy—toward Indians and African slaves—that would shape American imperialism in Latin America. For Indians, white supremacy justified taking Indigenous property in law, whereas for Blacks it justified making them property.[49] Mexicans complicated this dual-pronged racial project immeasurably. The question of whether Mexicans were more like Indians or more like Blacks was pervasive in Congress and the press in the 1840s, as debates raged about Texas statehood, the war with Mexico, and the ratification of the Treaty of Guadalupe Hidalgo.[50] Southerners were deeply ambivalent about the war and its spoils because they considered "the Mexican race . . . but little removed above the Negro."[51] William Watts Hart Davis of Missouri, who was appointed U.S. attorney for the New Mexico Territory in 1865, kept a revelatory travel journal, later published, in which he dismissed Pueblo Indians as "a primitive race." He criticized Mexicans because they were racially impure: "Here was a second blending of blood and a new union of races; the Spaniard, Moor, and the aboriginal were united in one and made a new race, the Mexicans," describing them as dark-skinned with "no present hope of the people improving in color."[52]

The question of how to categorize Mexicans arose repeatedly each time the question of New Mexico statehood was proposed in the sixty-two years it was an American territory. In the 1870s, the *New York Times* enshrined the stereotype of Mexicans as lazy and unfit to join industrious Americans: a front-page article referred to "Lazy Mexicans" in its headline and went on to call Mexican men "the very personification of tramphood, seldom or never turning his hand to the extent of sweating his brow." When statehood was debated again in the 1880s, the *New York Times* ran a front-page article that announced racist conclusions in its lengthy headline: "Greasers as Citizens. What Sort of State New-Mexico Would Make. The origin and character of the so-called 'Mexicans' of that Territory—their hatred of Americans, their dense ignorance, and total unfitness for citizenship—the women of New-Mexico."[53]

National Geographic described Mexicans and Mexican Americans as "lazy" and as "wetbacks," explaining the latter term as "a Texas expression for Mexicans who enter the United States without immigration inspection by swimming the Rio Grande."[54] Despite calling them lazy, *National Geographic* photographs showed industrious Mexican workers: cotton pickers in Arizona (1941) and spinach pickers in Texas (1945). In a 1928 article, the magazine drew a contrast between recent Texas history, in which the Texas Rangers carried out violent attacks on Mexicans and Mexican Americans, and conditions in 1928, when Texas's "trouble [was getting] enough Mexicans to pick her cotton, work her oil fields, mills, railway shops, shear goats and sheep, and gather the long trainloads of fresh vegetables and fruits shipped annually from the lower Rio Grande Valley."[55] In a 1920 article, the magazine, notwithstanding mixed metaphors, described Mexicans as "running to and fro apparently as aimlessly as the inhabitants of a disturbed ant-hill" because "they swarm up and down these lines to border towns, carrying women, children, birdcages, blanket rolls, and family utensils."[56] One is tempted to assume the author was ignorant of the just-concluded Mexican Revolution (1910–1920), which had in fact caused great upheaval, including greater migration to the United States, but this was not the case. The articles referenced were written by Frederick Simpich, former consul general to Mexico and, as of 1931, an assistant editor at *National Geographic*.

Simpich also wrote about Puerto Rico, extolling the benefits of American rule. In a nod to eugenics, he credited the United States with improving Puerto Ricans' health but said the Americans had done too good a job since too many people now were living into adulthood: "Under its ancient social order, mortality from disease kept the balance between population and food supply, but now all that is upset."[57] As noted in the last chapter, before and after he was president, William Taft wrote in a similar vein about how much better off Puerto Rico was due to American imperialism: "Without our fostering benevolence, this island would be as unhappy and prostrate as some of the neighboring British, French, Dutch, and Danish islands."[58] In 1930, after having served as president and chief justice of the U.S. Supreme Court, Taft criticized Puerto Rican nationalists as greedy:

> There are those who shout for independence there, and who are always wanting something in the way of enlargement of their powers or a recognition of their status . . . [but Puerto Ricans] were never so prosperous in their lives as they have been under the American government, and never so happy. They never had a government that approached it in efficiency, in the giving of health and opportunity for business, and the means of acquiring comfort."[59]

One can hear echoes of those words in President Trump's comments about Puerto Rico today, from a 2017 tweet that chided Puerto Ricans for "so little appreciation" after Hurricane Maria, to intervening in December 2019 to reduce Medicaid funding to Puerto Rico because "with the historical waste we have faced in Puerto Rico, additional funding was not needed or fiscally responsible," even as the island recovers from a damaging earthquake.[60]

National Geographic provides a window into early twentieth-century American exceptionalism. Colonialism and exploitation of migrant workers were lauded, as slavery had been for African Americans, for leaving Puerto Ricans better off than they had been. There was little regard for how Puerto Ricans contributed, directly and indirectly, to American security and economic well-being. By 1907, less than a decade after American occupation, Puerto Rico had an export industry valued at $24 million annually, virtually all of it controlled by American corporations.[61] Two decades later, a *National Geographic* article congratulated America's occupation of Puerto Rico, noting its strategic proximity to the Panama Canal, praising its exports consisting of sugar, rum, molasses, tobacco, and fruit and noting it was the world's eighth-biggest importer of American agricultural and manufacturing goods.[62] During the post-war expansion, Puerto Ricans contributed labor to the growing manufacturing and service sectors in the United States via the Farm Labor Program and Operation Bootstrap, previously described.

Mestizaje in the Wake of American Imperialism

The Jones Act of 1917 granted American citizenship to Puerto Ricans, allowing them to freely migrate between the island and the mainland, with full citizenship rights (including the right to vote for president) reserved for those Puerto Ricans who relocated to the mainland.[63] While the legislation was a victory for Puerto Rico, public debate over it exposed Washington's skepticism about Puerto Ricans' "racial fitness" for American citizenship and dashed hopes for statehood. Several scholars have concluded that an apparent increase in the island's

White population between 1910 and 1920 was due precisely to Puerto Rico's growing sense of racial inferiority.[64] In effect, a growing recognition of how White Americans viewed them as racially inferior resulted in substantial reclassification, between the two censuses, with census enumerators moving many Afro-Puerto Ricans from mulatto to White in 1920. In 1930, when U.S. census officials did away with the mulatto category, Puerto Rican enumerators again reacted by reclassifying additional Afro-Puerto Ricans as White instead of as Black, disregarding census instructions not to do so.[65]

Like other Latin American nations, Puerto Rico contested and negotiated its reality as an American colony by moving up and down and in between racial categories in the U.S. racial order. This continued after World War II, even as Puerto Ricans demanded independence or statehood. For example, beginning in 1960, the Puerto Rican government received permission from the U.S. Census Bureau to forego classifying the island's population according to race, in a move reminiscent of the Dominican Republic's decisions about its census. Interviews and memoranda from Puerto Rican census officials provide insight into what motivated their request: "The most adequate and convenient solution for our economic, social, and cultural reality is not to include the question about racial determination."[66]

Five decades later, the United States was unwilling to extend permission to omit collection of race data. By then, census information was no longer collected by enumerators; instead, race was determined via self-identification. A century after the American occupation, by 2000, Puerto Rico had become even whiter: 80 percent of islanders identified as White. Yet, for Puerto Rican migrants to the mainland in the same year, only 47 percent said they were White (with 40 percent self-identifying as "other," 6 percent as Black, and 8 percent as belonging to two or more races).[67] Scholars have explored alternative explanations to no avail (such as that Afro-Puerto Ricans migrated to the mainland, which has been shown not to be the case), instead concluding that the island's twenty-first-century racial self-identification is akin to Dominicans' widespread embrace of the Indio category, a reflection of idealized racialization in the shadow of white supremacy.

Racial gymnastics at the level of the state, including the anti-colonial state, have shaped race in Latin America. Consider Mexico, which was a twentieth-century leader across Latin America. Its agrarian revolution inspired leftist governments and grassroots populists across the globe. When it nationalized American- and British-owned oil and mining corporations in 1917, other Latin American countries were emboldened to demand greater accountability from multinational corporations. For three decades in the mid-twentieth century, Mexico produced films watched around the world, and especially in Spanish-speaking countries, even sending actors to Hollywood.[68] Mexico's intelligentsia similarly carried weight, especially as newly independent states sought to define themselves against earlier Spanish colonialism and ongoing American imperialism.

In 1925, as part of Mexico's effort to establish a cohesive national identity in the wake of its agrarian revolution, intellectual José Vasconcelos published *"La Raza Cósmica,"* or "the cosmic race," an essay that heavily influenced many nations in Latin America.[69] Vasconcelos, who served as Mexico's secretary of education from 1921 to 1924, asserted that Spain's contribution to the world was bringing together what he called the "four major races"—red, yellow, Black, and White—to produce "the fifth great race," the *mestizos* of Mexico. According to cultural studies scholar María Joséfina Saldaña-Portillo, the concept of *la raza cósmica* was "at once utopian and racist, democratizing and hierarchical."[70] It was utopian because it rejected Western notions of racial inferiority because of American notions of "miscegenation" and Spanish portrayals of racial combinations in eighteenth-century *casta* paintings showing the offspring of various pairings among Indians, Blacks, and Spaniards.[71] It was racist in that it presupposed the elimination of all other racial groups, up and down the racial hierarchy, as they melded into the catch-all *mestizo* category. By far the greatest impact—because of its large size—was on Mexico's Indigenous peoples, who, it was hoped by government officials, would disappear as time went on, becoming subsumed into the *mestizo* nation.[72] As a hegemonic idea, it promoted complete assimilation, inducing Indians to leave their peasant ways behind as they migrated to cities to become wage laborers, exchanging their *huaraches* for boots.[73]

Much like colorblind race ideology in the United States today, Vasconcelos's ideology of *mestizaje* as state policy operates to mask white supremacy and conceal racial subordination in Mexico of Indigenous people and Afro-Mexicanos. Anthropologist Shannon Speed, writing about Guatemala, calls out the ideology of *mestizaje* as ultimately oriented toward complete assimilation (and thus disappearance) of Indigenous people, even when embraced by populist leaders. She points to the progressive policies of Jacobo Árbenz, who as previously noted, rose to power in 1944 and then was removed by a CIA coup in 1954 after pursuing land reform and political rights for peasants, workers, and students. Even as a socialist, he viewed Guatemala's large and diverse (speaking more than twenty languages) Indigenous communities as a "problem" for nation-building for nationalism. Speed explains:

> Yet like other liberal governments of the era, particularly that of Mexico, the Árbenz government pursued indigenist policies of assimilation for Indigenous peoples, believing that it was in their best interest for them to modernize and become full citizens of the nation-state. The Árbenz government discursively invoked nationalism and the notion of a unified nation under a banner of "*Somos todos guatemaltecos*" (We are all Guatemalans). In 1945 the National Indigenist Institute was created to facilitate this process. Like other such institutes in Latin America (Mexico's was created in 1948), its goal was to solve the 'Indian problem' through assimilation and modernization.[74]

As for Afro-Mexicanos, they were already presumed marginal by the

1920s. Despite, as I have noted, the fact of extensive African slavery in Mexico over three centuries, Vasconcelos would have felt no need to write Afro-Mexicans out of the national history. Like other elites, he would have assumed that had been achieved long before independence from Spain via liberal sexual and marital couplings as well as *blanquea-miento* as a policy in the late colonial and early Mexican periods from 1800 to 1840.[75] A recent study of contemporary racial self-identification in Mexico, Brazil, Colombia, and Peru concludes that the four countries have succeeded in depressing their citizens' willingness to identify as Indian, Black, or White, instead incentivizing citizens to embrace *mestizo* identities even (perhaps especially) when they are either relatively light-skinned or dark-skinned.[76] As in other places in Latin America, this ideology of *mestizaje* coexists with white supremacy, especially because, as previously described, *mestizaje* itself was viewed as a path for eliminating or reducing the African and Indigenous populations.[77]

Sociologist Christina Sue explains that Mexico's nationalist, post-revolutionary ideology stands on a conception of Mexico as a nation without Blacks, in which "the marginalization, neglect or negation of Mexico's African heritage" thrives.[78] Sixty-year-old Silvia (a pseudonym Sue gave her) is a case in point. She lives in Veracruz, a port city on Mexico's Atlantic coast where slave ships carrying Africans landed in the sixteenth and seventeenth centuries. Sue interviewed Silvia multiple times, describing her as having "dark-brown skin and tightly curled hair"; Silvia used various terms to describe herself racially, including *mestiza*, *negra* (a Black woman), and *morena* (a brown woman).[79] She described one grandmother as a Spanish woman and, much later in the conversation, added that her husband, her grandfather, was a Black man. Silvia recounted her relationship with an American man, volunteering that his family opposed their relationship because she was Black. She and her sister related that their "White sisters" used to taunt them with racial epithets and that her father favored their lighter-skinned sisters with attention, gifts, and greater educational opportunities. Despite having been victims of racism in her own family (or because of it), Silvia shared that she would not be comfortable dating someone of her skin color or darker. She posed this question: "If I had a child, and he [the father] is Black and with me being Black, how is the baby going to come out?" Silvia went on to convey examples of racism among children at the daycare center where she was employed, adding that her coworkers favored those children with green eyes and light skin. At the individual level, Silvia's experience powerfully illuminates the realities of Mexico's anti-Black racism and the complexities it produces for racial identification.

In its first post-revolution census, Mexico used four racial categories: "*raza indígena*" (Indigenous race), at 29 percent of the population; "*raza mezclada*" (mixed race), 59 percent; "*raza blanca*" (White race), ten percent; and a catch-all "*otra raza*" (other race), coming in at less than 1 percent.[80] Mexico's valorization of *mestizaje* was emulated by many Latin American nations.[81] Between 1920 and 1930, Panama's Black population seemingly shrank, from 37 to 15 percent of the population. What actually happened was that census enumerators were directed to utilize new racial categories: *mulato* (Black-Spanish *mestizos*), which came in at 5 percent, and *indio*, which came in at 9 percent. The population went from 44 to 52 percent "*mestizo*" and 14 to 18 percent "White" in a decade, decreasing the percentage of Black-identified Panamanians.[82] In heavily indigenous Guatemala, 1892 census categories remained in place for a century: *indio* and *ladino*, the latter denoting a *mestizo* term unique to that country that was broad enough to encompass Indigenous persons wanting to or forced to assimilate.[83]

A comprehensive study of how twenty Latin American nations have conducted population censuses over two centuries suggests there recently has been a move away from the centering of the national subject as *mestizo*. While the valorization of *mestizaje* is alive and well, the study finds that many national censuses began collecting data on Indigenous or Black populations in the late twentieth century. One reason given by sociologist Mara Loveman is evolving international norms about the rights of minority populations. For example, the United Nations'

Convention on the Elimination of All Forms of Racial Discrimination has pressured nations to acknowledge race-based discrimination. Loveman also points to pressure applied by the World Bank and the International Development Bank on Global South nations to collect data on "minority" populations, as defined by race, indigeneity, and/or language usage. But another dynamic at play was the rise of identity-based social movements in the 1980s in response to repressive, anti-democratic trends in much of Latin America. Organizing for state recognition by Indigenous groups, drawing heavily on U.N. precepts, has been especially strong in Central and South America.[84]

Only the Dominican Republic and Cuba defy this trend. As noted, the Dominican government, as of the 2010 census, still refuses to collect any data on race. Cuba is a different story, one that shows the resilience of race across censuses conducted under Spanish and American colonialism and under rightist and leftist governments post-independence. Unlike the Dominican Republic, Cuba's plantation economy developed rather late, such that African slaves, forced there in the mid-nineteenth century, gained their freedom during the fight for independence from Spain in the late nineteenth century.[85] In fact, the abolition of slavery occurred because many former slaves were eager to fight against Spain, including a large number who were first- and second-generation Africans.[86]

Without their leadership and participation, Cuba would not have defeated Spain, but that did not prevent anti-Black racism after independence. Recall that Americans retained the right to intervene in Cuba after the Spanish-American War. The United States promoted racism, specifically incentivizing the Cuban government to disenfranchise Afro-Cubans. Under pressure from American corporations, in 1912, the Americans threatened a military invasion if Cuba did not suppress the Afro-Cuban political movement organized as the *Partido Independiente de Color* (the Colored Independent Party). When the Cuban military responded by arresting two hundred members of the 60,000-strong political party, days of protests resulted. In the end, the

Cuban government slaughtered 4,000 party members.[87] Incidents like this cast a long shadow, with the socialist government giving lip service to racial inclusion but, in fact, largely continuing to deny the reality of anti-Black racism.[88] As recently as the 2002 census, enumerators classified Cuba's racial population thusly: 65 percent White, 10 percent Black, and 25 percent mixed Black/White.[89]

At the turn of the twenty-first century, the Central American nations of El Salvador, Honduras, Guatemala, and Nicaragua responded to pressure from international funding agencies by incorporating census questions about Indigenous identity.[90] El Salvador switched to self-identification, adding an option for Afro-descent and adding both language and group membership as proxies for Indigenous status. Beginning in 2005, Nicaragua followed suit, although for group membership it offered a list of eleven Indigenous communities, along with the options "other" and "does not know." Honduras and Guatemala have the largest Indigenous populations in Central America, but instead of a membership approach, they added only a language question. In 2000, Mexico joined its neighbors in finally retreating from the "we are all *mestizos*" framework. For the first time it included questions about group membership and Indigenous languages in 2000 and, in 2010, incorporated additional questions about language. These questions included asking whether one has fluency or limited spoken or comprehension of Indigenous languages. The latter is especially important, because many so-called heritage language speakers may comprehend a parents' or grandparents' other language but not actually speak it fluently.

Early twenty-first century changes to national censuses are of a piece with growing consciousness, resistance, and pride among Afro-*mestizos* and Indigenous peoples across the Americas, including in the United States. In 2006, a traveling exhibit entitled "The African Presence in México: From Yanga to the Present," from the National Museum of Mexican Art, made its U.S. debut at the Mexican Fine Arts Center Museum in the Mexican American neighborhood of Pilsen in Chicago. The exhibit, which traveled to ten additional U.S. cities, specifically situated itself as a project of recovery and recognition: "For nearly 500 years, the existence and contributions of the African descendants in Mexico have been overlooked."[91] A decade previously, the Mexican government acknowledged the country's racism in the context of the United Nations International Convention on the Elimination of All Forms of Racial Discrimination. A national "survey of discrimination" followed, and then, a few years later, a public education campaign against racism. The survey and campaign, which included videos shown on television, social media, and in movie theaters, were overseen by the government's new National Council for the Prevention of Discrimination. The educational campaign provided accessible examples of everyday racism, ending with, "in Mexico, the majority of us say we are not racist," followed by the presentation of survey results showing the opposite.[92] Recognition of anti-Black and anti-Indian racism in Mexico is an important step forward—one that portends future impact on Latinos, since such a large proportion of them have origins in Mexico.

How Latinos Identify Racially in the United States

Does the way race is counted and idealized in Latin America affect the racial attitudes of Latinos in the United States? One might imagine this is the case for the 20 percent of Latinos who are themselves immigrants or the additional 10.5 million Latinos who are the children of at least one migrant parent.[93] But I make a different claim. I want to suggest that Latinos have unique responses—compared to Americans generally and compared to other people of color—to the question of racial self-identification apart from recency of migration. One place to explore Latinos' racial attitudes is in terms of their racial self-identification on the U.S. census, which since 1980 has included a so-called Hispanic/Latino ethnicity question.[94] By way of this configuration, the race question does not include a Latino option, reflecting the census mantra, "Latinos can be of any race"—White, Black, American Indian, or Asian

American, as well as a combination of multiple races. Later in the book, I will return to questions about the census, specifically taking up the decision to bifurcate race from Latino ethnicity beginning in 1980.

For now, let us focus on this astounding fact: 99.8 percent of Americans who are not Latino easily select one or more census racial categories as those with which they self-identify. Yet, for each census between 1980 and 2010 (the last year available when this book went to press), between 37 and 43 percent of Latinos rejected every possible race category (including the option to select two or more of them, available since 2000). Instead, 4 out of 10 Latinos consistently opt for "other" to describe their race.[95] This trend may reflect the imprint of the African, Indigenous, and Spanish *mestizaje* characteristics of Spanish colonial society reinscribed as *blanqueamiento* by post-colonial governments. In this sense, it may reflect Latinos' resistance to self-classification as Indian or as Black—subscribing to the logic of "anything but Indian" and "anything but Black." At the same time, those who choose "other" also reject self-identification as "White."[96] We ignore these other-race Latinos at our peril since, if the four-decade trend continues with the 2020 census, "other" will be the nation's second-largest racial category, after White, chosen by some 24 million Latinos.

Although Indigenous ancestry varies across the Spanish Caribbean, Central America, Mexico, and elsewhere in Latin America, there are economic reasons to expect U.S. Latinos to be, on average, more likely than those who stayed behind to be Indigenous or *Indo-mestizos*. Especially in Mexico and Central America, rural, land-based Indigenous and *Indo-mestizo* populations have borne the brunt of economic displacement from American corporate, military, and other imperial intervention. Yet just under 3 percent of Latinos identify racially as "American Indian and Alaska Native," although another 3 percent fall into the "two or more races" category, perhaps including Indian. We would expect Guatemalans, an estimated 50 percent of whom are Indigenous Maya, to choose to identify as American Indian, but less than 2 percent of Guatemalans select American Indian as their race, while more than half choose "some other race."[97] These low numbers are consistent with internalized anti-Indigenous racism, but they also may reflect a rejection of a census category labeled "American Indian," the connotation of which may have little to do with Mayan notions of difference that have nothing to do with tribal organization in the United States.[98] This seems to be borne out by examining only foreign-born Latinos; using the regional categories used in chapter 1, we see that no group of foreign-born Latinos has more than 1 percent racial identification as American Indian: Mexico (0.8 percent Indian), Central America (1 percent Indian), and Caribbean (0.2 percent Indian).[99] Yet, for these same Latinos, "other" race is nearly as appealing as it is for U.S.-born Latinos: Mexico (33 percent), Central America (38 percent), and Caribbean (14 percent).[100]

The experiences of Maya people in the United States hint that their indigeneity matters on the ground, if not on the census form. While some scholars emphasize that the racialization and racism Maya experience in the United States is analogous to that experienced by Latinos generally and Mexicans specifically, they have in fact endured specific targeting. For example, two of the largest ICE raids during George W. Bush's two terms targeted Maya, whether intentionally or inadvertently. In New Bedford, Massachusetts, during the 2007 raid at the Michael Bianco factory, 300 workers were arrested, the vast majority of whom were Maya, while the 2008 Agriprocessors raid in Postville, Iowa, led to the arrest of 400 workers, 290 of whom were deported to Guatemala, the majority of them Maya.[101] Maya migrants came to the United States as long ago as the 1940s, as braceros from southern Mexico, and, as is still the case today, their exploitation as immigrant Mexican workers was compounded because they spoke neither English or Spanish fluently.[102] In cities like Phoenix, where in the early 2000s the Mexican American population of 52,000 dwarfed the combined population of Central Americans (at less than 15,000), Central American Latinos sometimes "opt to 'pass' for Mexican . . . [adopting] Mexican sayings, accent, and dress styles" in order to blunt the harsh discrimination they would otherwise face.[103] Patterns of racial identification reflect peoples' choices, but those choices are severely constrained for the least powerful Latinos.

When it comes to Latinos' self-identification as Black, we see great variation by national origin, region, and national origin combined with foreign birth. For the latter, consisting only of those Latinos born in another country, we see the highest rate of Black self-identification for those born in the Caribbean, at 45 percent, and then numbers far smaller: the South American–born identify as Black at 5.4 percent, Central American–born identify as Black at 3 percent, and Mexican-born Latinos identify as Black at 0.3 percent.[104] The fact that almost half of Latinos born in the Caribbean say they are Black despite trends in the Dominican Republic, Puerto Rico, and Cuba that suggest an official whitening project, is puzzling and deserves further analysis. Six percent of Puerto Ricans on the mainland self-identify as Black, compared to 8 percent for Dominicans.[105] Under Spanish rule, both countries saw their Indigenous populations decimated and the importation of high numbers of African slaves. Both have national racial narratives that seek to maximize non-Black ancestry and minimize African roots. It is certainly the case that anti-Black racism—historically rooted in Spanish colonialism but also a prominent feature of the twentieth-century post-independence nations of Latin America—influences Latinos' willingness to identify as Black, even when they know others perceive them as Black. For instance, one study found that twice as many Dominicans in New England say other Americans see them as Black than self-identify as Black.[106]

For Latinos overall (native-born and foreign-born), data from the 2018 American Community Survey show that just under 5 percent of Latinos identify as Black, with significant national origin differences.[107] For example, Dominicans were nearly twelve times as likely as Mexican Americans to identify as Black. Recall the Dominican census official who explained the unwillingness to collect race data as due to inaccurate responses because those who are "Black" would say they are "White." Perhaps the willingness of Dominican Latinos to claim their

Black heritage in the context of the United States reflects the recognition of American racism and the desire to avoid cognitive dissonance. For Mexican American Latinos, the few who identify as Black may well reflect the erasure of *Afro-mestizos* over the course of both Spanish and American colonial projects. Despite these national origin differences, there appear to be even greater differences according to region of the United States in which Latinos live. More than twice as many Dominicans in Florida as in New York/New Jersey select the "White" category. A parallel dynamic exists for Puerto Ricans: those who live in Florida are much more likely to select "White" (70 percent) than those who reside in New York/New Jersey (45 percent). It is telling that self-identified whiteness is more popular among those living in the former Confederacy, suggesting that Latinos who live in the South may, in fact, adopt whiteness as a defense to racism.[108]

Similarly, there are pronounced regional differences among Mexican Americans with respect to selecting "other" race. Mexican Americans in more liberal California are more likely to identify as "other" (53 percent) than are those in more conservative Texas (36 percent), and California's Mexican Americans are likewise less likely to self-identify as White (40 percent) compared to Mexican Americans in Texas (60 percent). Similarly, Salvadorans and Guatemalans in California self-identified as "other" much more often than those groups who live in Texas, who disproportionately identified as "White." Such regional differences suggest that census racial identification may say more about regional racial hierarchies than about how race is organized in Latin American–sending countries. On the other hand, Cubans and Argentinians are considerably more likely than Mexican Americans who live in Texas to self-identify as White, at rates above 80 percent. And Dominicans self-identify as "other" at the same rate as Californian Mexican Americans, at 59 percent.

Despite these rich patterns, the Census Bureau generally has approached those who select "other" race as doing so in error. For example, in 1990, the census simply folded all those who self-identified as other race into White. This is an astounding example of the racial state at work. For most of the census's history, its role has been to police racial categories,[109] so what interest would it have in increasing the number of "White Hispanics"? The census is invested in maintaining the categories as they exist, and so the "other" Latinos are confounding. After again receiving very high numbers of "other" race Latino self-identification in 2000, census officials proposed entirely eliminating the option of "some other race." But they had to contend with Puerto Rican congressman José E. Serrano (D-NY), who at the time was the ranking Democrat on the Appropriations Subcommittee. Serrano, who is phenotypically light-skinned with wavy dark hair and a big moustache, threatened to block funding for the 2010 census unless it included the other race option. He faulted the census for not reflecting "the realities of race in America today," pointing out that Latinos do not fit readily into American census categories but that did not make their racial choices invalid.[110]

Various researchers have attempted to figure out what 19 million Latinos think when they self-identify as "other" race, rather than, like the census, assuming these choices reflect "wrong answers." Is "some other race" a *mestizo* category otherwise absent from how the United States racially classifies people? Or does "other" capture Latinos' sense that their racial identity is more fluid compared to that of "real Blacks" and "real Whites"? To be sure, racial identity is dynamic for many Americans, such as those who are biracial or multiracial. Perhaps some Latinos with deep *mestizo* roots behave similarly to the biracial person who sometimes chooses one parent's race and at others choose the other parent's race; both are authentic states of who they are, but at a particular stage in life (childhood versus college years) or in a particular context (a government census questionnaire versus an in-group party), one or the other may resonate more.[111] Phenotype may be especially relevant; one study found that 66 percent of Latinos, faced with a question format parallel to the census, chose "some other race," but that skin color made a significant difference. Those whom interviewers rated as "very dark-skinned" identified as "Black" 3 percent of the time, as

"White" 25 percent of the time, and as "some other race" 72 percent of the time. Those whom interviewers rated "very light-skinned" identified as "some other race" 63 percent of the time and "White" 36 percent of the time.[112] Unfortunately, this study did not assess phenotype beyond skin color, thus failing to capture Latinos' diverse bases for racial identification (consider the Dominican categories that include "Indio" as a racially mixed reference).

In a nationally representative study of Latinos, sociologist Nicholas Vargas found that 42 percent of Latinos said their race was White and 50 percent said it was "other race." Another question he asked was whether other Americans see the study participant as White; only 6 percent of Latinos answered affirmatively, with only 2 percent of those who self-identified as White previously saying non-Latinos see them as White.[113] This research fundamentally challenges the assumption that Latinos who self-identify as White are, in fact, truly White, instead suggesting they have a tenuous attachment to whiteness at best. In an economic study comparing the incomes of Latinos with phenotype and racial self-identification, researchers found significant differences by national origin and nativity.[114] All of those surveyed were Latinos born outside the United States who possessed "legal permanent resident" status—this coveted immigration status also known as "having a green card" is a step closer to becoming a naturalized citizen, the opposite end of the spectrum of undocumented migrants. Green card holders are disproportionately better educated, and the study found that a stunning 79 percent self-identified as White. This study used different categories than the census, specifically omitting "other" race, which could have had the effect of increasing the number of White-identifying participants. The numbers who identified as American Indian were slightly greater than those who identified as Black, although both combined were only 7.5 percent; the remaining 14 percent refused those racial categories (disproportionately selected by Dominican Latinos). Those participants who self-identified as White were more likely to be light-skinned and also Cuban or of South American origin. Even controlling for national origin, education, and English literacy, the study finds that darker-skinned Latino immigrants earned less than their lighter-skinned peers. This last finding suggests that, try as they might to "pass" as White, only a small minority of Latinos are able to credibly claim to be White.

Returning to the fact that eight out of ten Latino immigrants with green cards self-identified as White—a much higher number than native-born Latinos—we might think of their racial claim as aspirational rather than descriptive. These new immigrants on their way to American citizenship aspire to full inclusion in American society, as citizens, thus as White. Some evidence for such an interpretation comes from a comparison of Latino immigrants to their American-citizen children. Children of Central American immigrants self-identified their race as "Hispanic/Latino" between 44 and 62 percent, depending on national origin, whereas their parents did so in the range of zero to 8 percent, by national origin. More than one-third of Cuban American children said their race was Latino, while only 1 percent of their parents did so.[115] As Latino children learn their racial place in their communities and in the nation at large, they readily grasp what their parents may not: that the White-over-Black racial hierarchy in the United States means that they do not belong in either category. For the U.S.-born children of Latino migrants, their racialized Latino identity grows out of their sense of exclusion.[116]

Sociologist Julie Dowling's life history interviews with Mexican American women in Texas suggest that, for some, the costs of divergence from the "White" category, symbolic or not, might be prohibitive. She found that those who lived near the Mexican border were much more likely than those living farther from the border (in the Dallas area) to self-identify as "White" when asked about their race (in a question format that mirrored the census). Dowling concludes that the Latinas she interviewed "who identify as 'white' cling to whiteness not in spite of but because of their position as [members of] a stigmatized group. However, these 'white' Mexican Americans are not generally recognized as White by others. Hence, it becomes quite clear that they do not truly 'own' whiteness as it is not a validated social identification for them."[117] Dowling posed additional questions, finding that they yielded considerable cognitive dissonance for the women. In a question designed to get at how others view them racially, she asked two questions: how others in their town would label them in terms of race or ethnicity and whether anyone had ever asked them what their race or ethnicity is.[118]

Consider this story offered by one of her subjects, Mari Bredahl (née Ramírez), who self-identifies as White and is married to a non-Latino White man. At the time of the interview, Mari was a teacher in her fifties who described herself as the daughter of Mexican immigrants on her mother's side and the granddaughter and great-granddaughter of Mexican immigrants on her father's side. She told the story of arriving to her central Texas college in the 1970s, "horrified" to encounter signs in the windows of local restaurants saying, "We refuse to serve Mexicans!" She went on to describe meeting her White college roommate for the first time: "When she saw me, that I was her roommate, she nearly died. . . . She just took one look at me and walked out of the room. I mean it didn't bother me that much. I have a lot of self-confidence. Maybe for someone who did not have a lot of self-confidence it would bother them."[119] In what sense is it not devastating to know your new college roommate is repulsed when they discover you are Mexican American? Yet Mari has spent decades telling herself it was no big deal. Despite sharing this story, she told Dowling she had never experienced discrimination. For some subset of Latinos who choose "White" on the census race question, they may well be invoking whiteness in a defensive, rather than possessory, sense.

Conclusion

Colorism—the favoritism for lighter-skinned members of the same racial group—among African Americans was confirmed as far back as 1860: census records for 15,000 free Blacks showed that those who had one White parent earned 50 percent of the income of Whites, whereas those with two Black parents earned 20 percent of the income of Whites.[120] A recent review of the literature showed robust findings linking better outcomes to lighter-skinned compared to darker-skinned members of the same group, including twenty-three studies of colorism among African Americans (showing differences in marriage, income, education, occupation, wealth, political ideology, arrests, and criminal punishment) and twelve studies of colorism among Latinos (showing differences in marriage, income, education, occupation, and residential segregation).[121] In another study, this one focused on younger Latinos with ties to Puerto Rico, the Dominican Republic, and Cuba (who were therefore, on average, more likely to have African ancestry), those who were dark-skinned were significantly more likely to report discrimination by police, at work, in housing, and in public accommodations such as restaurants and stores.[122] At the same time, those Latino national origin groups with extensive African slavery have been especially eager to police the White-over-Black boundary; one study found that those most likely to be identified by non-Latinos as Black were most likely to embrace a Latino identity in contra-distinction to a Black identity.[123] Likewise, the Dominican example reveals that Latinos sometimes embrace Indigenous identity as a way to push away their African roots.[124]

According to Mérida Rúa, a Latino studies scholar, claiming a broader Latino identity has sometimes offered escape from specific disadvantages associated with Puerto Rican identity more specifically given its association with blackness: "'Hispano' and 'Latino' was considered preferable to 'Puerto Rican' because of the stigma attached to this population in New York, and later, in Chicago."[125] This has been especially prominent in Miami, where a tight-knit, White-identified Cuban community both created and then reinforced segregation between it and the African American community.[126] Among Cuban Americans themselves, White-over-Black racism has been observed with respect to the treatment of the second-wave Cuban migrants from the 1980 Mariel Boatlift—who were disproportionately Afro-Cuban—by mostly White-identified Cubans who migrated in the 1960s and 1970s.[127] Of course, distancing from African Americans is not unique to Latinos, with research showing that West Indian immigrants and young adult children of immigrants in New York actively sought to make non-Blacks aware that they were different and "superior."[128] Some studies have found that African Americans and Latinos have racial dynamics in common. One study comparing colorism among Blacks and Latinos in the context of crime found that darker-skinned men in both groups were more likely to be arrested.[129] It was this very *mestizaje* that allowed Puerto Rican migrants to the mainland in the post–World War II period to build coalitions with African Americans, Whites, and other Latinos, capitalizing on a "hybrid" identity.[130]

It is the case that Latinos and African Americans both are victims of white supremacy but also the case that Latinos benefit by situating themselves as a buffer between Whites and Blacks. In the latter position, Latinos perpetrate anti-Black racism.[131] The South Central Los Angeles riots of 1992, which followed the jury's acquittal of the Los Angeles Police Department (LAPD) officers who beat Rodney King, are an example of the former and also a situation in which Latino participation in the riot was largely erased. The LAPD targeted both Latinos and Blacks in an economically depressed area, arresting 5,633 people within six days, revealing an assault by the city's power structure that is hard to imagine occurring in any other part of Los Angeles County.[132] Those arrested included 477 undocumented immigrants, whom the LAPD turned over to the Immigration and Naturalization Service (the precursor to ICE), in violation of city policy at the time; most were Mexican nationals, but immigrants from El Salvador, Guatemala, Honduras, and Jamaica also were deported.[133] Latinos and non-Latino Blacks each were 50 percent of those arrested (Latinos were 35 percent of those arrested for property crimes such as looting and 42 percent of those arrested for curfew violations).[134] The riot was portrayed, in the media and government reports, as a Black-on-Korean conflict, while Latinos were written out of the story, despite being 30 percent of those killed and owners of 40 percent of the businesses damaged in the unrest.[135] South Central was perceived as African American, but the 1990 census showed it had a Latino population of 55 percent, compared to an African American population of 24.5 percent, including 9 percent of Latinos who self-identified as Black (an increase from 1.6 percent Black Latino in 1980); this was nine times as many Black Latinos as in the city of Los Angeles.[136]

Increasingly, Latinos are calling out those in their community unwilling to name and fight anti-Black racism. Writing in *Salon*, journalist Aura Bogado called out Latino racism in dating and mating:

> When we begin dating, some of us are told that we have a duty as Latinos to *"mejorar la raza,"* which means "to improve the race." . . . Dating can lead to marriage, which can lead to children, so the message we are expected to internalize is that Latinos should literally become as white as possible over time. "Improving the race" can mean dating and marrying whites only (including white Latinos)—and specifically staying away from indigenous, Black, Asian, or mixed potential mates; in this hierarchy, white is the most desirable condition, while Black is the least.[137]

An academic study points to the same dynamic, but refuses to call it racism, instead using the euphemism of "racial blind spots."[138]

Others call for Latinos to own up to "their collective blackness," invoking the American racial order as having three tiers, with Whites at the top, "collective Black" at the bottom, and "honorary Whites" in between the two.[139] In this construction, Latinos may choose, depending on their phenotype, which of the three to inhabit. But this thinking gives too much credence to individualized mobility at the cost of ignoring the American racial hierarchy's ability to simultaneously incorporate and oppress buffer groups such as Latinos. Is this the "Latin Americanization" of race coming north to the United States, as sociologist Eduardo Bonilla-Silva asserts, or is this the core link between Latin

America and the United States, between colony and metropole? Certainly, the middle category, whatever we choose to call it, is essential for maintaining white supremacy because this category, ever capacious, does the very critical work of holding the boundary against the collective Black. Given what we know about colorism and other intra-racial inequalities, the middle group is fluid and diverse enough to encompass some upper-class, light-skinned probably biracial Blacks as well as groups judged to be "not Black and not White" like Latinos and Asian Americans.

At the same time, some Latinos will be placed in—or choose to go into—the collective Black by virtue of their phenotype as Black or Indigenous (or both) or their life experience—such as the Latinos oppressed and arrested during the Los Angeles rebellion, who disproportionately to Latinos in other neighborhoods identified as Black. In particular, today there is a renaissance of Afro-Latino cultural production.[140] A number of writers have focused on rap and hip hop as key sites for the African diaspora, including Puerto Ricans and other Latinos.[141] For Raquel Rivera, it is not a question of Black or Puerto Rican becoming ascendant, but, rather, rejecting the White/Black binary in both Latin America and the United States in favor of a "wide variety of intermediate racial possibilities."[142] Others emphasize that the racialized cultural production of the past few decades had precedents in the formation of a Nuyorican identity in the 1970s and 1980s, with such institutions as the Nuyorican Poets' Café of Manhattan's Lower East Side (or Loisada).[143] Even earlier, formations in Latin jazz, salsa, and other music of the mid-twentieth century in New York showed the Afro-Latino diaspora as a force even when race was not formally named.[144]

3

THE ELUSIVE QUEST FOR WHITENESS

Content to be white for these many years, now, when the shoe begins to pinch, the would-be-intervenors wish to be treated not as whites but as an "identifiable ethnic group." In short, they wish to be "integrated" with whites, not blacks.

—Federal Judge Ben C. Connally, siding with a school district defending a Mexican American challenge to segregation, 1971[1]

Go up the road and bury him with the n****** and Mexicans.

—Jimmy Bradford, cemetery caretaker, Normanna, Texas, 2016[2]

Although separated by forty-five years, these two quotations expose the dilemma for Latinos that has existed for as long as they have lived in the United States: in the American racial order, where do they fit? For many, the question is, are they more like Whites or Blacks? In his important study of Mexican, Black, and White cotton sharecroppers in central Texas, historian Neil Foley captures this in-between racial status: "Mexican sharecroppers . . . were subject to segregation in schools, neighborhoods, churches, and public facilities, as were more permanently settled African Americans. . . . [They were] in the ethnoracial middle ground between Anglo Americans and African Americans, not white enough to claim equality with Anglos and yet, in many cases, white enough to escape the worst features of the Jim Crow South."[3] In this chapter, focusing on the twentieth century, we consider precisely how Latinos came to be in this middle ground and what the implications are for how we understand race in the United States. There is a throughline from the last chapter to this one: individuals, organizations, and social groups must engage with the racial state, creatively finding their place on the official racial map in ways that offer relative protection and that, at least sometimes, ring true to their everyday realities.

Much of the story takes place in huge, sprawling Texas, where the South meets the Southwest—where white supremacy as it affected Latinos and African Americans first overlapped. Recall that the mostly southern White Americans who accepted Mexico's invitation to settle what is now Texas brought their slaves with them, in defiance of Mexico's abolition of slavery in 1829 (thirty-three years before the Emancipation Proclamation). White Americans, who by the early 1830s outnumbered Mexicans, declared the Texas Republic in 1836, and in the first full decade that Texas was a state, from 1850 to 1860, there was a threefold increase in its slave population. The stories here take us through the central core of Texas, a triangle formed by Dallas, Houston, and San Antonio—three of the ten most populous U.S. cities. At the northern tip of the triangle is Dallas (and Oklahoma north of it); Houston (and Louisiana east of it) is southeast of Dallas; and San Antonio is southwest of Houston, at the southwest corner of the triangle.

Both historically and today, San Antonio is symbolic of Mexican Texas. It is the gateway to the Rio Grande Valley, an agricultural region that runs from south of San Antonio to the most southern point in the continental U.S. The Valley, as it is known, is bounded to the east by the Gulf of Mexico (with the city of Corpus Christi a major coastal hub) and to the west by the Mexican states of Coahuila and Tamaulipas. This is the heartland of Latino Texas, the birthplace of Mexican American civil rights organizations like the League of United Latin American Citizens (LULAC) and the American G.I. Forum. The former was founded in the 1920s, following the model of the NAACP, as a membership organization divided into local chapters (which LULAC calls councils). In 1929 Mexican American men formed Council #1 in Corpus Christi; today the organization has 132,000 members. Nineteen years later, also in Corpus Christi, Mexican American World War II veterans formed the American G.I. Forum. As the General Infantry abbreviation suggests, it is a civil rights organization specifically dedicated to fighting for Mexican American veterans, who—despite their disproportionate (compared to Whites) enlistment during World War

II, death in combat, and receipt of decorations for bravery—faced racial discrimination when they returned home to Texas, including exclusion from funeral homes and cemeteries.[4]

The epigraph includes a quote from Jimmy Bradford, the White caretaker of the only cemetery in Normanna, Texas, in a county settled in the 1840s by Whites from South Carolina and Mississippi. When Dorothy Barrera, the White widow of Pedro Barrera, sought burial for her Latino husband of forty-four years in their hometown cemetery, Bradford told her to take Barrera's body to a cemetery for Blacks and Mexican Americans in another town.[5] Barrera refused, instead electing cremation and a campaign for justice that means Pedro Barrera will go down in the history of the ongoing fight for racial justice in the Lone Star State. Despite being a majority-minority town of 121 people—43 percent Latino, 4 percent Black, and 12 percent biracial—deceased people of color could not be buried there until a 2016 civil rights lawsuit.[6] Faced with a lawsuit from the G.I. Forum, and a wave of unfavorable television and newspaper coverage, the Normanna Cemetery Association settled the lawsuit, agreeing to provide burial plots without regard to race in the Rio Grande Valley community.[7]

For students of Mexican American history, the Barrera case conjured an eerie similarity to a case more than a quarter-century earlier labeled "The Felix Longoria Affair" by the *New York Times*. U.S. Army Private Felix Z. Longoria was killed in combat in 1945, two weeks after he arrived in Luzon, the Philippines. Longoria, who was born and raised in the Rio Grande Valley town of Three Rivers, Texas, was awarded the Purple Heart and the Combat Infantryman Badge, but his body was not recovered until 1949. At that time, his widow Beatrice Longoria sought to hold a memorial for her husband at the Rice Funeral Home, knowing he could only be buried in the town's "Mexican cemetery."[8] Tom Kennedy, who owned the town's only funeral home, refused the booking, complaining that Mexican Americans "get drunk" at funerals and that his business would suffer were he to accept her business: "I don't dislike the Mexican people but I have to run my business so I can't do that. You understand the whites here won't like it."[9] As it did in 2016, the newly formed American G.I. Forum intervened to protest. After contacting elected officials and the press, the Latino civil rights organization assembled thousands to read aloud a January 12, 1949, telegram from Texas's freshman Senator Lyndon Johnson. LBJ had arranged for Longoria to be buried with honors at Arlington National Cemetery.[10]

A few months after Longoria's burial at Arlington, the Texas legislature held hearings on the matter. Their purpose was not to vindicate the rights of Longoria or Mexican American servicemen generally; instead, Texas Dixiecrats perceived Johnson as too liberal on race relations. They called Johnson home to testify, hoping to show he had contrived the entire Three Rivers hoax in order to curry favor with Mexican American voters.[11] At Johnson's side to advise him during those hearings was attorney Gus García, who five short years later made history as the first Mexican American to argue before the U.S. Supreme Court. In *Hernandez v. Texas*, García and other Latino lawyers represented Pete Hernández, who had been convicted of murder and sentenced to life in prison. At the time, there were few Latino college graduates, much less attorneys. Unlike African Americans, Latinos did not face *de jure* segregation, and they never developed a segregated education system they themselves controlled. The system of higher education institutions today known collectively as historically Black colleges and universities (HBCUs) has produced generations of college graduates, teachers, professors, and attorneys, including many of the most elite African American professionals in the twentieth century.[12] For Latinos, aside from Puerto Rico, which developed a substantial system of higher education, there has been no sizable college-educated Latino middle class until recently.

Without college graduates, historically, there were few doctors, lawyers, or intellectuals among Latinos, and this produced challenges with initiating civil rights litigation efforts on behalf of Latinos. This is not to say that African American, White, and Asian American attorneys have not sometimes advocated on behalf of Latinos, but it is to say that

Latinos historically faced great challenges finding lawyers (especially if they required Spanish fluency to communicate with their monolingual-Spanish speaking clients) and launching lawsuits to protect their rights. By the time Pete Hernández's case made it to the Supreme Court, he had four Latino lawyers, the youngest of whom, John DeAnda, went on to be the first Latino appointed a federal judge in Texas. The *Hernandez* lawyers walked a tightrope between claiming their Mexican American client's rights were violated because Mexican Americans were excluded from the jury pool in his case and maintaining that Mexican Americans were White under Texas law. More technically, they alleged that Jackson County jury commissioners had violated the Fourteenth Amendment by excluding Latino citizens from the pool of potential jurors.[13] In that sense, Latinos' early civil rights victories came on the backs of Blacks because Latino litigants and attorneys did not seek to address racism more generally, as it impacted both Latinos and African Americans.[14] This chapter explains why Latinos sought to have it both ways until the late 1960s, when they adopted a "minority" approach in seeking enforcement of civil rights.

School Segregation and Latino Activism

Residential segregation has sometimes been a predicate for school segregation. In the Southwest, as Whites settled in places where they were outnumbered by Mexican Americans, they built towns or neighborhoods that separated the races, though usually by custom rather than by law. Residential segregation began in New Mexico and California in the nineteenth century.[15] Examples from Texas include a Rio Grande Valley town founded in 1915 with two separate White and Mexican sides, as was typical. As late as the 1970s, the town's one Catholic parish segregated Anglos to pews on the left and Mexican Americans to pews on the right.[16]

In New York City and Chicago, Latino residential segregation looked different given earlier African American/White segregation. The 71,000 Puerto Ricans who migrated to the United States between 1900 and 1944 settled primarily in New York City's working-class neighborhoods like Chelsea, East Harlem, the Lower East Side, the West Side of Manhattan, and the Brooklyn Navy Yards.[17] By the 1920s, East Harlem had become known as "Spanish Harlem" or "El Barrio."[18] Sociologist Jorge Duany reports that Puerto Rican neighborhoods "developed alongside African American neighborhoods" and were racially as diverse as the Puerto Rican population of New York City, one-third White and two-thirds Black or *mulato* in the 1940s.[19] Both Puerto Ricans and Mexican Americans arrived in small numbers in Chicago in the early twentieth century. Historian Lilia Fernández argues that it was White flight from urban Chicago in the 1960s and 1970s that made room for Latinos in the city.[20] "White flight" occurs when Whites leave a neighborhood to escape increasing numbers of racial minority neighbors. White flight was associated with court-mandated school desegregation in the wake of *Brown v. Board of Education*, the 1954 Supreme Court decision outlawing separate schools for Black and White children.

In response to court-ordered busing to achieve integration, between 1960 and 1980, Chicago's White population plummeted to less than 20 percent, while its African American population increased to 40 percent and its Latino population climbed to 20 percent.[21] Latinos moved into the least desirable White neighborhoods, those adjacent to African American neighborhoods, thus becoming a physical buffer between predominantly Black neighborhoods and "better" White neighborhoods that mirrored their in-between status. According to Fernández, "Mexicans' and Puerto Ricans' racial ambiguity spared most [of them] from the more sustained racial exclusion or immediate racial turnover [of neighborhoods] that African Americans experienced. . . . [They] often served as a 'buffer' between blacks and whites, a liminal group that constituted the transitional zone between rigid racial borders."[22] The same pattern has been observed nationally with Latinos and Asian Americans having replaced Whites in urban neighborhoods.

African Americans remain segregated from Whites, with most urban "integration" occurring between Blacks and Latinos, on the one hand, and Blacks and Asian Americans on the other.[23]

In the Southwest, the historical segregation of Mexican Americans in public accommodations, including restaurants, movie theaters, and swimming pools was of a piece with residential segregation.[24] It, in turn, produced the school segregation of Mexican American children, though their supposed inability to speak English often provided the false justification. Lawsuits demanding the integration of Mexican American children, sometimes in combination with African American plaintiffs, illustrate the depths of anti-Latino racism in the region that was formerly Mexico. Of the Southwestern states, the U.S. Civil Rights Commission found in the 1970s that Texas ranked worst in segregating Mexican American children.[25] Education scholar Richard Valencia identified all thirty-five desegregation lawsuits between 1920 and 1985 involving Mexican Americans. Fully two-thirds were in Texas, with another 20 percent in California.[26] These cases reveal how Latinos straddled the line as a group that was neither Black nor White but that experienced substantial and systematic educational segregation.

In a 1935 case, Adolfo Romo Jr. sued on behalf of his four children, who were forced to attend an Arizona school where every teacher was in training as a student-teacher.[27] At that time, the Supreme Court's decision in *Plessy v. Ferguson* provided the governing law: the "separate but equal" doctrine allowed school districts, cities, and states to separate the races so long as facilities were purportedly equal.[28] The *Plessy* court refused to invalidate Louisiana's requirement that "colored people" and Whites travel in separate cars of trains (except when they were attending to Whites as servants) under the Equal Protection Clause of the Fourteenth Amendment. Homer Plessy, who was seven-eighths White and one-eighth Black, argued the law was applied in an arbitrary manner (since he was sometimes allowed to ride in the White car) and reflected the state legislature's intention to subordinate African Americans. In response, the Supreme Court pronounced its "separate but equal" doctrine that segregated public facilities were constitutional so long as they were roughly equal, setting in motion lawsuits over whether racially segregated facilities were, in fact, equal. The Arizona case was notable because a federal judge sided with the Mexican American parents and children, finding that "the Mexican school" was not comparable to the White school, thus violating *Plessy*.

One year after its 1929 founding, LULAC sued the Del Rio, Texas, school district. Located deep in the Rio Grande Valley on the U.S.-Mexico border, the town operated separate schools for White and Mexican American children. LULAC's lawyers argued that, since state law provided only for segregation of Black children, the school district could not lawfully separate Mexican American children. Instead of attacking all racial segregation, LULAC essentially created a division between Latinos and African Americans by arguing that Mexican Americans were protected from segregation, unlike Blacks, because they were White. The school superintendent testified that he separated the Mexican American from the White children for good cause—because the former missed substantial portions of the school year by joining their parents as migrant farmworkers and because they could not speak English well enough to keep up with the White children.[29] The judge ruled that segregation based on such reasonable educational grounds such as these was lawful.[30] Under Texas law, school instruction was required to be exclusively in English, so this 1930 case effectively signaled to Texas school boards that they could legally use language as a proxy for segregating Mexican American children.[31]

A year later, in 1931, in California, the Mexican American plaintiffs in Orange County had better luck when they argued straight-up discrimination in a similar school scenario.[32] The town of Lemon Grove, located east of San Diego fifteen miles north of the Mexican border, built a new "Mexican school" when the Latino population in the town's elementary school reached a tipping point of 44 percent.[33] Parents organized themselves as the Comité de Vecinos de Lemon Grove (the Lemon Grove Neighbors Committee) and contacted the Mexican consul in

San Diego, who introduced them to two White attorneys, one of whom spoke Spanish fluently.[34] The school board made arguments similar to those in the Del Rio case: Mexican Americans needed a separate school to undergo "Americanization" because of their English language deficits. Judge Claude Chambers, a state judge, turned these excuses on the defendant school board, arguing that the best way to achieve those goals was to educate Mexican American children with White children, who could teach them English.[35] The judge also noted that he was especially impressed with one witness for the plaintiffs, Roberto Álvarez, a grade school student who testified in perfect English.

Legal scholar Derrick Bell has argued that, in the wake of World War II, courts felt pressure to take school segregation and other civil rights cases more seriously. The dual factors of greater awareness of the wrongs of racism given the rise of Nazi Germany and the weight of international pressure on the United States as a racial state supporting apartheid led to pro-plaintiff rulings in segregation lawsuits, including *Brown v. Board of Education*.[36] *Mendez v. Westminster*, an Orange County, California, case, is illustrative.[37] This was the first federal ruling to declare unconstitutional the segregation of Latino children; it was upheld on appeal by the Ninth Circuit Court of Appeals in 1946. *Mendez* also represented a turning point in that Latino and African American civil rights groups collaborated on the case, including the attorneys who would go on to argue *Brown v. Board of Education*. Yet it was not cited by the Supreme Court in *Brown* in 1954. Whereas in *Brown*, the question was one of *de jure* segregation of Black children, there was no comparable California law that mandated segregation of Latino children. Instead, it was a matter of *de facto* segregation, racial segregation by practice rather than by law, with school officials' reliance on proxies for racial status, such as the ability to speak fluent English or the fact that a student missed part of the school year to travel with their migrant farmworker parents. The plaintiffs' expert in *Mendez* foreshadowed the arguments made in *Brown*: "Segregation, by its very nature, is a reminder of inferiority, of not being wanted, of not being part of the community."[38]

Back in Texas, Latinos sought to extend *Mendez* there. First-grader Minerva Delgado was one of nineteen Mexican American plaintiffs who sued in federal court a century after the Treaty of Guadalupe Hidalgo ended the U.S.-Mexico War in 1848. LULAC and the G.I. Forum teamed up to file the case against four different school districts, hoping to end the segregation of Mexican American children once and for all. Minerva's parents wanted her to attend the school closest to her home, but the superintendent of Bastrop Independent School District refused because neither she nor her parents spoke English.[39] The plaintiffs made two claims: first, that segregation of Mexican American children was invalid because no state law authorized it; and, second, that Plessy's separate but equal logic applied to Blacks but not to Mexican Americans because, they claimed, Mexican Americans were White.[40] In 1948, the federal judge ruled in favor of the plaintiffs, finding that separate White and Mexican schools violated the Fourteenth Amendment's equal protection guarantee and giving the school district fifteen months to rectify the situation. The judge, however, left the school superintendent an out: the school was allowed to place Mexican American children in a separate classroom on the same campus "in the first grade only."[41] This surely was a "reminder of inferiority" that would shape children's entire school career.

Meanwhile, the Supreme Court's 1954 decision in *Brown v. Board of Education* changed the legal avenues for African American and Mexican American parents and children seeking justice. Attorney and future judge James DeAnda won two hard-fought school desegregation cases in and around Corpus Christi in the years following *Brown*. In *Hernandez v. Driscoll*, White and Mexican American children attended the same school, but Mexican American children were tracked into different classes, where they were forced to take twice as long as White students to complete the first two grades of school.[42] In other words, it would take Latino children four years to complete first and second grade and, in the same time, White students completed the first through fourth grades. The school superintendent blamed Mexican American parents for not teaching their children to speak English, and he brazenly asked the judge to require the plaintiff parents to speak exclusively in English to their children, a feat he knew was impossible. The judge saw through the school district's pretext—one designed to discourage Mexican American children to drop out of school before beginning junior high. By 1967, another school district—Odem Independent School District, in a town fifteen miles from Corpus Christi—made the switch to a different kind of language argument as the basis for separating Latino children.[43] The schools claimed that, in order to best educate Mexican American children, they needed to be taught exclusively by teachers who were bilingual in English and Spanish. The federal judge once again sided with the Latino plaintiffs.

In *Cisneros v. Corpus Christi Independent School District*,[44] De Anda represented both Mexican American and African American families, arguing it was not sufficient merely to "integrate" the plaintiffs' children while leaving White children unaffected by desegregation. The judge concluded that Mexican Americans were "an identifiable ethnic-minority class" protected under *Brown v. Board of Education*, one recognizable on the basis of "language, culture, religion, and physical characteristics."[45] This 1970 case marked the death knell for the "other White" strategy in Texas and also made history as the first to recognize the *de jure* segregation of Latinos. While segregation pre-*Brown* was *de jure* for Blacks, no state had similar laws for Latino students; instead, Mexican Americans in the Southwest were segregated by practice, often based on language-related issues. But those language pretexts could be either *de jure* (by law—either explicit law such as a statute or law in terms of a written policy) or *de facto* (by practice, by custom). In the Corpus Christi case, the judge ruled that the district's stated policy of how to achieve post-*Brown* desegregation constituted *de jure*, and thus illegal, segregation. The school's written desegregation plan combined African American first and third graders at one school with Mexican American second and fourth graders from another school to achieve desegregation—a technique known as "pairing."

Just because Latino plaintiffs stopped arguing they were White as the basis for challenging segregation did not mean school districts defending these lawsuits did the same. In New York City, in the late 1960s, African Americans were still suing to achieve the integration promised by *Brown*. Historian Sonia Song-Ha Lee finds that, although some Puerto Ricans engaged in intense competition with African Americans over war on poverty resources, many continued to insist they were White.[46] She concludes, however, that White New Yorkers, in the 1960s and 1970s, whether politicians or everyday people, saw Puerto Ricans as non-White alongside African Americans, with both groups shaping White "New Yorkers' notions of 'race,' 'ethnicity,' and 'minority' in the civil rights and Black Power eras."[47] In 1968, Black parents pressed for integration; the school district contended they had achieved integration in a Spanish Harlem elementary school because both Puerto Rican children and African American children attended the school. School officials claimed that since Puerto Ricans were White and African Americans were not, the school was racially integrated. Black and Puerto Rican parents responded with a united, well-publicized protest campaign.[48]

Houston school officials made a similar argument in the early 1970s, when they integrated African American children with Mexican American children, whom they said were White.[49] Specifically, they used the pairing strategy that had been found unconstitutional in Corpus Christi: where children from one school in certain grades would be paired with children from another school in different grades. Since schools were based in neighborhoods that in Houston were largely segregated between Whites, Blacks, and Mexican Americans, the "pairing plan" was designed to shield White children from desegregation, while combining schools that were predominantly Black and Latino. The strategy was viable only in school districts with Whites, African Americans, and Latinos and rested on residential segregation; it represented a way to formally comply with court-ordered desegregation without making White children "suffer" for it. Just before school started in August

1970, school officials used a waste paper basket lottery to decide which individual Black and Latino children would be bused away from their neighborhood school. To be clear, the school board did not act on its own initiative. Federal judge Ben C. Connally forced it to do so, devising the pairing plan to settle a desegregation lawsuit filed by African American parents and the local NAACP.

Responding to Connally's plan, NAACP members met with a Latino parents' group called the Mexican American Education Council, asking for their support to appeal the court's plan. In response, Mexican American parents went to court, seeking to formally intervene in the case (given the lawsuit's timing, it was too late for them to become plaintiffs). Connally was incensed, perceiving the parents' action as a personal affront. Connally came from a powerful Texas family, the son of U.S. Senator Tom C. Connally (D-TX, 1929–1953), whom a 1943 British intelligence document described as having typical Southern "prejudices."[50] The superintendent of schools was outraged, saying, "I don't know what a Mexican is," presumably to affirm the idea that Mexicans were as White as he was.[51] Connally was furious at the Latino civil rights leaders seeking to insert themselves into the case, accusing them of wanting to be White when it was convenient and racial minorities when it was not: "Content to be white for these many years, now, when the shoe begins to pinch, the would-be-intervenors wish to be treated not as whites but as an 'identifiable ethnic group.' In short, they wish to be 'integrated' with whites, not blacks."[52] For Texas bluebloods like the Connallys, the world around them was crumbling—or, at least, their ability to maintain White Anglo-Saxon power against the growing tide of Black and Brown resistance was in question.

The litigation continued for three more years, during which time thousands of Latino parents boycotted the public schools beginning in August 1970. Instead, they sent their children to *Huelga* Schools," staffed by volunteer teachers, run by parent committees, and located at Catholic Churches and community centers. *Huelga* means "strike" in Spanish, but the connotation is steeped in resistance to oppression;

it likely reflected parents' solidarity with farmworker labor movements occurring at the time in Texas and California. Mexican Americans as a substantial population were new to the city of Houston in 1970, and most of them would have had personal experience as farmworkers or the children of farmworkers. Education scholar Augustina Reyes, who was a young teacher in the *huelga* schools, reports that 2,000 parents showed up to the first community school in fall 1970.[53] In the end, Latinos and African Americans won a school desegregation decree that required Houston school officials to classify both groups as distinct minorities and require White children to participation in desegregation.[54] The Houston and other school segregation victories were no panacea for Latinos, just as *Brown* did not provide one for African Americans. Today most Latino children attend schools that are majority-Latino and almost all of them attend schools with negligible numbers of White children.[55]

Racism and the English-Only Movement

One of the reasons Latino parents could readily mobilize around the *huelga* schools was that there was an ongoing crisis in education. In Houston in 1970, 87 percent of Mexican Americans dropped out before graduating from high school.[56] In most of the Southwest, Mexican American children were not allowed to speak Spanish at school and faced severe punishment when they did so. As the school desegregation cases show, schools often used the fact that Latino children spoke limited English as an excuse to hold them back in school or force them to attend segregated schools. Yet the United States has never had an official language. Indeed, in the early twentieth century there was a vigorous movement of private schooling in the German language that resulted in a Supreme Court case upholding parents' right to educate their children in the language of their choice.[57] The way some politicians talk, however, you could be forgiven for thinking English the nation's official language.

In 2015, candidate Trump criticized candidate Jeb Bush for speaking Spanish, saying "In this country, we speak English, not Spanish."

For Latinos, repeated efforts to prevent them from speaking Spanish over two centuries are of a piece with school segregation, which so often was putatively based on English deficiency. Stand-up comedian Paul Rodríguez used to regularly tell a joke that made fun of the so-called English-only movement: he enters an elevator with two people speaking Vietnamese and interrupts them to say, "you're in America now, speak Spanish!"[58] The modern anti-Spanish push began in 1981, when Senator Samuel Ichiye Hayakawa (R-CA, 1977–1983) proposed a constitutional amendment to make English the official language of the United States; twenty-eight states have passed some version of an official English law or resolution since then.[59] The movement both gained and lost supporters due to its close links to organizations such as the Federation for American Immigration Reform (FAIR), which favors restricting immigration from Mexico and Central America. FAIR founder John Tanton, whose father was a Canadian immigrant, funded the push to make English the nation's official language as well as the Remembrance Project, which organizes those whose relatives allegedly have been killed by undocumented immigrants. Not long before his death in 2019, Tanton's report "Latin Onslaught" revealed his long suspected ties to the White nationalist movement.[60]

Language imperialism also was part and parcel of American colonialism. Among the first laws promulgated by the Americans in Puerto Rico was the mandate that all education be in English; the law was not changed until 1930. In 1912, Arizona and New Mexico took very different approaches to the Spanish language in their new constitutions. New Mexico reflected its majority–Mexican American population (and electorate): it declared two official languages, Spanish and English, and barred discrimination on the basis of language. Arizona, by contrast, made speaking English a requirement for holding office and made English the state's official language.[61] Today's anti-Spanish crusade has spun off variants of official English, including the drive to institute

English-only state laws and policies in schools and workplaces. In California in 1998, English-only advocates succeeded in enacting Proposition 227, a measure called "English for the Children" that banned bilingual education.[62] As sociologist Manuel Pastor put it, the law and campaign for it represented "fear that Latinos were resisting assimilation and that California was slipping back to its once-Mexican roots."[63] Significantly, the law did not ban schools' ability to offer foreign languages as enrichment (often endorsed by well-off White parents), but only public schools' programs for English learners who, of course, are disproportionately immigrants or their children. California voters overturned the law twenty years later, after a generation of limited-English speaking children were saddled with it.

The response to an English-only initiative in Florida that targeted Cuban Americans serves as a fascinating comparison to California. In 1980, Miami-Dade County voters enacted a law making English the official language. In response, according to sociologists Alejandro Pórtes and Rubén Rumbaut, "Cubans laid claim to the city," replacing the county commissioners who had supported the law with Cuban Americans by 1985 thus launching the congressional careers of several Latino politicians.[64] Cubans could not, however, have achieved this feat had they not received refugee status when they fled Castro's 1959 revolution. The first wave of Cuban immigrants arrived in the United States with capital because the most wealthy Cubans fled in the first decade (when Cuba lost 10 percent of its population). By the time the English-only law was enacted, Cuban Americans owned 28,000 (mostly small) businesses, and by 2007, they owned more than 250,000 businesses, including controlling more than half of all residential construction in the Miami metropolitan area.[65] Cuban refugees received benefits that have not been enjoyed by most Latino immigrants: public assistance (welfare); resettlement assistance; English-language courses; health benefits, among others. Most importantly, refugees have the right to become legal permanent residents a year after arriving, thus leading to their eventual naturalization as U.S. citizens with rights to vote and hold office—giving Cuban Latinos the power to boot out English-only politicians.

Harry Pachón, a Cuban American who grew up among Chicanos in East Los Angeles, founded the National Association of Latino Elected Officials in 1976. He described language as the strongest glue across Latinos, regardless of party or national origin, by which he meant issues like bilingual education, the right to speak Spanish, the need for government publications in Spanish (including ballots), and, especially, unity against the English-only movement. He used the example of a national English-only group targeting "their 'number one enemy.' . . . What does it mean to a Republican, right-wing Cuban to be called 'enemy number one' by a right-wing organization simply because she wants to speak in Spanish?"[66] The English-only cause's "enemy number one" was Ileana Ros-Lehtinen, who had galvanized opposition to the Florida English legislation. Ros went on to become the first Hispanic woman elected to Congress, and, in 1989, became the first Republican ever elected to Congress from Florida, retiring in 2019 after serving three decades in the House. Ros was born in Havana and is a staunch anti-Castro Republican, but she is also a never-Trumper.

Federal bilingual education programs, first enacted by Congress in 1968, were designed to improve the graduation rate of Latinos. At that time, Puerto Rican and Mexican American students had drop-out rates of 90 percent in many school districts.[67] Later, being bilingual in English and Spanish came to be a source of pride for many Latinos, rather than a stigma as it had been for Latino school children who came of age prior to that time. This is why bilingual education became a lightning rod, both for Latinos who favored it and non-Latinos who opposed it. Today's English protection laws reveal the broader anxieties about Latinos "taking over." While expressed as frustration about having to press a button to hear telephone information in English, the real worry is that white cultural dominance is slipping away. The anxiety has little to do with reality, given that research shows that, among Latino adults, 72 percent of immigrants speak mostly Spanish, whereas by the third generation (that is, the grandchildren of immigrants), 78 percent speak mostly English, though 22 percent are still bilingual.[68]

Racial Violence against Latinos

The violence Latinos have suffered based on their identity as Latinos has played a central role in the racial logic of white supremacy. Upon becoming a state a century ago, Arizona named its state police the Arizona Rangers invoking the Texas Rangers, infamous for their brutality toward Mexican Americans.[69] In his comprehensive history of Mexican Americans in Texas, David Montejano traces the Texas Rangers' widespread murder and harassment of Mexican Americans in the nineteenth and early twentieth centuries. Along the entire length of the border, the Rangers used intimidation and violence in order to secure the transfer of ranch lands into the hands of White settlers. While some Mexican ranchers were killed outright, others were persuaded to leave of their own accord, as the following account by a Mexican rancher shows:

> The cry was often heard, "We have to make this a white man's country!!" It would not be difficult to establish the fact that many well-to-do natives of Texas, of Mexican origin, were driven away by Rangers, who told them "If you are found here in five days you will be dead." They were this way forced to abandon their property.[70]

The Rangers played a major role in the enforcement of chattel slavery in Texas by tracking runaway slaves who sought refuge in Mexico and targeting Mexicans accused of aiding them to escape bondage.[71] After the Emancipation Proclamation, the Texas Rangers turned their sights directly on Mexican Americans in what scholars have labeled as "tantamount to state-sanctioned terrorism."[72] Historians now conservatively estimate that six hundred Mexican Americans died by lynching between 1848 and 1928 in what was formerly Mexico. Despite its much larger Mexican American population, New Mexico had only forty-nine lynchings, compared to Arizona's fifty-nine, even with a much smaller Mexican American population. California had 188 Mexican lynchings, but, to no one's surprise, Texas topped the list with 282.[73] There is no question that the Texas Rangers crossed the lines between enforcing state law, carrying out extra-legal lynchings, and terrorizing the Latino population.

Only recently, under the banner of the "Refusing to Forget" project, has there been a collective reckoning for how "Mexicans were intimidated, tortured, and killed by hanging, shooting, burning, and beating" by those charged with ensuring public safety, for whom "a culture of impunity prevailed."[74] One such effort in 2017 led to the unveiling of a state historical marker near Edinburg, Texas, in the Rio Grande Valley, that acknowledged the Texas Rangers' 1915 *matanza* (massacre) of hundreds (and, according to some reports, as many as 1,000) of Mexican descent persons. They were killed for being bandits, even though those murdered included a local postmaster and a school teacher. The real motive appears to have been to steal valuable ranch lands for Anglo settlers. Texas Rangers called in to testify about the matter said Mexican Americans were prone to violence and disloyal to the United States.[75] A report from the Texas legislature, written after an investigation in the wake of the massacre, concluded that the Texas Rangers had been lawless rather than lawmen: "Many of the men of the ranger force pride themselves in their reputation of being quick with their guns and desiring to have the reputation of bad men rather than faithful and efficient officers of the law."[76]

It was a Mexican American state senator from the Rio Grande Valley, José Tomás (J.T.) Canales, who in 1915 demanded the investigation of the Texas Rangers. He called for a "reorganization" of the Rangers, perhaps because it was not politically feasible to demand abolition of the state law enforcement branch. The legislative investigation and report heralded the end of the Texas Rangers' reign of terror, causing the force to be reduced from 1,300 to 100 men. Canales's great nephew,

Texas state representative Terry Canales spearheaded remembrance of this period of Texas history, channeling his uncle's courage in calling the Rangers to account. Canales compared the massacre to present day Texans' continuing efforts "to minimize the struggle of ethnic minorities' quest for civil rights."[77] Canales later invoked the 1915 massacre during his floor speech against Senate Bill 4, signed into law early in the Trump administration, which allows Texas state and local police to question the immigration status of those detained or arrested and punishes government officials who refuse to cooperate with ICE (i.e., by saying their city will be "a sanctuary" from federal immigration enforcement). Canales compared today's attitudes toward Latinos to the Rangers' past behavior, saying, "It is shocking to me that a century [after the 1915 massacre], we are still having to fight laws that are prejudiced against any Texan."[78]

Even as lynching has become a rarity, Latinos, like African Americans, have experienced disproportionate everyday violence from police for the past century. After World War II, Latino veterans, as has been noted, experienced racial discrimination on a daily basis. Unlike their parents, who were more likely to have been born in Mexico, these second-generation Mexican Americans were less apt to tolerate discrimination without fighting back. Ongoing police brutality was an important site for their resistance. One such incident was the Sleepy Lagoon murder trial in Los Angeles. In early 1943, seventeen Mexican American youths were convicted of serious crimes, including first-degree murder, in what was "the largest mass conviction in California history." A police officer testified before the grand jury that Mexican American men were "biologically prone to violence." As if to confirm the claim, the judge who presided over the trial refused to let the defendants cut their hair or change their clothes, despite the fact they had spent several months in county jail by the time of the trial. During this period, the *Los Angeles Times* published articles about the "zoot suiter menace"—a reference to the style of dress popular with some Mexican American and African American young men. Over the course of several summer days in 1943, the Zoot Suit Riots unfolded. White servicemen dressed in uniform attacked young Mexican American men dressed in the zoot suit style, as the police watched, refusing to intervene.[79] The original trial, the public and press characterizations of Mexican Americans, and the riots all served to imprint the idea that Mexican American men were inherently deserving of police and vigilante violence. These events were portrayed in the play and then the 1981 film *Zoot Suit*, written and directed by Luis Váldez.

In Los Angeles, it was uniformed servicemen who beat Latinos with impunity, but, in Texas, even uniformed Congressional Medal of Honor recipients were not immune from police abuse—if they were Mexican American. Speaking at an academic conference in 2004, federal judge James DeAnda—one of the lawyers who successfully fought school districts so that Latino children would not be segregated—recalled an incident of police brutality against a fellow veteran. In 1945, Sergeant Macario García was in the wrong restaurant at the wrong time. De Anda tells the story:

> They wouldn't serve him because he was Hispanic even though he was wearing his Congressional Medal at the time. And somebody said, "You're going to have to leave." As he did so, he tipped a glass of water over on the table and there were two [sheriff's deputies] in the restaurant at the time. They took him outside and beat the hell out of him and filed on him for assaulting an officer. . . .[80]

In the same year in the Rio Grande Valley, police watched as White teens beat Benigno Aguirre, at nineteen already back from World War II. Aguirre was attacked in 1945 in San Angelo, a town in the Rio Grande Valley. Aguirre and his friends Pete Gonzales and Rudy Salazar were out on a Saturday night when they were chased by a dozen White teenagers. His friends got away, but they caught Aguirre, who weighed only 115 pounds, and fifteen boys pummeled him, leaving him for dead.[81] Miraculously, Aguirre survived after surgery to repair his cracked skull followed by thirty-two days in a coma.

More than five decades later, Aguirre still feels daily physical pain from the beating; the psychological wounds persist as well. Even as an elderly man, he has no trouble recalling how the police facilitated the attack against him in a conversation with sociologist David Montejano:

> The mayor and most of the police force didn't like Mexicans—*para mí eran del* Klan [to me, they were like the Klan]. The police would escort the Anglo boys to the barrio as if this was a sport. The white boys admitted that the police had them doing this kind of stuff. The police would step in if the Mexicans tried to fight back. When they beat me up, the police were nearby.[82]

Aguirre's assailants largely escaped legal consequences despite the fact that he and his friends identified all fifteen assailants. It is surprising they were held to account at all, given that the city's police, prosecutors, and courts were rigged to favor Whites. The beating hit a nerve in San Angelo's Mexican American community, with several middle-class Mexican Americans and the local LULAC chapter pressing the case— perhaps because the victim was a World War II veteran or perhaps because similar beatings had happened too many times without repercussions. The district attorney finally sought indictments for assault with intent to murder against twelve teens (Aguirre is still irked that the remaining three were not charged), but the grand jury returned only one indictment for aggravated assault, a misdemeanor. Seventeen-year-old Leon Hunter Jr., the poorest of Aguirre's White assailants, pleaded guilty and paid a $125 fine.[83]

Like other towns in the Rio Grande Valley, social relations between Whites and Mexican Americans in 1940s San Angelo reflected ingrained racism that pervaded every facet of life. Mexican American men worked in the least-desirable jobs in sheep ranching and farming, while Mexican American women did domestic work or took in laundry or other menial piecework at home. In a town of more than 25,000 people, Mexican Americans were one-quarter of the population. Despite Mexican Americans serving in World War II and being disproportionately recognized for their bravery,[84] they returned home to blatant racial exclusion in Texas. Whites routinely denied them service at restaurants, bars, barbershops, hotels, and motels and at drugstore lunch counters. Mexican American senator Dionisio "Dennis" Chávez (D-NM, 1935–1962), the first Latino elected to federal office in the United States, introduced civil rights legislation to help those returning servicemen and others. A full two decades prior to the passage of Title VII of the Civil Rights Act of 1964, Chávez sought to prohibit racial discrimination at work. Chávez conducted whistle-stop hearings in 150 Texas towns, where Mexican American witnesses testified before his subcommittee about the widespread discrimination they experienced.[85]

Crime and policing serve as key sites for racializing Mexican Americans and other Latinos as non-White and racially subordinate, akin to the central place of criminalization in maintaining the oppression of African Americans. At least since the early twentieth century, Whites have asserted that Mexican, Mexican American, and Puerto Rican men have a propensity for criminal activity and violent behavior. *De jure* efforts to criminalize Mexican Americans go back to California's Greaser Act of the 1850s, by which time White Americans already outnumbered Mexicans by more than five to one. The law allowed for "greasers"—"the issue of Spanish and Indian blood"—to be punished if they were not "peaceable and quiet."[86] In a similar vein, nine Southern states enacted anti-vagrancy laws that allowed police to arrest newly freed slaves, who would then face incarceration and the prospect of labor as convicts without compensation.[87]

One of the results of Latinos' historical claim that they were White is that many states and cities, even today, do not gather or report statistics about Latinos or other groups beyond Whites and Blacks. In the area of crime and punishment, this has been of particular importance, often preventing Latinos and their advocates from proving racial profiling and related patterns. A notable exception was the fundamental role played by quantitative data in challenging and ultimately declaring unconstitutional the New York Police Department's notorious stop-and-frisk policy. The policy originated in 1994 with the election of Mayor Rudy Giuliani, who campaigned on a law-and-order platform.[88] The NYPD's Street Crimes Unit operated in plain clothes and unmarked cars, targeting "high crime" areas, but, in fact, data show that the best predictor of stops was a high proportion of Blacks and Latinos living in the neighborhood.[89] Neither was stop-and-frisk a crime fighting tool: in the program's early years, out of 45,000 stops, police had probable cause to arrest less than one quarter. Instead the program appeared to serve as everyday harassment of young men of color in public humiliation rituals that constituted racism by state actors. The National Congress for Puerto Rican Rights' Justice Committee, led by Puerto Rican activist Richie Pérez, called for an end to stop-and-frisk in the mid-90s.[90] Buttressed by a comprehensive report by the state attorney general, Perez and company were primed to succeed in their lawsuit, but then 9/11 occurred. The terrorist attack provided cover for law enforcement at the local, state, and federal levels to undertake extreme actions violating personal liberty in the name of national security.[91]

Instead of ending stop-and-frisk, the NYPD expanded it, even as a federal court ordered it to collect and monitor data on the program. The data showed that in the five years following 9/11, 85 percent of those stopped by police under the program were African American or Latino. Of those stopped, only 12 percent resulted in arrest, a considerably lower rate than pre-9/11. In 2008, a second class-action lawsuit was filed, defining those in the "class" to include all persons who since 2005 "have been, or in the future will be, subjected to" the NYPD's stop-and-frisk policy "in the absence of a reasonable, articulable suspicion . . . including those stopped on the basis of being Black or Latino."[92] Judge Shira A. Scheindlin in 2013 found that Blacks and Latinos were more likely than Whites to be stopped, even after controlling for a number of factors—including the frequency of crime in an area, the number of police patrolling an area and its socioeconomic characteristics—and that racial disparity existed across precincts and census tracts. She also found that Latinos were 95 percent more likely than Whites to be subjected to use of force and that Blacks were 14 percent more likely than Whites to be subjected.[93] Based on these and other findings in her 195-page decision, Scheindlin found stop-and-frisk unconstitutional and ordered the NYPD and the City of New York to end it. At the time of the ruling, then Mayor Michael R. Bloomberg vowed to appeal the ruling, accusing the judge of bias. Six years later, as a candidate for the Democratic Party's nominee for president, Bloomberg apologized for making stop-and-frisk a centerpiece of his twelve-year mayoralty.[94]

Whiteness Claims: Co-optation or Resistance?

The example of the Latino/African-American coalition to end stop-and-frisk is not surprising at the end of the twentieth century, when it started, or at the beginning of the twenty-first century, when it succeeded. But in the post–World War II decades, such a coalition would have been not only unlikely, but probably impossible given the context of the White-over-Black racial regime. In the early 1950s, an unlikely team of lawyers made civil rights history: Mexican American lawyers Gus García, Carlos Cadena, John Herrera, and James DeAnda. They began by searching for a "good" case to challenge the state of Texas for its exclusion of Mexican Americans from the jury box. Only American citizens have the right to serve as jurors and, as such, wholesale exclusion from this fundamental right violates the Constitution's Equal Protection Clause. At the same time, a criminal defendant has the Sixth Amendment right to be tried by an impartial jury.

The legal team eventually settled on representing Pete Hernández, recently convicted of murder and sentenced to life in prison by an all-White jury. Hernández worked at a filling station in Edna, Texas, southwest of Houston and northeast of Corpus Christi, in the triangle of central Texas. Most Mexican Americans in Edna picked cotton for a living, although the man Hernández was convicted of killing, Joe Espinoza, was not a farmworker but instead a labor contractor who matched workers with farmers. The case provided the opportunity to argue both that their client's Sixth Amendment rights had been abridged and that Mexican American citizens' rights as potential jurors had been violated. Because the killing arose from a verbal altercation at a tavern and Hernández had no prior troubles with the law, his lawyers thought they had a chance of winning on appeal.

Despite the fact that 15 percent of Jackson County citizens had Spanish surnames, not a single one had ever been called for jury service. Hernández's attorneys eventually made it to the U.S. Supreme Court, but they had to sell a lot of tamales to get there. Local LULAC chapters funded the litigation with tamale sales, spurred to action in one Texas town after another. García and his team published articles in the Spanish-language press and delivered rousing calls to action on Spanish-language radio stations. Though they argued their client—and Mexican American citizens in the county—had been discriminated against in violation of the Fourteenth Amendment, they held on to the valuable fiction that Mexican Americans, unlike African Americans, were White. Hernández's legal team presented statistics and other evidence to show that Mexican Americans in Jackson County were discriminated against as "a separate class," but their refusal to say Mexican Americans were not White almost cost them victory. Like the school desegregation cases in New York and Texas, the defendant in this case, the state of Texas, argued that, precisely because Mexican Americans were White, there had been no discrimination: Hernández was White, and White jurors decided his fate.

The *Hernandez* litigators presented an especially dramatic piece of evidence during the appellate arguments. In a highly unconventional move, a member of the legal team was sworn in to testify; he was asked whether he had gone to the restroom in the courthouse during the just-concluded recess. It was thus revealed that the courthouse had segregated men's restrooms, one reserved for White men and one specifically designated for African American and Latino men—as the men's room signage put it "Colored Men and *Hombres Aquí* (Men Here)." Perhaps they also asked where the attorneys stayed at night; they would have told the judge that it was not safe for Mexican Americans to be in the area after sunset, so that they drove the 100 miles back and forth to Houston each day.[95] We know the first question and its answer made an impression on the justices because they specifically invoked it in their unanimous opinion. Chief Justice Earl Warren, the former governor and attorney general of California, was likely the only one of nine justices who had familiarity with Mexican Americans. As governor he signed into law repeal of the state's school segregation statute.[96] As noted above, California law mandated that Black, Indian, and Chinese children be educated separately from Whites, but its demise was triggered by the 1946 *Mendez v. Westminster* ruling regarding the *de facto* segregation of Mexican American children. For the other justices, the evidence that Mexican Americans were, in this instance, segregated with Blacks would have been a powerful way to understand Mexican Americans as deserving of the law's equal protection.

Hernandez appears alongside *Brown* in the 1954 Supreme Court volume, and Warren, who as chief justice controlled which justice authored which opinion, wrote both opinions. His punchline was compelling in its bluntness: "It taxes our credulity to say that mere chance resulted in there being no members of this class among the over six thousand jurors called [in the county] in the past 25 years."[97] How the court reached that conclusion says much about how Blacks and Whites remain the baseline comparator to any other group seeking constitutional protection. The court declared that the Fourteenth Amendment is not concerned exclusively with a "'two-class theory'—that is, based upon differences between 'white' and Negro." The quote marks around "white" are telling, given that the *Hernandez* brief does not concede Mexican Americans are *not* White but, rather, that they are a different kind of White. In short, he gestured to the sensibilities—and sensitivities, no doubt—of Mexican Americans, who claimed that they were unconstitutionally discriminated against *and* that they were White.

Chief Justice Warren acknowledged that racial categories are social constructs when he wrote, "throughout our history differences in race and color have defined easily identifiable groups which have at times required the aid of the courts in securing equal treatment under the laws. But community prejudices are not static, and from time to time other differences from the community norm may define other groups which need the same protection."[98] To say that "race and color" are dynamic ("not static") and that they just as surely reflect "community prejudices" acknowledges racism as process and hierarchy that some have argued is absent in *Brown*.[99] Warren concludes that "whether such a group exists within a community is a question of fact," thus contrasting the Fourteenth Amendment's automatic, universal protection of African Americans with the case-by-case protection of other groups. To say that whether a group other than Blacks will secure equal protection depends on convincing a judge that "community norms" are such that the group is stigmatized or disadvantaged vis-à-vis the dominant racial group is a substantial hurdle, especially given skeptical judges like Connally in the Houston school case. In *Hernandez*, the team of Latino lawyers presented a host of social and demographic data to support the view that Mexican Americans, while White by law, were treated adversely in ways that warranted constitutional protection.

Latinos responded in various ways to the context of their categorization and treatment within the system of white supremacy. None were predictable or progressive in any linear sense. For example, when Lyndon Johnson was the young head of a New Deal jobs program—the Texas National Youth Administration—in the mid-1930s, he made sure the "vast majority" of South Texas Mexican American participants "were properly classified as 'white.'" Johnson's was a political calculus: Texas's all-White Democratic Party primary meant that only Whites could vote. Johnson and Congressman Maury Maverick, of San Antonio, spoke to President Roosevelt about the problem of the "colored" label keeping some Mexican American "New Dealers" from voting; shortly thereafter, FDR ordered federal agencies to designate Mexican Americans as White.[100] In a previous job, Johnson worked for Congressman

Richard Kleberg (D-TX), a third-generation heir to the massive King Ranch in South Texas. Kleberg's cousin once bragged that, in an earlier era, the ranch policy was to deduct the poll tax from the paychecks of its Mexican American *vaqueros* (cowboys) "until the men had voted for the landowners' candidates under the foreman's watchful eye."[101] What is critical is that African Americans had neither opportunity; when in 1937 Blacks lobbied for the abolition of the poll tax, LULAC refused to support them. LULAC lobbied for the designation of Mexican Americans as White so that they could vote in Texas's so-called White man's primary. Both moves reveal how Latinos' precarious status as White furthered the subordination of Blacks.[102]

LULAC's embrace of the term "Latin American" at its 1929 founding in South Texas was, at base, obsequious to the portion of the White power structure that did not want to think about "Mexicans."[103] In particular, the claim distanced the group's aspiring Mexican American founders, who conceived of themselves as more American than Mexican and prided themselves on their distinctiveness from Mexican immigrants. The term Latin American also reflected their claim to be "White" in Texas, which necessarily was simultaneously the claim that one was "not Black." As historian Neil Foley notes, "To claim whiteness fully and convincingly, LULAC emphasized the importance of maintaining the color line between its members and African Americans and urged members not to associate with Negroes."[104] María Joséfina Saldana-Portillo offers a more charitable interpretation, emphasizing that LULAC members' "daily lives [were] charted by violence, denigration, and discrimination."[105] In such a world, the cloak of whiteness was welcome when it could be worn.

World War II, the Nazi genocide of Jews, and the ramping up of the African American civil rights movement all called the old LULAC strategy into question. Two examples illustrate the dilemma, which eventually catalyzed a growing gulf among Mexican Americans. In 1943, LULAC joined the Mexican Consulate in supporting state legislation to shore up Latinos' inclusion in the White category. The Caucasian

Race–Equal Privileges Resolution passed the Texas legislature and was signed by the governor. Texas pols and agribusiness desperately needed to convince Mexico to end its boycott of the then-new wartime program to supply short-term Mexican laborers (the Bracero Program), and the Mexican government sought a way to protect its young, usually Indigenous workers from exploitation and discrimination. As a resolution, the measure carried little weight, but its symbolic significance was momentous. It once again showed Latinos that they could find protection by claiming whiteness. Foley put it well when he characterized the resolution's importance as an assumption that Mexicans are "members of the Caucasian race, which they were only in some legal, pseudo-scientific, and ethnographical sense; but practically no Texan regarded Mexicans, particularly *bracero* farm workers as white."[106] By 1964, when the United States ended the Bracero Program, cotton growers had found a better solution: 78 percent of cotton was machine harvested.

What is most damning about LULAC's endorsement of the resolution was that it displayed a willingness to sacrifice African Americans, making Latinos complicit in White-over-Black oppression. Like LULAC, the G.I. Forum—the veterans' group that fought the refusal to bury Mexican Americans in 1949 and 2016—has been accused of capitulating to Whites. Faced with a 1957 request to support African Americans in their fight to have the *Brown v. Board of Education* ruling enforced in Texas, G.I. Forum leader Manuel Ávila was adamant: "I can already hear the Anglos saying, 'those n***** lovers.' . . . To go to bat for the Negro, as Mexican Americans, is suicide."[107] In its best light, we could interpret the statement as a calculated recognition of the depths of White racism in regard to both African Americans and Mexican Americans. Seen in another light, the statement's pitting of "us" against "them" is striking. As political strategy, the position failed to take account of Latinos' long-term interests, given that, in combination with African Americans at that time, they were one-third of the state's population (today they are more than half). Whether they were motivated by the long view that their fate was tied to that of African Americans or doing the right thing, Mexican American lawmakers in Texas's lower house uniformly defied the G.I. Forum in support for *Brown*. In the state senate, Henry B. González, a Mexican American politician who would go on to represent San Antonio and the surrounding area in Congress for thirty-nine years, joined them. He filibustered for thirty-six hours to successfully kill the segregationist legislation.[108]

Ambiguities and contestations emerge as the defining features of Latino racialization in America. In the post–World War II era, Latino leaders danced around whiteness, at times self-defining as White as a defensive move and at others trying mightily to reinforce the boundary between themselves and African Americans. Whatever the circumstances, the result was Latinos' complicity in enforcing the White-over-Black racial logic, giving the upper hand to "real" Whites once more. James DeAnda's legal brief to end to the segregation of Mexican American children was pragmatic, arguing both that *Brown* protected Mexican Americans against exclusion and that, under *Hernandez*, they were a different class of Whites.[109] An early Mexican American scholar, University of Texas Professor George I. Sánchez, was an expert witness for Latino plaintiffs in many school desegregation lawsuits, but he was inconsistent in his embrace of the strategy of whiteness in contrast to siding with Blacks in anti-racist coalition.[110] In one instance in 1959, Sánchez corresponded with NAACP Legal Defense Fund attorneys about possible joint efforts. Saldaña-Portillo examines his playfulness about Mexican Americans' whiteness, which she terms "an ironic undoing of whiteness."[111] Although Sánchez at this point in time still advocated deploying whiteness as a shield, he suggested in the letter that, once Whites had made the mistake of letting Mexican Americans into their club, other racial groups would not be far behind; yet he admitted that this tenuous whiteness amounted to very little protection for Mexican Americans.

By the 1970s, Latinos ran headlong into the limitations and contradictions of claiming to be White. In his history of the Chicano Movement in East Los Angeles between 1966 and 1978, Ernesto Chávez charts the rise and fall of the Black Panther-influenced Brown Berets, the anti–Vietnam War Chicano Moratorium Committee, and a radical labor organization known as CASA (Centro de Acción Social Autóno-mo).[112] All three shared a radicalized youth base, one that rejected whiteness and demanded Whites' recognition as a distinct racial minor-ity. While some have portrayed the rise of the Chicano Movement as a sharp break with the past,[113] there were continuities between the radi-cals and their parents' generation. For example, Edward Roybal in 1949 became the first Mexican American elected to the Los Angeles City Council in the twentieth century.[114] Campaigning for Black votes in 1948, Roybal said: "Our skin is brown, our battle is the same. Our vic-tory cannot be but a victory for you too."[115] During his first term he fought housing discrimination, at one point posing as a homebuyer in order to reveal a real estate developer's refusal to sell to Mexican Ameri-cans, African Americans, Japanese Americans, and Jews.[116] During his time on the council, Roybal cast the lone vote against mandatory reg-istration for "Communists and other subversives," called out the police chief's characterization of Mexican Americans as "wild tribes," endured a political opponent's accusation that he had pulled a knife on him, and narrowly lost the fight to establish the city's Fair Employment Practices Commission.[117]

In New York City, Puerto Ricans formed the Young Lords, an organization modeled on the Black Panthers. In the summer of 1969, they galvanized Puerto Ricans—and other New Yorkers watching television—by burning a huge pile of trash in East Harlem to protest the city's neglect of their neighborhood. "It was the drama of that high pile of garbage burning in the middle of the street that hot summer evening," said Jose Ramon Sanchez, "It was the feverish image of rage and defiance in the faces of old and young Puerto Rican men and wom-en."[118] In New England and Illinois, there were twenty-eight riots by Puerto Ricans between 1964 and 1971.[119] Puerto Ricans struggled, like Mexican Americans, as a group in between White and Black.[120] As Lilia Fernandez put it, "*brown* stands in as a placeholder that captures the malleable meaning assigned to the social difference most Mexicans and Puerto Ricans are believed to embody."[121]

In Chicago, it was up to Latinos to deploy the notion of brown rather than White or Black as a racialized state of being. Once settled in large numbers in Chicago, would Latinos swing, in the 1983 mayoral election, toward the Democratic Party establishment or toward Harold Washington, an African American who espoused a progressive Rainbow Coalition vision? Eight of ten Latino voters supported Washington in the general election, and even more voted for him when he was re-elected in 1987. Some credit "the alliance of the Young Lords, Young Patriots, and Black Panthers" as the source of Washington's success.[122] He campaigned to elect the first Latinos who broke into Chicago politics, such as former congressman Luis Gutiérrez (D-IL, 1993–2019), elected alderman in 1986.[123] Beyond those who voted for him, other Latinos who, due to age or citizenship status, could not vote were nonetheless swept up in the interracial alliance for civil rights, gender equality, and social justice Washington began.[124]

As for the Chicano Movement, its most profound legacy was its politicization of young Mexican Americans, whether high school or college students in the 1970s. More than 10,000 high school students in and around Los Angeles walked out of school to protest Chicanos' low rate of high school graduation, the failure to hire Mexican American teachers in predominantly Mexican American schools, and the curriculum's neglect of Mexican and Mexican American history and culture.[125] These school walkouts inspired others across the nation, as well as a groundswell of new college and university organizations, some of which persist today as sites for the social and political integration of first-generation-to-attend-college Latino students, such as El Movimiento Estudiantil Chicano de Aztlán, or MEChA (which in 2019 voted to change its name to Movimiento Estudiantil Progressive Action). Latinx students have continued to be at the political vanguard, as when, in 1994, thousands walked out of school to protest the anti-immigrant law known as Proposition 187. Less than twenty-five years later, those teen protestors had become local and state politicians—like Kevin de León, who, as leader of the California Senate, ensured the passage of laws to welcome and protect immigrants from ICE raids and other increasingly harsh federal enforcement. Speaking on Prop. 187's twenty-fifth anniversary, in 2019 de León affirmed that "What 187 did is spawn a new generation of politicians. There's no question about it. There's no ambiguity. There's no vagueness. There's no room for misinterpretation."[126]

4

TO COUNT, WE MUST BE COUNTED

I felt like I needed to ask Kennedy to forgive me for not being able to stop those bullets. . . . I never owned a suit in my life, and so when I wore the suit and stood in front of his grave . . . I felt important. I felt American.

—*Juan Romero, who as a seventeen-year-old busboy cradled a dying Robert F. Kennedy, 2018*[1]

I grew up the only Mexican kid in my neighborhood. . . . I was made to feel like a third-rate citizen. But I used to read about the Smithsonian, think about what an amazing place it is—and now they have my machine.

—*Mariano Martínez, Latino restaurateur and inventor of the frozen margarita machine, circa 2010*[2]

Juan Romero and Mariano Martínez came of age in Los Angeles and Dallas, respectively, at roughly the same time, but their lives were starkly different. Born in the Mexican state of Sonora, Romero's family settled in East Los Angeles in the early 1960s, then the heart of Latino Los Angeles. Strictly speaking, East Los Angeles lies outside Los Angeles city limits, in an unincorporated area of Los Angeles County that begins just west of downtown Los Angeles. A series of neighborhoods bounded to the east by the municipalities of the San Gabriel Valley, East L.A. sprouted in the early twentieth century as home to workers who were, due to racially restrictive covenants, not allowed to own homes in many Los Angeles neighborhoods. What we know today as "South Central Los Angeles"—more accurately South Los Angeles County—developed in the same way: Latinos, African Americans, Jews, and Japanese Americans lived in both areas before they came to have identities as Black, for South Los Angeles, and as Mexican, for East L.A. Both areas are characterized by industrialization (replete with environmental hazards) and bear the brunt of Los Angeles's massive freeway system (another source of toxic exposure), making them affordable places to live.[3]

When Romero's family moved there, East L.A. was home to the largest concentration of Latinos in the United States (and the second largest concentration of Mexicans in the world). That made it home, as well, to the Chicano movement, which sprouted in public schools like Garfield High School and Roosevelt High School, where in 1968 thousands of Mexican American students and a handful of Latino teachers boycotted school to protest racism. Romero attended Roosevelt by day and worked by night at the Ambassador Hotel in downtown Los Angeles, just over the bridge from East L.A. In 1968, Senator Robert F. Kennedy was seeking the Democratic Party nomination for president; after voting closed in the California primary, he addressed supporters at the Ambassador Hotel with Dolores Huerta, the labor activist, standing behind him.[4] He won by a few percentage points, thanks, some say, to Mexican American voters.[5] After the speech, Kennedy took a service elevator so as to exit via the kitchen, where Romero shook his hand right before he was fatally shot. Cradling Kennedy's head so it wouldn't touch the floor, blood running through his fingers, Romero placed his rosary in Kennedy's hand, hoping the ambulance drivers would allow him to keep holding it. A *Los Angeles Times* photographer captured the moment and the iconic photo appeared on front page newspapers across the globe. Romero became recognizable as the brown-skinned busboy holding another dying Kennedy brother, but his reality as an unskilled laborer until he died in 2018 never changed.[6]

Mariano Martínez had a very different life. He is the great-grandson of Mexican Americans born in Texas. His grandparents and parents on both sides were small business owners, operating family-style Mexican restaurants. Hoping to ensure he would receive a high-quality public school education, his middle-class parents were the first Latinos to integrate the all-White development of Lakewood, a metropolitan Dallas suburb. Martínez, far more privileged than Romero, dropped out of college, taking several years to play electric guitar in garage bands. He settled down in 1971, as he puts it, opening his eponymous restaurant in a Dallas suburb (now one of six locations in Texas). Unlike his parents' and grandparents' restaurants, Martínez sought a higher-end ambience—he wanted customers to hire a babysitter, have a margarita in the bar before dinner, another one while eating, and another in the bar after dinner.[7] The bartenders could not keep up with the high demand, leading Martínez to invent the frozen margarita machine based on 7–11's Slurpee machine. His original machine is now housed in the Smithsonian's American History collection. Meanwhile, Mexican food has gone from tamale carts in Chicago and New York in the 1920s to Taco Bell to fine cuisine: "It's been conquest by a thousand tacos, a million tamales, and a hell of a lot of salsa, which surpassed ketchup as America's top-selling condiment back in the 1990s," as Gustavo Arrellano, a journalist and author, puts it.[8]

On one level, Romero's and Martínez's stories of racial exclusion dovetail. Both came of age in the late 1960s, a time of great political awakening and radicalism among some Latinos, but neither one was politically engaged as a young man, despite their treatment as second-class Americans because they were Latino. Only at the end of his life, wearing a suit for the first time, as he stood at Bobby Kennedy's gravesite at Arlington National Cemetery, did Romero feel truly American, as he put it. As for Martínez, even relatively late in life, he still juxtaposed his greatest triumph—having his frozen margarita machine in the Smithsonian—with the pain of racial exclusion he experienced as a child.

In a way, Latinos collectively have experienced the same vicissitudes of exclusion and inclusion. In the 1960 election, they were first courted by a presidential campaign. Lyndon Baines Johnson (LBJ) narrowly lost the Democratic nomination to John F. Kennedy (JFK), but joined the ticket as the vice-presidential nominee. The campaign's "Viva Kennedy Clubs" were the JFK-LBJ ticket's effort to mobilize Mexican American voters in Texas and California.[9] At the time, Texas's Democratic and Republican parties, like other southern states, still ran all-White primaries: primary contests in which only Whites could vote, a way of undermining the Voting Rights Act, which constrained states at election time but did not affect private organizations like political parties. In California, there was no such mechanism, but both political parties had long neglected Mexican American voters. Political parties, at the institutional level, reflected the exclusion Romero and Martínez felt at the individual level.

The clubs were JFK's introduction to Mexican Americans, and he gave them credit for his narrow win over incumbent Richard Nixon in Texas.[10] LBJ, in contrast, was well acquainted with Mexican Americans. When he was first elected to Congress in 1949, he won narrowly with such strong Mexican American support that his opponent alleged voter fraud that was never proven.[11] Johnson's connections to Mexican Americans ran deep. Though he was from a middle-class family in the Texas Hill Country, between Austin and San Antonio, Johnson attended Southwest Texas State Teachers College (now Texas State University) in San Marcos, Texas, an hour's drive northeast of San Antonio. Johnson later described struggling to afford college (he said he showered and shaved at the gym), and took a year off to earn enough money to complete his studies. In that year, he was a full-time teacher at the segregated school for Mexican Americans in the town of Cotulla, in the heart of the Rio Grande Valley. He also worked closely with Mexican Americans as director of the Texas National Youth Administration in the 1930s. He had a history of supporting Black civil rights, too; in 1954, LBJ was the only Southerner in the Senate who refused to sign onto the "Southern Manifesto," which challenged *Brown's* mandate for school desegregation.[12] After Kennedy's assassination in 1962, President Johnson drove the Democrats' transformation from the party of White segregationists to the party of the soon-to-be non-White majority.

Voting Rights, Protest Politics, and the Politics of Incorporation

We rightly conceive of the 1965 Voting Rights Act (VRA) as a supplement to the Fifteenth Amendment to the Constitution, which guaranteed freedmen the right to vote. It has also had tremendous significance for

Latinos. Speaking before a televised joint session of Congress to promote the proposed law, LBJ singled out the impact it would have on
Mexican Americans. He invoked his year teaching, four decades previously, at "the Mexican school," describing "the pain of prejudice" in his
students' eyes. "It never occurred to me in my fondest dreams that I
might have the chance to help the sons and daughters of those students
and to help people like them all over this country. But now I do have that
chance—and I'll let you in on a secret—I mean to use it."[13]

Sure enough, Latino civil rights organizations have sued states, counties, cities, school boards, public utility districts, and community college
districts across the nation to enforce the VRA in order to protect the
rights of Latino voters. As early as 1966, the Supreme Court upheld
the new law's mandate that the absence of English literacy could not be
the basis for voter exclusion as applied to mainland Puerto Ricans.[14] In
California, the VRA and a state version of the law have utterly transformed the political landscape. The late Joaquín Ávila, the author of the
California VRA and the most prolific litigator of voting rights cases for
Latino plaintiffs, linked ongoing struggles to enforce voting rights to
the continuing legacy of slavery:

> The institution of slavery is so ingrained in the DNA of this
> country [that] it is difficult to completely excise it. That's
> why you have to have strong measures like the federal Vot-
> ing Rights Act and the California Voting Rights Act and
> you have to have a very committed cadre of voting rights
> activists, with passion, fighting every instance of voting dis-
> crimination.[15]

Enforcement under the federal and California voting rights laws has
fundamentally reshaped California politics, leading predominantly
Latino state senate and assembly districts to elect fully 20 percent of
state lawmakers and 15 percent of city councilors state-wide.[16]

Latino politics in the 1960s reflected two strands that sometimes
intersected: protest politics and electoral politics. The decade saw the

rise of labor organizing among Latinos in Texas and California. In Texas, hundreds of farmworkers, backed up by high school and college students, conducted "the minimum wage march" from the Rio Grande Valley to the capitol in Austin, leading to passage of the state's first minimum wage law.[17] In California, Dolores Huerta and Cesar Chávez sought to unionize farmworkers, garnering the national spotlight in 1968 when the United Farm Workers Organizing Committee (UFWOC) called for a boycott of grapes as a way of supporting those who harvested the fruit under grueling conditions. The strikers eventually claimed victory—two-thirds of California grapes would be grown under UFWOC labor contracts—but that was after a bruising strike, including a twenty-five day, 340-mile march from Delano in California's San Joaquin Valley to the state capitol in Sacramento.

After that march, Chávez began the next leg of the strike with a twenty-five-day fast. He was joined by Bobby Kennedy, with a priest who gave them communion; afterwards, Kennedy praised Chávez as "a hero of our times." During this fast, Chávez received a telegram of support from Dr. Martin Luther King Jr., just a month before King was assassinated in Memphis on April 4, 1968. Two years later, on Labor Day in 1970, police arrested Chávez during a lettuce strike in Salinas. Both King's and Kennedy's widows, Coretta Scott King and Ethel Kennedy, respectively, visited Chávez in jail.[18] By 1980, the farmworkers union had 60,000 members, but by the end of that decade, membership had slumped to fewer than 10,000.[19] In one sense, this was a victory: growing numbers of Mexican Americans were moving out of agricultural labor into other, better-paying jobs. Seen in another light, however, the UFW's success brought about its demise, in that its successful advocacy for stronger federal and state protections of agricultural workers eventually led growers to turn to a cheaper, more vulnerable class of workers—undocumented Mexican migrants, who came north in ever-larger numbers after 1970.[20]

Huerta's and Chávez's efforts to improve the lives of farmworkers nevertheless had considerable impact on Latino political success. Initially, their tactics relied on protest politics like those of the Black

Civil Rights Movement—marches, boycotts, strikes, fasts, and so forth. Arrests during these protests generated media attention, galvanizing both elite and popular sympathy for the farmworkers. Similarly, young people in Boricua (Puerto Rican) and Chicano (Mexican American) communities organized at the grassroots level in urban environments. These two strands of more radical political mobilizing eventually gave way to the more moderate politics of incorporation, perhaps as a testament to the impact of protest politics. Political inclusion may have been inevitable as high school and college students grew up and started families. Like unionized farmworkers, maybe they, too, drifted from working-class to middle-class jobs. Perhaps inclusion was the result of larger political dynamics and a withdrawal, by many, from the most contentious debates around racial equality, free speech, the Vietnam War, and women's liberation.

Put another way, it seems the political mainstream co-opted "the Puerto Rican elites," who took up positions in White economic and political institutions.[21] Reflecting on the transformation from more radical "Chicano" to more mainstream "Hispanic" politics among Mexican Americans, the late Raul Yzaguirre put it this way: "What militants did was open a lot of doors for middle-class and upper-class Hispanics."[22] Yzaguirre, then the leader of the National Council of La Raza, situated himself as an activist who had been politicized by the late-1960s Chicano movement. The National Council of La Raza, whose name invokes Vasconcelos's "la raza cósmica," was an organization founded in 1968 as a radical alternative to LULAC. Just recently, the group changed its name to UnidosUS (*unidos* in Spanish means united) in order to reach young people and a wider segment of the Latino population, beyond Mexican Americans. Its website explained the logic of the name change as follows:

> Our previous name paid tribute to Chicano activism born in the Southwest back in 1968, during the heyday of the civil rights movement. . . . Through three years of one-on-one meetings, surveys and 18 focus groups across the country, we found that our previous name didn't resonate with

the people that we were trying to reach—in particular those who don't remember the civil rights movement or weren't raised in communities that used the term [la raza].[23]

Former New Mexico governor Bill Richardson is a case in contrast to Yzaguirre. Richardson, the son of a Mexican-born mother and a White American father, grew up in a Boston suburb and was far less charitable about "the militants," as Yzaguirre termed them. "The word Chicano had a bad connotation. . . . [We] can open more doors with Hispanic."[24] Then a congressman (D-NM), Richardson went on to serve in the 1990s as President Bill Clinton's United Nations ambassador and then secretary of energy, before serving two terms as governor of New Mexico (2003–2011). His biography epitomizes the kind of middle-class Latino who benefited from the legacy of Chicano activism to which Yzaguirre refers.

A utilitarian reason politicians and elected officials embraced Latino or Hispanic identity was that it allowed them to speak jointly, using one term, about Mexican Americans, Puerto Ricans, and Cubans—groups previously seen as minor players in regional politics who had little hope of gaining national attention. Congressman Matthew Martínez (D-CA), who represented East Los Angeles from 1980 to 2000, shared this pragmatic outlook. Born in 1929 in a Colorado mining town, Martínez's Mexican American parents moved to East Los Angeles before he began elementary school. After serving in the Marines until 1950, he went on to complete trade school and start a furniture upholstery business before serving as a local and then a state elected official. For Martínez, Latinos were wise to play up "the misconception" of a united voting bloc, because it made it more likely they would not be ignored. He astutely captured the role that non-Latinos play in creating a sense of shared fate: "If you're in New York, you're [my] color, and you speak with an accent or speak Spanish, you're [assumed to be] Puerto Rican. By and large, throughout the United States, the non-Hispanic doesn't make a distinction between a Puerto Rican, a Cuban, an Ecuadoran, a Bolivian, a Salvadoran, you name it."[25] Martinez's story is all the more interesting because, in 2001, he was defeated by a considerably more progressive Latina candidate, Hilda Solís, whom Obama later appointed secretary of labor. Solís portrayed Martínez as out of touch with his constituents, and, as if to confirm it, he changed his registration to Republican after losing to her in the Democratic Primary.[26]

At one level, the reason Martínez gave—that non-Latinos saw Latinos as "all the same"—is consistent with the claims-making by the young radicals in the Boricua and Chicano movements. They were motivated by the same discriminatory treatment, the same perception of White racism. One 1980s survey of Latino elected officials (including all of those in Congress) found that 84 percent credited their experience of racial/ethnic discrimination the catalyst for their political activism. Seventy percent of them reported their father had not completed more than eight years of schooling, and 60 percent reported their father's occupation as laborer or skilled laborer (the survey did not ask about mother's education or occupation).[27] Yet Martínez's rationale also describes the sociological notion of racial group assignment, as opposed to self-identification, by others: racially (and in a host of other ways), we are who others think we are, and that, in turn, shapes our racial self-identification.

Creating Racial Categories and Sorting People into Them

Whether as mainstream politicians or grassroots activists, Latinos wanted a seat at the national table, whatever the issue being served up and whether the host was a Democrat or Republican. They were beginning to get that seat in the 1970s, as each presidential administration also worked hard to manage their racial inclusion. The decennial census provided one way to do so. The racial state uses all the means it has to create racial categories and then sort people into them, both historically and today. The racial state, whether in the United States today or colonial governments in the past, must work hard to make races and sometimes to unmake them; it doesn't happen automatically or in a self-executing way. Elites must perpetually wrestle with race and how to govern racially subordinated populations. As the story of the making of Latinos as a race shows, however, this is not merely moving chess pieces around on a racial chessboard. Racially subordinated groups have a long history of resisting racial domination, but the process does not always unfold in a linear way but, rather, is full of twists and turns, unintended consequences, and pregnant with possibilities that emerge when one side is caught off guard.

The official sorting mechanism in the United States is the census, the painstaking population count undertaken each decade by the federal government. Ostensibly, the purpose of the census, as specified in Article 1, Section 1 of the U.S. Constitution, is apportionment: "Representatives and direct Taxes shall be apportioned among the several States which may be included within this Union, according to their respective numbers. . . . The actual enumeration shall be made . . . every subsequent Term of ten Years" (capitalization in original).[28] Since 1911, the 435 seats in the House of Representatives, the more democratic of the two branches (since each state, without regard to population, gets two senators) have been allocated according to census results. Of course, the Constitution's original sin was that apportionment of "the people" did not mean counting all people the same. For, as the late Supreme Court Justice Thurgood Marshall put it, the Constitution's words "we the people" did not include everyone: "When the Founding Fathers used this phrase in 1787, they did not have in mind the majority of America's citizens. . . . On a matter so basic as the right to vote, for example, Negro slaves were excluded, although they were counted for representational purposes—at three-fifths each."[29]

The three-fifths clause, as it came to be known, did not appear in the precursor to the Constitution, the Articles of Confederation. The three-fifths clause emerged as the centerpiece of the Constitution's support for slavery in order to secure the South's support for the new federal government. Its purpose was "magnifying Southern political power" by

allowing fewer numbers of White Southerners to gain greater representation in the House by partially counting enslaved Blacks for apportionment purposes.[30] The results predictably were that, of the first sixteen
U.S. presidents, twelve were Southern slaveholders.[31] Native Americans
also featured in the Constitution's apportionment compromise: Indians who remained tribal members ("Indians not taxed") were not to
be counted, while Indians who lived with the colonists would be. The
Constitution's apportionment clause thus reveals that race and racial
categorization have been at the heart of the nation since the founding.

More precisely, how racial categories have been defined, added, and
transformed via the federal census reveals its role in promoting and
upholding white supremacy. The census has been a key tool of the racial
state, allowing for the manipulation of categories of people deemed fit
and unfit to be included in a nation long-imagined as White and as inevitably White-dominated. By looking at key censuses since the nation's
founding in 1790, we see how race is socially constructed and yet how
racial divisions over time, come to be taken for granted as natural and
inevitable, rather than as created and malleable. The state, via the census, produces race, and race and racism produce the census, in a dialectic
feedback loop. From at least 1790 to 1970, "whiteness and power motivated the addition and removal of racial groups, the names for racial
groups, and the use of census officials to observe and record the race of
participants," as sociologists have said.[32] For the past half-century, since
the passage of modern civil rights laws, another major role of census
data has been to document racial inequality,[33] although as the debate
over the 2020 census indicates, there continues to be fierce debate about
this purpose.

Up until 1970, the federal government hired "enumerators" to conduct
the count of the population. Typically White and male, they were privileged members of the community (they had to be literate) who would go
house to house talking with the head of household to obtain information about the residents of the house. They followed instructions from
the federal government, examples of which I describe. Researchers have

reviewed old census records, learning that enumerators' original tallies were sometimes adjusted by their supervisors, offering yet another layer in the state's racial management. One imagines these interactions—how the enumerators situated the individual and his or her family, taking cues from their living situation, occupation, and residential neighborhood to classify them according to race, only to be subject to further subjective review by a higher-up. Both the original tallies and then final, cumulative state results eventually were submitted to Washington. The entire process was loaded with inconsistency in how race was determined, variation from place to place as well as from one decade to another, because, as historian Patricia Cline Cohen put it, "legions of counters, armed with their individual interpretations," logged their racial impressions.[34]

Apart from the introduction of categories like Mulatto, racism was apparent in every census. For the first few decades of censuses, enumerators were required to sort only Whites by gender and age, hinting at White racial superiority. The census of 1820 finally incorporated age categories for slaves (though still not gender), but the age categories differed from those for Whites because they were designed to assess the economic value of slaves as property and as a labor force.[35] Just as they are today, some early censuses were captured by partisan interests, such as the controversial 1840 census (which took a record five years to tabulate).[36] The 1840 results purported to show that northern Blacks were more likely to suffer from insanity than southern Blacks, which slave owners—including those holding federal office—claimed confirmed that slavery was, in fact, better than freedom for African Americans. Abolitionists instead argued that the results were due to counting errors at the local level compounded by sloppy practices at the federal level. The 1840 controversy led Congress to require that future censuses be conducted by statistical experts. Today, hundreds if not thousands of statisticians are employed by the Census Bureau.[37]

A tour through 150 years of census history on race will reveal how the racial state made race, decade by decade, by defining racial categories, and sometimes by unmaking race.[38] For example, in the 1850 census, Washington added the category "mulatto" as a racial option—as Cline notes, leaving "enumerators to make a judgment based on inspection of skin color" that resulted in the same individual being classified as Black in some censuses and as Mulatto in others.[39] As new categories were added and old ones removed, the same process occurred in repeated cycles. Over time, the racial taxonomy of the nation came to be taken for granted as natural.

The 1850 census would have been the first in which Latinos were counted, both because of the admission of Texas as a state in 1845 and the involuntary incorporation in 1848 of 115,000 Mexicans who overnight became American citizens. The first Mexican Americans, then, were to be counted in the 1850 census, but whether they were classified as White, Black, or Mulatto varied from place to place. In New Mexico Territory, where Spanish-speaking enumerators were hired simply because there were few White Americans, Mexican Americans were marked White. *Afro-mestizos* and *Indo-mestizos* might well have led Mexican Americans to be counted in each of the three categories (White, Black, Mulatto) although it is impossible to know for sure, other than via the painstaking study of a local community's census results in a given year. Factors such as a person's status and wealth would likely have influenced their categorization by enumerators. Given the dearth of Whites in the vast territory between California and Texas, Mexican Americans would have conducted the enumeration there; but in those two states, White enumerators likely would have had little incentive to accurately count Mexicans, especially those living in regions isolated from White settlements.

In 1860, for the first time, the census included "Indian" as a racial category, and it is possible that, depending on the local context, large numbers of Mexican Americans would have been counted in this category because it included only Indians living outside Tribal Nations. Whites were the unspecified default category, with enumerators instructed to indicate "color" as follows: "In all cases where the person is black without admixture insert the letter 'B'; if a mulatto, or of mixed blood, write 'M'; if an Indian, write 'Ind.' . . . is very desirable to have these directions carefully observed."[40] These new instructions may well have reflected the slavery debate, recently heightened by the Supreme Court's opinion in the Dred Scott case, decided in 1857. Scott argued that he and his family were no longer slaves because his owner, Dr. John Emerson, had taken them numerous times into states and territories that did not allow slavery. Scott's case became a referendum on slavery more generally; an activist Supreme Court went far beyond where it needed to go to decide it. The court invalidated the Missouri Compromise, the 1820 law in which Congress, with respect to new territories, allowed slavery south of the thirty-sixth parallel but banned it north of there, and it also declared that neither free nor enslaved Blacks could ever be American citizens.[41]

By the 1870 census, the Civil War had come and gone, Lincoln had issued the Emancipation Proclamation, and the Radical Republican Congress (devoid of representation from the defeated Confederacy) had enacted civil rights laws as well as the Thirteenth, Fourteenth, and Fifteenth Amendments to the Constitution—all in order to protect the newly freed slaves from all manner of oppression by state and local governments. Despite this tsunami of change, the census kept its definitions of Black and Mulatto the same, as if nothing had changed. In contrast, it added "Chinese" as a category under "color," reflecting increasing hostility toward Chinese immigrants. California led the nation in anti-Chinese laws by taxing "foreign" miners in the 1850s and, three years before the federal Chinese Exclusion Act of 1882, prohibited the employment of Chinese laborers. This was the first national origin addition to the census race categories, but it would not be the last. By the next census, Japanese laborers had been recruited to the West Coast to fill the void left by the Chinese Exclusion Act. In response, officials added "Japanese" to the race options to which census enumerators could assign people.

By 1890, then, the notion of race had expanded to include Asian status, in addition to the categories Indian, Black, and Mulatto. But the last census of the nineteenth century also saw the addition of two new categories further specifying blackness in terms of blood quantum—"quadroon" (one-quarter Black) and "octoroon" (one-eighth Black). On the one hand, the inherent incoherence of racial classifications becomes transparent with the conflation of national origin and ancestry via blood quantum. On the other hand, however, the pretense that census enumerators in every state would use the same criteria to ascertain who was and was not one-eighth, one-quarter, one-half, and "all" Black suggests White elite anxiety about racial "purity" and degrees of racial "mixture." By this time, the heyday of Radical Republican political ascendancy—as expressed in civil rights laws and constitutional amendments to protect the freed men and women—had been replaced with the "compromise" between the two major parties. The withdrawal of federal enforcement made way for increasingly brutal state and local laws restricting the rights of African Americans.

White anxieties were on vivid display in *Plessy v. Ferguson*, the 1896 Supreme Court case that issued the "separate but equal" doctrine, essentially nullifying the Equal Protection Clause of the Fourteenth Amendment.[42] As I have noted, Homer Plessy's status as mixed race, ancestrally seven-eighths White and one-eighth Black, was crucial. Plessy's lawyer argued that it was impossible to consistently enforce the segregation law, the essence of the argument being that racial classifications were inherently unstable, making enforcement arbitrary.[43] A vivid illustration was Plessy's arrest: it had to be orchestrated, given that, based on his appearance, no train conductor would have forced him to leave the White car. In a seeming blindness to this context, the Supreme Court doubled down, giving license to Jim Crow segregation.

Four years later, the 1900 census categories reflected—much as some of the Latin American censuses we have examined—the racial state's effort to disappear mixed-race African Americans by removing the tri-partite blood quantum Black categories of Mulatto, quadroon, and octoroon, leaving in place the more easily administered category "Black." Race is unwieldy at the best of times, explicit instructions to census enumerators notwithstanding. Reflecting this reality and perhaps reflecting some dissent about the elimination of the African American mixed-race categories a decade earlier, the 1910 and every census since then has provided a catch-all "other" option for racial categorization. This is at once a transparent concession to the precarity of racial classification and enumerators' human fallibility but also, in the post-1970 self-identification era, an opportunity to resist the state's imposition of racial categories, as the story of so many Latinos' preference for "other" showed earlier in the book.

In 1917, Congress created the infamous "Asiatic barred zone," thereby effectively extending the previous exclusion of Chinese laborers to immigrants from virtually all Asian countries. Legal scholar Bill Ong Hing has pointed out that the only Asian immigrants not subject to the ban were those from the Philippines and Guam, ironically enough, because nineteen years earlier they had gone from being Spanish colonies to American colonies.[44] In addition, the 1917 ban made an exception for students, teachers, and merchants from Asian countries, though that loophole was closed in the 1924 naturalization act.[45] Three years later that antipathy to Asians was visible in the 1920 census. For the first time, the census included three new Asian racial categories as options for enumerators: "Filipino," "Hindu," and "Korean." In 1924, as previously noted, Congress revamped the immigration laws to reinforce the nation's identity as White. Specifically, national origin quotas were pegged to the 1890 census results in order to allow greater migration from Northern and Western Europe, and less migration from Southern and Eastern Europe. It was necessary to utilize stale census data in the law precisely because of the huge influx of immigrants from Southern Europe (Italy in particular) and Eastern Europe (especially Jews) between 1891 and 1923. In comparison to today, when Jews, Italians, and other Europeans are assumed to be White, this law shows precisely how the boundaries of whiteness have been contested and expanded.

At the same time, even historically and despite the clear preference for some Europeans over others, no European national origin ever became a census race/color category. Yet many Asian national origin categories and one Latin American category (Mexican) were census race options. This may indicate limits to the thesis that the White category is flexible enough to incorporate successive groups. U.S. censuses have variously looked to national origin, as with Asian categories nonetheless listed under "color," and blood quantum, as with the varying degrees of "admixture" of White ancestry for African Americans, in an effort to rationally categorize what is irrational and socially constructed. But these techniques have never been applied to Europeans.

Mulatto reappeared as an option in 1920, suggesting continuing disagreement over who was and was not African American. In large part, these shifts in how to categorize Blacks, at least within the confines of the national census, revealed anxiety about marriage and sexual unions across racial categories in the antebellum era.[46] Prior to the founding of the United States, bans on White and Black sex and/or marriage existed in Delaware, Georgia, Louisiana (then a French colony), Maryland, Massachusetts, North Carolina, Pennsylvania, South Carolina, and Virginia.[47] At the nation's founding, these laws worked jointly with the legal edifice of slavery, which, of course, perpetuated slave women's subordination by mandating that children born to slaves inherit their mother's slave status, even when their fathers were White slave masters. For African Americans, both an intensive blood quantum approach and the one-drop rule of African descent are consistent with the evolving priorities of white supremacy at particular historical moments. The hypodescent rule, under which any amount of Black ancestry made one "Negro" under the census, evolved only after the Supreme Court issued its "separate but equal" ruling in *Plessy*.[48] Given the racist patriarchy of sexual dynamics under slavery, blood quantum had a certain logic, but after slavery, a new agenda emerged: easy enforcement of *de jure* segregation of the races. When the Supreme Court validated segregation as passing muster under the Fourteenth Amendment's Equal Protection Clause, it was a massive green light to states in the Midwest, North, and West to enact such laws. A blood quantum approach would have made segregation impossible to enforce, whereas a crude way to classify via the legal fiction of the one-drop rule was useful to white supremacy.

By and large, over the course of American history, the children of

White and Indian unions have become successively White, in contrast to the children of Whites and African Americans.[49] For example, in 1924 Virginia lawmakers recognized the "Pocahontas exception" for the definition of who was White versus Indian: one-sixteenth or less Indian blood made one White.[50] Similarly, a kind of reverse one-drop rule became the norm for Mexican Americans in the late nineteenth and early twentieth centuries.[51] At least for some Latinos, one drop of blood from a distant Spanish ancestor was partly the basis for classification as "White."

Historically, this was formalized in census instructions such as this one from 1940: "Mexicans are to be returned as white, unless definitively of Indian or other nonwhite race."[52] It is notable, however, that these instructions—the first that ever expressly instructed enumerators on how to classify Mexicans—came about because of a starkly different approach to identifying Mexican Americans a decade before. In 1930 the national origin term "Mexican" appeared as an option for "color" with this instruction to enumerators: "Practically all Mexican laborers are of a racial mixture difficult to classify, though usually well recognized in the localities where they are found."[53] The deep roots of Latinos as descendants of Indians, Africans, and Spaniards are here acknowledged with the upshot that the enumerator will, in effect, know a Mexican when he sees one. The 1930 and 1940 instructions are inherently unstable, producing extensive variation by state and region—and the incentive to "pass" as White.

At the same time, Mexican Americans clearly had a tenuous hold on "whiteness," one that could be revoked from one decennial census to another. Despite lasting for only a single census, the classification of "Mexican" as a racial option had lasting impact. The intention in defining Mexican Americans as racially "Mexican" was to allow for their efficient deportation. Riled up by politicians and newspapermen who scapegoated Mexicans for the Great Depression, federal, state, and county law enforcement officers conducted raids in majority-Latino workplaces and neighborhoods in the early 1930s. Deportations decimated the Mexican American population of Texas, causing a 40 percent reduction between

1930 and 1940.[54] California lost a third of its Mexican population to "voluntary" departures or government deportations during the same period. It was later confirmed that confidential name and address data from the 1930 census was used, in violation of government regulations regarding the use of census information, to identify Mexican Americans and Mexicans in order to deport them.[55] In the Texas cities of Dallas, San Antonio, El Paso, and Houston (among others), officials relied on the 1930 census data to reclassify Mexican Americans as "colored."[56] As described previously, Latino civil rights leaders protested these abuses, and in 1940 the only change to census racial options was the removal of the Mexican category. In this way, Latinos held onto a formalistic census-White status, one that, as we have seen, failed to correspond to their actual social experience as a racially subordinated group.

Modern Census Race-Making

Inevitably, it is easier to grasp the racial state's deployment of the census for nation-building and race-making as a historical phenomenon. While it is harder to see in our own lifetimes, it is no less present. For instance, as noted, the 1970 census was a watershed moment because the Census Bureau switched from a system of third-party racial classification by enumerators to a system of racial "self-identification"—strictly speaking, the identification of all household members by one person in the household. Scholars have described this switch as a reflection of the state's need to collect demographic data in order to enforce the Civil Rights Act of 1964 and the Voting Rights Act of 1965.[57] As a companion to census data, the Office of Management and Budget (OMB) also compiles race data, and provides guidelines for racial classification that certain employers, colleges, and universities, and others who receive federal funding must use in their data gathering. At present, the OMB recommends using six mutually exclusive "self-identified" race/ethnicity options: White; Black; American Indian or Alaskan Native; Asian; Native Hawaiian or other Pacific Islander; and Hispanic.[58] Both census and OMB classifications have received greater congressional scrutiny since 1970—the time at which state and federal revenue-sharing took off as the model for per capita federal spending to support state governments in education, housing, and other areas.[59] Along with the apportionment function, these changes put considerable pressure on the executive branch to avoid systematic population undercounts.

Some have emphasized the shift from third-party racial categorization to self-identification as the government's support for "identity expression" that is decoupled from how others see one's race.[60] Legal scholar Rachel Moran saw this at work in the successful push to allow the selection of more than one race starting with the 2000 census. Advocates drafted "A Bill of Rights for Racially Mixed People" calling for multiracial people to be allowed to "openly express their loyalty to more than one group and freely cross racial boundaries to choose whom to befriend and love."[61] Something like free expression—unfettered from how one is seen and classified racially by others—was at work when, after the change to self-identification on the census in 1970, the American Indian population increased by 48 percent (relative to an 18 percent increase for the overall population).[62] Some of this increase no doubt resulted from the poor ability of enumerators to accurately classify Native Americans before 1970, especially those who lived outside of reservations.[63] But it also reflected the identity-expressive function of some Whites who claim a distant Indian ancestor. For Whites in particular, the desire to claim a more expressive symbolic ethnicity has recently been fueling the surge in commercial DNA testing.[64]

With the embrace of formal racial equality by all three branches of the federal government between 1948 and 1970, it became untenable to continue the "near obsession with maintaining the lines among races, specifically with political, economic, and social concerns about safeguarding Whiteness and maintaining the racial hierarchy."[65] It does not, however, follow that the census role in race-making over the nation's first two centuries ended with the switch from enumerator identified race to self-identification. The option to select more than one racial category, starting in 2000, has presented the census with a puzzle. How should census officials both honor the choices of self-identified multiracial persons while also maintaining the usefulness of race data for the enforcement of civil rights laws, federal funding and apportionment as mandated by Congress? This has at times meant that the census opted to "reclassify" individuals who identify as biracial (while individuals have the option of selecting "two *or more* races," most select only two). The four most common "double-race" combinations, in order of prevalence, are: Indian/White, Asian/White, Black/White, and Indian/Black. In 2000, people who self-identified as such were reclassified as Indian, Asian, Black, and Black, respectively![66]

Recall the widespread phenomenon of Latinos choosing "other" race discussed previously. After both the 1990 and 2000 censuses, officials instructed bureau statisticians to reclassify Latinos who rejected census race categories by instead selecting "other." They used a technique called "hot-decking" to reclassify self-identified "other" Latinos as White or Black, depending on how other Latino adults in their household self-identified (as White or Black) or how their Latino neighbors self-identified (as White or Black).[67] When Puerto Rican Congressman José Serrano challenged the Census Bureau for not taking Latinos' self-identification seriously, it was precisely this kind of practice he was calling out. This example hints at more going on than mere substitution of the historical wrongs of enumerator-based classifications with the "correct" self-identification of race, since the government still has the power to adjust the classifications.

Critics also point to the fact that the census is fundamentally political. Consider the move in 1980 to initiate counting Latinos as a national group. The story begins with President Johnson's establishment in 1967 of the first federal entity tasked with addressing Latino interests, the Interagency Committee on Mexican American Affairs.[68] As vice president, Johnson led JFK's initiative on equality in employment, and he received pressure from Mexican Americans in response to early 1960s data showing that African Americans composed 98 percent of the more than 4,000 discrimination complaints against government contractors, while "Spanish-surnamed people" made up the remaining 2 percent.[69] After the 1970 census results were released, Latinos claimed a severe undercount. Parties ranging from congressional representatives of California, Texas, and New York to Latino civil rights organizations attacked census accuracy and pressured all three branches of government. The Mexican American Legal Defense and Education Fund (MALDEF), the litigation-focused Latino civil rights organization modeled on the NAACP Legal Defense Fund, filed suit on behalf of other civil rights and community organizations, seeking the Census Bureau's admission that the "Spanish-speaking" population had been undercounted. Although the case was dismissed, it generated pressure for change, including from the U.S. Civil Rights Commission.[70] In response, in the early 1970s, census officials began a multi-year investigation of how to more accurately count Latinos.

How to do so was not obvious given the 1930 debacle and Latinos' fraught claims to whiteness. What is more, there was no commonly agreed-upon linguistic term for Latinos, since each national origin subgroup had a regional base. Nor was there a nationally accepted conception about the basis for Latino racial identity, as there was for African Americans. Whereas Black racial classification has been historically on the basis of recognition of phenotype (especially skin color), for Latinos, the indicators of racial group membership—and the corresponding bases for racial discrimination—are more varied. I am not saying skin color and other indicia of phenotype (e.g., hair texture, facial bone structure) are irrelevant for how non-Latinos classify Latinos, only that other factors enter the mix as well. For example, a recent survey of Latinos showed that four in ten have experienced discrimination in the past year, whether due to looking Latino, speaking Spanish in public, or being told to go back to their country.[71] Prior to 1980, the Census Bureau collected information on Spanish surname, speaking Spanish at home, and birth or parent's birth in a Spanish-speaking country or Puerto Rico on various long-form questionnaires (e.g., sent to 5 percent or 15 percent of the population in between complete census counts) in certain regions (e.g., the Southwest).[72]

Standing alone, each of these methods of determining who is (and is not) Latino is both under- and over-inclusive—routinely including people who are not, in fact, Latino as well as excluding those who are by other means Hispanic. Yet these conceptions of Latinos have continuing relevance today. One's Spanish surname (or even Spanish first name) may trigger discrimination on paper, say, on a home loan application or on a resume, and may act as a booster when combined with how one "looks." In other words, one may see someone as racially ambiguous, but then, when one learns their surname, may categorize that person as Latino and thus discriminate against them. Language, whether in terms of one's inability to speak English, one's accent while speaking English, or one's speaking in Spanish may trigger discrimination over the phone when, say, inquiring about a rental apartment, or as pretext for a hiring or promotion decision, as with an employer's claim that customers would not comprehend someone with "your accent."[73] Latinos report that national origin, whether one's place of birth or the place of birth of one's parents, is frequently the basis for discrimination. For Latinos and Asian Americans, the assumption that, because of the way one looks, one is from another country—the assumption that one is a perpetual foreigner—continues to be a powerful dimension of racialization. Depending on the context, each of these or their operation in combination serves to mark Latinos as racial others. Yet in an era of self-identification, post-1970, they each were, at different moments, proxies for self-identification even if poor proxies.

In response to criticism over the undercount of Latinos in 1970, the Census Bureau formed an advisory committee consisting of Cuban, Puerto Rican, and Mexican American civil rights leaders.[74] The committee suggested adding a Latino category to the race question, on par with the currently listed categories.[75] In early 1979, however, committee members received word that the census had decided to go in a different direction.[76] Instead of adding Latino to the race question,

Leo Estrada—perhaps the very first Mexican American statistician employed by the census and until his death in 2018 a University of California, Los Angeles professor—was told to inform the committee that the 1980 census would ask all persons whether they were Latino (and, if they answered affirmatively, ask them to further specify their national origin). It would include the same race question as in 1970 (without a Latino option) alongside the new so-called "Hispanic ethnicity" question.[77]

The reason: opposition from bureau experts charged with accurately counting the African American, American Indian, and Asian American populations. According to Estrada, those experts relied on internal studies of how adding a Latino race option would cause a decline in the count of African Americans (because some Puerto Ricans in New York might switch their designation from Black to Latino), a decline in the count of American Indians (because some Mexican Americans in Tucson, Arizona, might switch their designation from Indian to Latino), and a decline in the count of Asian Americans (because some Filipinos in the San Francisco Bay Area might switch their designation from Asian American to Latino). The latter was of special interest—to Asian Americans and to cities and regions with large Asian American populations—because 1980 also was the first time Asian was included as a racial category, rather than the earlier, less inclusive national origin categories previously discussed. In short, according to Estrada, it was the "minority" interest groups who opposed expanding race to include a Latino category.

Despite his account, the conventional interpretation for the incorporation of a separate question about ethnicity rather than incorporation into the race question has been that Latino leaders themselves rejected self-definition as a racial group separate from Whites. I first heard this explanation in 1985 directly from Cuban American Ed Fernández, the first head of the newly minted Department of Ethnic and Spanish Statistics at the Census Bureau.[78] This account fits squarely as a continuation of the "other White" strategy in litigation over civil rights.

Yet it also obscures the role of non-Latino racial minority groups themselves policing racial boundaries. At the same time, I have no doubt
that there were some Latino leaders who advocated to continue treating
Latinos in ethnic rather than in racial terms, especially more politically conservative Cuban Americans, Mexican Americans, and Puerto
Ricans. It certainly was the case that, for some time before the 1980
change, some in Washington and the advertising industry, dominated
by Cuban Americans, had pushed the census to recognize "a common
Hispanic culture or identity," and claim more consistent with the Hispanic ethnicity question than with a Hispanic racial category.[79] In the
end, their interests converged with those of non-Latino minority interests within the census.

The 1980 count led to mainstream recognition that Latinos existed.
They were now a national group, "the second-largest minority," as some
put it. That, in turn, triggered the provision of federal funding and social
services by government and nongovernmental organizations to combat
Latinos' relative low education, high poverty, and concentration in poor
housing stock. It prompted national political parties to take Latino voters more seriously, though criticisms persist forty years later that the two
major parties continue to neglect Latino voters.[80] At the same time, the
fact that White nationalists could now point to the tangible reality of
increasing numbers of Latinos in the nation prompted a racist backlash
that ignored the census emphasis on "Hispanic ethnicity" and that has
only grown since 1980.

Outside the sphere of politics and government, one of the immediate private sector uses to which the new census data was put was in
the marketing industry. Specifically, census data drove the creation and
then expansion of an entirely new subset of the American advertising
industry. Cuban American–owned advertising firms seeking to develop
television, billboard, or other media campaigns for every type of product
touted the size of the Latino market with pitches like this: "Today 50%
of all bookings at Radio City Music Hall are Hispanic artists. Salsa out-
sells ketchup in the Midwest. Nachos beat hot dogs at movies. What's
happening? Simple. A cultural and marketing phenomenon known

as the U.S. Hispanic market."[81] By 1983, the five largest advertising agencies in New York City had Spanish-language divisions.[82] By 1984, armed with census data, the Spanish-language television network now known as Univision had conducted market research to conclude that "a blurring of differences" had occurred, making "Hispanic Americans more conscious of themselves" as one group rather than only as Mexican Americans, Puerto Ricans, or Cuban Americans.[83] Of course, Univision's research was self-interested, designed to spur the sale of television commercial time to mainstream American corporations.

Early advertising aimed at Latino consumers focused on "the big three" cultural traits: Spanish language, Catholicism, and the family.[84] As Latino studies scholar Arlene Dávila has noted, this portrayal is inherently conservative, fostering conformity and traditional gender roles while seeking to box-in Latinos as "traditionalists," in contrast to the framing of African Americans by advertisers as "trendsetters."[85] Both stereotypes depend on emphasizing certain components of large, diverse groups and downplaying others. The same was true in casting Latino actors, according to one advertising executive interviewed by Dávila: "What they want is the long straight hair, olive skin, just enough oliveness to the skin to make them not ambiguous. To make them Hispanic."[86] In short, Latino actors who "look" too Black or too Indigenous need not apply, despite the prevalence of those phenotypes among the majority of Latinos due to *mestizaje*. These stereotypes have been shared by Spanish-language news producers, who prefer news anchors with light skin and lighter hair who speak a certain kind of Spanish: "Mostly upper-class Mexican Spanish . . . whereas Caribbean Spanish is hardly heard in generic advertisements" or network programming.[87] More research needs to be conducted to examine how advertising marketed to Latinos who do not communicate primarily in Spanish replicates or rejects these trends in marketing and programming on Spanish-language media.

One sector where marketing to Latinos still is relatively new is the Hollywood box office. For example, one creator of movie trailers who described entering that market after 2010 emphasized themes like family, saying in reference to an animated film: "The last thing you wanna do is scare . . . Hispanic moms."[88] Whether they have their own in-house Latino marketing teams or hire from "multicultural" divisions of the major advertising firms, Hollywood has become increasingly attentive to Latino moviegoers. A recent example is Disney/Pixar's 2017 *Coco*, an animated fantasy set in Mexico in the context of Dia de los Muertos, or the Day of the Dead celebration that occurs on the first of November. The film is beautiful and won the 2018 Oscar for Best Animated Film. It has grossed more than $807 million, including $209 million in the United States and $190 million in China.[89] The story plays out the stereotypes of Latino family orientation and religiosity and uses some Spanish even in the English-language version. Indigenous scholars have criticized the film for its embrace of *mestizo* rather than Indigenous-looking characters and for appropriating social practices rooted in Indigenous Mexican communities.[90] Clearly, there is no escape from questions of racial identity in mainstream cultural production and its marketing to Latino consumers and consumers in general.

Latinos and the 2020 Census Controversies

Despite the clamor to allow Americans to select multiple racial identities on the 2000 census, only 3 percent of people did so in 2010. This was a higher percentage than the previous decade, when half as many people did so. Latinos were more than twice as likely as non-Latinos to do so, perhaps a testament to the Latin American history of social and sexual mixture among Indigenous people, African slaves, and Spanish colonizers. Another interesting divergence between Latinos and others, as discussed in an earlier chapter, is their preference to self-identify as "other" on the census race question. In the four decades for which data is available—1980, 1990, 2000, 2010—between 37 and 43 percent of all Latinos chose "other" race rather than White, African American, Native American, Asian American (or some combination of those). In 2010, whereas only 0.2 percent of non-Latinos chose "other" race, 39 percent of Latinos selected that as their race. Census officials predicted fewer Latinos would elect "other" given the ability to select multiple racial categories in 2000, but that was not the case.[91] Once again, census statisticians underestimated Latinos' dissatisfaction with census-race choices, but no longer do they have the option of using methods like hot-decking. In fact, the census reported, in the context of smaller samples between the short-form census every decade, that, since 2010, the share of Latinos selecting "some other race" has continued to grow.[92] "Other" Americans will be the second-largest racial group, after Whites, in the 2020 census, again confounding census officials.[93]

This result is problematic because it effectively challenges the census race framework as illegitimate or, at a minimum, not an accurate reflection of a large portion of the American population. As a result, the Census Bureau was set to change the 2020 census form: it proposed eliminating the Hispanic ethnicity question in favor of including Latino/Hispanic as an option on the race question (along with the ability to specify national origin identification).[94] The census also proposed adding the category "Middle Eastern and North African" as a race option in 2020. Both proposed changes reflect how census racial classifications have lagged behind on-the-ground changes in racial identity at both the individual and collective levels. Some of those of Middle Eastern descent, especially younger people and/or more recent immigrants, reject the current census approach classifying them as White.[95]

The Census Bureau's recommendation to eliminate the separate Latino ethnicity question and instead incorporate Latino as an option on the race question emerged after years of surveys, telephone re-interviews, and focus group interviews with eight hundred Latinos.[96] In 2015, the Census Bureau mailed or emailed another 1.2 million households, testing one of two question formats adding Latino as a race option. The 2015 testing, which was the basis for the recommendation that Latino be folded into the race question for 2020, tested three different options: (1) "the separate question"—a separate Latino ethnicity and race question without Latino (replicating the status quo, 1980–2010); (2) "the combined question"—elimination of the Hispanic ethnicity question coupled with adding Latino as a race option; and (3) "the combined question-plus"—elimination of the Hispanic ethnicity question coupled with adding Latino as a race option, along with asking additional information about national origin.

The results were virtually the same for each combined question formats (options 2 and 3 above): less than 1 percent of Latinos chose "other" in comparison to the 37 to 43 percent who have selected other from 1980 to 2010 under option 1, the status quo. For options 2 and 3, more than 70 percent of Latinos self-identified *only* as Latino without selecting one or more additional race options. These Latinos told census officials things like "I like this [new] question. I found myself more easily."[97] Under option 1, in contrast, respondents frequently continued to choose "other" in a high proportion; Latinos who answered yes to the Hispanic ethnicity question then answered the race question in one of the following ways: Latino and other race (39 percent), and Latino and two or more races (38 percent), and Latino and White race (16.5 percent).[98] Thus, option 1 did not yield a reduction in the selection of "other" race and, thus, would continue to raise questions of accuracy and reliability in the data. Meanwhile, regardless of which of the three options was utilized, those Latinos who reported Black race alone or American Indian race alone did not change in the 2015 sample questions.[99]

As career census officials saw it, there was no downside to making these changes. Trump's secretary of commerce, Wilbur Ross, had other ideas.[100] In January 2018, Ross announced he had rejected the proposed additions of Latino and Middle Eastern as race options. One reason he gave was that it was too late to make changes given that the 2020 census forms would soon have to be printed; this despite the fact Ross sat on the recommendations for almost a year. Two months later, Ross directed the Census Bureau to include a question about citizenship on the 2020 short-form census.[101] Ross explained (and later testified under oath) that Attorney General Jeff Sessions had requested the addition of the question in order to better enforce the Voting Rights Act. In seven different lawsuits, a combined eighteen states, many cities, and several Latino civil rights organizations sued to block the addition of the citizenship question.[102] The plaintiffs argued that the addition of the question would cause a massive undercount of Latinos and Asian Americans because undocumented immigrants would refuse to complete the census form for fear they would be targeted by ICE. The question also would affect mixed-status households; that is, those with a combination of citizens (or legally authorized immigrants) and also undocumented migrants. The lawsuits further argued that, more generally, Latinos and Asian Americans who are citizens would be discouraged from completing the census questionnaire because they would, in 2020 and beyond, distrust the census generally.

Several federal judges sided with the plaintiffs in a handful of lawsuits, and one case made it to the Supreme Court. In a five to four opinion authored by Chief Justice John Roberts, the court refused to allow the citizenship question, labeling Ross's explanation about voting rights enforcement "contrived."[103] During oral argument on the case in 2019, Justice Sonia Sotomayor pressed the federal government lawyers on their reaction to the story of a person who experienced the citizenship question during testing; he was so frightened by the mock citizenship question that he walked out of his own home during the interview, leaving the census worker there alone. Most court-watchers concluded, after oral argument, that the court would, along conservative-liberal lines uphold Ross's discretion to include the citizenship question.[104] Although he denied it under oath, secretary of commerce Ross was found to have lied about exchanging emails about the citizenship question with, among others, Stephen Miller and Kurt Kobach. Miller is Trump's aggressively anti-immigrant aide who has repeatedly been identified as aligned with White nationalists.[105] Kobach, the former secretary of state and failed gubernatorial candidate in Kansas, was appointed co-chair of Trump's short-lived Presidential Advisory Commission on Election Integrity. He was charged with investigating the "millions" of Latino voters—presumably unauthorized immigrants—whom he claimed voted fraudulently for candidate Hillary Clinton in 2016.[106]

In fact, it was fraud of another nature that apparently motivated the proposal to include the citizenship question, which had not been asked on the census short form since 1940. The real reason for the question's addition was a brazen attempt to undercount Latinos, in order to produce a reapportionment process that would yield fewer Democratic congressional districts based on the 2020 census. The mastermind of the plan was now-deceased GOP consultant Thomas Hofeller, whose nickname in Republican circles was "the Michelangelo of gerrymandering," a reference to his expertise in drawing legislative districts, at the federal and state levels, that capitalize on racially polarized voting by political party.[107] Far from helping to enforce the right to vote, the inclusion of a citizenship question was designed to suppress Latinos' voting rights, since they vote three to one for Democrats, while promoting Republican candidates.[108] Hofeller's stock in trade was as a redistricting consultant, working to keep states (including North Carolina and Texas) red, even as their Latino and African American populations swelled.

A trove of documents and emails released to plaintiffs by Hofeller's estranged daughter reveals that he had meticulously laid out a plan precisely to use a census citizenship question to depress the Latino population so as to decrease the number of new majority-Latino congressional districts in states with large Latino populations including California, Florida, New York, and Texas, where 60 percent of all Latinos live.[109] Without those new districts, more congressional seats in majority-White states with rural populations would result.[110] Data contained on four external hard drives and eighteen thumb drives confirm that, not long before he died, Hofeller communicated his plan to officials in both the Justice and Commerce Departments. At the time the lawsuit against the government by the state of New York and others was argued in the Supreme Court, Hofeller's documents had not been made public. But between oral argument April 23, 2019, and the court's decision in June 2019, his records became public, generating substantial media attention. In fact, before the Supreme Court issued its ruling, but after oral arguments in the case, a judge in one of the cases already had agreed to reconsider, based on the Hofeller documents, his earlier judgment in favor of the Commerce Department; had this played out in the context of a Supreme Court opinion allowing the question, it could have meant the justices would have felt the need to revisit the issue (potentially creating a serious delay in starting the 2020 census).

The Trump administration's proposed citizenship question and its decision to reject the addition of a Latino race category should be seen as closely linked. Certainly, they signal the ongoing nature of the census as a site for the racial state to produce race and racial classifications. Yet they also reflect an overarching desire to limit Latinos' full and equal participation in American life. In this sense they reveal the inherently political nature of the census. The proposal to incorporate Latino as a category on the race question coupled with elimination of the Hispanic ethnicity question would have, I contend, generated great enthusiasm for the 2020 census. It would have unified Latinos to the extent that some Latinos see a gulf between "white Latinos" and other-race Latinos, while still allowing Afro-Latinos and Indo-Latinos to claim multiple racial self-identities. Given President Trump's anti-immigrant, anti-Latino rhetoric and actions, it is no leap to conclude he would find antithetical any census questionnaire revisions that would increase Latinos' group solidarity and sense of belonging in America.

With the fight over the citizenship question behind us for 2020, at least, the focus now must be on encouraging Latinos' full participation in the census and then ensuring congressional districts are fairly apportioned based on those population results. In the meantime, nothing prevents school board, local, or state governments from expanding the right to vote to residents who lack federal citizenship, as some municipalities already have done.[111] While they are not as loyal to the Democrats as African Americans, who vote Democratic 90 percent of the time, Latinos, like Asian Americans, vote for Democrats 75 percent of the time. Jews are the only White ethnic group with that degree of partisan loyalty to the Democrats, so the party finds itself dependent on people of color. In contrast—and this is what Hofeller knew, and what

Trump knows all too well—White women are only slightly more likely to vote Democratic than Republican, and only 40 percent of White men do so. For the time being, this math is fine for the GOP, since older, economically better-off Whites vote at much higher rates than younger, less well-off, voters of color.[112] But it is only a matter of time, given demographics, that the Republican Party well runs dry.

CONCLUSION

Thanks to a Trump presidency, Americans are more aware than ever before of anti-Latino racism. From his candidacy announcement at Trump Tower in June 2015, when he labeled Mexican men rapists to re-election campaign rallies in 2019 where he approvingly acknowledged chants that "shooting them in the legs" was the best way to stop Central Americans seeking asylum, Trump took overt racism from the Republican fringe to mainstream retail politics.

That fringe—if it ever was truly fringe—is encapsulated by three books published early in this century that parlayed census data about the browning of America into fear and loathing of those who are brown. The ideas in these books seem to have influenced Trump and others in his inner-circle, including Steve Bannon and Stephen Miller. In 2004 Simon & Schuster published *Who Are We? The Challenges to America's National Identity* by Harvard political scientist Samuel Huntington.[1] Prior to the fall of the apartheid regime, Huntington advised South African president P.W. Botha on security measures.[2] After 9/11, he came up with the phrase "clash of civilizations"—rhetoric upon which the worldwide attack on Muslims in the "war on terror."[3] In *Who Are We?* Huntington argues that immigrants from Latin America will not assimilate, culturally or linguistically, and thus forever change the character of the great Anglo-Saxon U.S.A. for the worse. Like Trump, he expresses disdain for cosmopolitan global elites who have no need for nationalism or borders.

Huntington's manifesto was bookended by two screeds by Republican stalwart Patrick J. Buchanan that say it all in their titles: *The Death of the West: How Dying Populations and Immigrant Invasions Imperil Our Country and Civilization* (2001) and *State of Emergency: The Third World Invasion and Conquest of America* (2006).[4] These *New York Times* bestsellers stoked fears about the Latino menace from within (witness frightening census data). Buchanan coined the phrase "anchor baby" in his first book as a derogatory reference for Mexican women who supposedly cross the border to give birth so that their children will be American citizens by birth. In a chapter called "The Aztlan Plot" in the 2006 book, Buchanan alludes to the Chicano mythic origin story, exhorting, "They are coming to conquer us."[5] No right-wing nut, Buchanan worked for three Republican presidents (Nixon, Ford, and Reagan) and himself sought the GOP nomination three times (1992, 1996, and 2000). Apparently oblivious to Mexican Americans' over-representation as World War II and Vietnam veterans, Buchanan touts his ancestors' Confederate service (along with his membership in the Sons of Confederate Veterans)— without disclosing he was an ROTC dropout in college and avoided Vietnam by obtaining a 4-F deferment for "reactive arthritis."[6] Wikipedia rightly has an entry on Buchanan's anti-Semitism, but not one for his anti-Latino racism.[7]

Early in 2018, Trump rhetorically asked an Oval Office audience gathered to discuss immigration policy, "Why are we having all these people from shithole countries come here?" He was referring to El Salvador, Haiti, and all of Africa, but the press coverage of the president's comment focused almost exclusively on how the off-color remark reflected anti-Black racism. In reducing racism to White-over-Black oppression, we erase El Salvador, the Americas, and Latinos simply because we so often do not get where Latinos fit. Trump, however, was well aware of the impact his comments had, for both African Americans and Latinos. After briefly denying he had made the comment, his aides soon switched to predicting the shithole quote would resonate with Trump's base.[8] It did so only because anti-Latino racism is intelligible to the public, conflated as it is with fear of Latino demographic ascendancy, "illegals" flooding the southern border, and rhetoric about violent gangs from El Salvador.[9]

A linked rhetoric—more megaphone than dog whistle—pervaded Trump's visit to Puerto Rico in the wake of Hurricane Maria in August 2017. His ignorance of the island's status as an American territory was overshadowed by his flippant assertion that the hurricane had done little damage, offered as he tossed rolls of paper towels to hurricane victims at a San Juan shelter.[10] Almost two years later, as another hurricane was bearing down on Puerto Rico, Trump's tweets revealed his lack of remorse. Seemingly ignorant of a huge grassroots protest movement that culminated in the resignation of the Puerto Rican governor and Trump ally Ricardo Rosselló,[11] the president called the island "one of the most corrupt places on earth" and warned fearful Puerto Ricans they would be lucky to receive aid as in 2017, which he mischaracterized as "more than any place has ever gotten." In this scenario, Trump conjures Puerto Rico as the stereotypical welfare mother, undeserving of public assistance and seeking one more dole-out. San Juan Mayor Yulín Cruz, who clashed with Trump during his first visit, warned Trump to shut up and "make way for those of us who are actually doing the work on the ground."[12]

Trump's drumbeat of hate is, at a minimum, correlated with greater violence toward people of color and immigrants (or those perceived to be immigrants), especially Latinos—and, quite possibly, has *caused* greater violence by legitimizing the open expression of racism. At the close of 2019, the FBI issued its annual crime report, concluding that violent hate crimes—violent crimes committed against victims because of animus based on race, religion, sex, sexual orientation, or transgender status—reached a sixteen-year high in 2018.[13] Hate crimes with Latino victims were up in 2018 (2019 data is not yet available). For all groups, these numbers undoubtedly undercount such crimes, and we should expect that, the more vulnerable the victim, the less likely they are to report the crime because they fear retaliation or have become inured to daily intimidation. Certainly, this is the case for undocumented migrants, who face violence and harassment from private individuals as well as the increased threat of workplace raids that lead to deportation and permanent separation from their U.S. citizen relatives. Such victims are fundamentally perceived by the dominant society as undeserving, as compared to victims who are American citizens and especially compared to victims in places of worship, such as the Charleston AME Church in 2015 and the 2018 Tree of Life Synagogue in Pittsburgh.

It is telling that the increase in hate crimes occurred concurrently with the ongoing, multi-year decline of crime nationally. That suggests that these crimes—which are, to emphasize, the tip of the iceberg—represent something fundamentally different from "crime" as we normally understand it. The FBI data shows that these are interpersonal crimes. In 2018, property crimes reflecting hatred, such as racist graffiti or vandalism, dropped by 19 percent. But crimes that reflect the (alleged) wrongdoer's willingness to directly confront another person increased: the intimidation category was up 13 percent, simple assaults were up 15 percent, and aggravated assaults were up 4 percent. Another study, relying on the FBI data, found that hate crimes rose dramatically in 2018 in three Texas cities with large populations of Latinos, immigrants, and Latino immigrants. Such crimes in 2018 were up nearly 200 percent in Houston, 150 percent in Dallas, and 100 percent in San Antonio.[14] This pattern is not surprising given the history of racism in Texas combined with the current political climate in which those on the right are emboldened to both express hatred and enact violence. As LULAC president Domingo García says, "There's a direct correlation between the hate speech and fear-mongering coming from President Trump and the right wing of the Republic Party with the increase in attacks against Latinos."[15]

Trump's August 2019 visit to El Paso, Texas, three days after the slaughter of twenty-two people—eighteen of whom were Latinos or

Mexican citizens—in a Walmart by a self-described White nationalist was telling.[16] Trump ignored requests not to visit El Paso, such as one by city councilor Cassandra Hernández, who, on the eve of his visit, said he "is not welcome here," where "people are afraid to be Hispanic."[17] Trump's visit the next day was mostly out of the public eye, with some speculating that those victims still hospitalized refused to meet with him. Trump forced a photo opportunity with an infant whose parents died in the Wal-Mart massacre. In the photo, first lady Melania Trump holds the brown baby, the president smiles and gives a thumbs up, while the baby's dead father's mother and brother flank the Trumps. To me, it was a sad reminder of the irony of everyone's willingness to capitalize on tragedy. In an unauthorized video from El Paso, Trump is shown regaling a doctor and other hospital workers with stories about how big his rally was the last time he visited the city. Hundreds of protestors gathered outside the hospital, including one brown-skinned, gray-bearded man wearing a T-shirt with a Vietnam veteran's logo who held up a mock "wanted" poster of Trump instead labeled "El Paso's Biggest Criminal." Meanwhile, Patrick Crusius will face the death penalty for the El Paso murders.[18]

What's at Stake?

Inventing Latinos offers an account of how Latinos came to be. The story includes individual and organizational agency but highlights the power of the racial state, larger forces in the political economy, and the shape-shifting nature of racism to reemerge in new and different forms in response to changing conditions. Racism works best when it is taken for granted, when its structure and scaffolding are more or less invisible. In this way, the racial state is not seen as a contradiction to our constitutional commitment to equal treatment under the law, to the rule of law.

Consider how Latinos came to be constituted as a racially subordinated group in the United States. American imperialism in Latin America created racialized inequality that for 175 years has produced economic displacement followed by a steady migration to low-wage U.S. jobs. As a racial group, Latinos have occupied a middle tier in the U.S. racial order, neither fully White nor fully Black, in part due to their European ancestry. At the same time, an idealized notion of *mestizaje* (itself a product of the racism inherent in colonialism) has obscured the lived reality of colorism and racism experienced by Latinos with visible African or Indigenous ancestry. A by-product of the former has been for Latinos to leverage their Spanish heritage as a way to claim whiteness; yet most Latinos themselves realize others do not see them as White, making this claim elusive. Latinos' collective ambivalence about occupying an in-between middle racial category has played out in the political domain, alternating between accommodationist versus insurgent leaders and organizations.

The case of Latinos reveals more general truths about how racism works in America. White supremacy persists, even as it changes in response to ruptures in the racial order such as the abolition of slavery, migration patterns (such as the turn of the century migration of southern and eastern Europeans who, over time became part of an expanded White category), the mass protest movement for civil rights of the mid-twentieth century, the formal end of Jim Crow laws, the late-twentieth-century mass migration of Central American and Mexican migrants because of civil wars and economic displacement in their home countries, and the current demographic transition to a nation in which Whites will no longer be the majority. Each of these (and many others) caused a rupture for white supremacy that, in turn, produced a recalibration of the racial order along with evolving racial categories. During these periods of transformation—call them electric shocks to the racial state—a host of factors must align to jump-start the shocked system in order to reset white supremacy. We have seen how the common sense of anti-Latino racism came to be entrenched as a national phenomenon after decades as a parochial, regional problem.

In part due to the federal government's decision in 1980 to begin counting them, Latinos came to be viewed as natural and inevitable in the American racial cosmology of the twenty-first century. But merely a racial-state decision to add Latinos to the recipe and stir would not have resulted in a fundamental transformation of the racial landscape. Historical antecedents included centuries of Spanish colonialism in Latin America, U.S. imperialism and colonialism there, and the mid-twentieth-century dynamics of Mexican Americans and Puerto Ricans serving as a buffer group between Whites above them and Blacks below them in the racial hierarchy. Nor would this transformation have occurred without Latinos themselves playing an active role in this process. For example, when Latino civil rights organizations demanded, in the first place, that Latinos be counted accurately in the decennial census they wrote history. Likewise, the many Latinos who insist, via self-identification as "other race," that they occupy a distinctive racial category are seizing power.

To be sure, the White power structure controls the definition of racial categories, whether new ones or changed ones, but such processes do not occur in a linear, uninterrupted progression from point A to point Z. For one thing, Whites and White-controlled institutions do not always agree or coordinate; like the racial-state itself, they are not monolithic. For another, racially subordinated groups just as surely contest and negotiate with the White power structure, sometimes advocating for a broadening of the White category to include them. Who is "White" and, thus, what it means to be both "White" and "non-White" change along with demographics, transitions in the political economy, and evolving ideas about what constitutes race and racism. In short, racial projects are pliable; they can be purposed to make people more free and equal—that is, for an anti-racist agenda—or they can be a force for greater oppression. This quality of elasticity means that, where race is concerned, the results are bound to surprise—like an unchoreographed, three-dimensional chessboard, with moves and counter-moves amidst changes that could not have been predicted. But chaos does not reign forever. Instead, racial logics become more or less solidified (but never set in stone, unable to transform), and always protecting Whites as the unquestionably dominant racial group.

In order to understand and combat racism writ large, we must know the histories of specific racial groups like Latinos. That includes understanding the varied components of Latino racialization, such as ingrained tropes of foreignness: the presumption that all Latinos are immigrants (coupled with willful blindness to the fact that the vast majority of Latinos are native-born citizens), and its complement, the presumption of illegality—the notion that Latinos lack basic human rights simply because they live here without formal documentation. It includes understanding how the language of "ethnicity" rather than "race" promotes Latinos' distinction from African Americans. In an ethnic framing, national origin operates as a powerful sorting tool. For example, since Mexican Americans are so predominant, seven out of ten Latinos, the remaining Latinos are sorted relative to them. This means that Cubans (at least the first wave who migrated in the sixties and seventies), Argentinians, and other South Americans have higher status and typically are more White-identified than Mexican Americans. On the other hand, those Latino national origin groups with, on average, more Indigenous and/or African ancestry—like Central Americans, Dominicans, Puerto Ricans, and post-1980 Cubans, fall below Mexican Americans. Of course, the "Mexican" category is itself diverse, as intragroup colorism and racism show.

In an analogous way, phenotype, especially skin color, operates differently among Latinos than it does among African Americans. Since they are a buffer group, Latinos have more likelihood of passing for White in a world in which the vast majority of African Americans do not. The dynamics of U.S.-style colorism and Spanish colonial race mixture and race mobility (*blanqueamiento*) intersect to provide less economic mobility for dark-skinned Indo-Latinos and dark-skinned Afro-Latinos. For those in the middle and those on the lighter end of the skin color spectrum, however, additional racial markers operate, allowing some Latinos to pass for White and foreclosing that option for others. These factors include language and accent, Spanish surname, region of residence within the United States, residential neighborhood within a city (are they in or out of place?), and occupation in (or out of) segregated, low-wage employment sectors. Language itself broadly includes speaking only English, speaking some combination of English and Spanish (Spanglish), speaking accented English, speaking only Spanish, speaking Spanish as a second language after an Indigenous primary language, among other dimensions. Language, then, operates as a proxy for Latino race, blocking one's ability to pass for White even when other factors might make it plausible. Contemporary reliance on language factors ignores the historical school segregation of Mexican Americans, even as it reflects both historic and ongoing campaigns to suppress speaking Spanish in schools, workplaces, and public spaces.

In addition to understanding anti-Latino racism, we must also make visible the interconnected racial logics that show how one racial logic (targeting Latinos) supports another racial logic (targeting African Americans) in the service of white supremacy. One resulting feature of Whites' deployment of Latinos as a wedge against African Americans has been Latinos themselves strategically claiming whiteness as a shield against racism. This pattern followed on post–Spanish-colonial Latin American nations' tendency to elevate an idealized *mestizaje* as a strategy to eliminate Indigenous and African people, while marginalizing those who would not participate in their own disappearance.

Consider the place of anti-Latino racism within the broader context of the late twentieth-century backlash by the Whites to the legal and cultural reforms of the civil rights movement. As sociologists Michael Omi and Howard Winant have said, the 1979 landslide victory for Ronald Reagan "provided political justification for the rightward trend in social policy. Racial policy was dramatically affected. The Reagan administration demonstrated its opposition to affirmative action, reconstituted the U.S. Civil Rights Commission in order to fight 'reverse discrimination,' relaxed or eliminated government action against racist practices and institutions, and in general attempted to reverse" the impact of the civil rights movement.[19] Thus, at just the moment Latinos came to be counted as a national racial minority group in 1980, race became both more and less salient—more salient because the conservative backlash unleashed greater anti-Latino racism and less salient because the legal protections for racial recognition plummeted.

What Is to Be Done?

We are at a turning point that goes to the very core of who we are as a nation used to thinking of itself as the conscience of the world. Instead, in 2020, the United States is widely known as a country that separates migrant children from their parents, deporting the latter and detaining in squalid conditions the former. The Supreme Court has allowed the Trump administration to fashion asylum rules that flout international norms and make a mockery of a commitment made in the wake of World War II to "never let this happen again." Many of the 20 percent of Latinos born in other nations, and another 12 percent who are their minor children, live precarious lives, vulnerable to exploitation at work, crime victimization, harassment in the public sphere, and residence in poor neighborhoods where they attend segregated, under-funded public schools and are more vulnerable to environmental harms.[20] In particular, the one-third of Latino immigrants who are undocumented—6.8 million or 47 percent of the total 10.5 million undocumented population—live in constant vigilance, fearing ICE raids at work and at home, afraid to report crimes against themselves or their neighbors to the police, and making plans for sudden separation from their children and partners.[21]

Both of these numbers—the overall undocumented migrant population and those who are Latino—have decreased significantly since the pre-Great Recession high, when undocumented persons composed 4 percent of the American population.[22] Of course, fear and vulnerability are not limited to the undocumented, as if they lived quarantined from the rest of society.[23] Consider that nearly 17 million people in the United States live in mixed-immigration-status families—families with at least one family member who is a U.S. citizen or legal migrant and at least one who is without legal permission to be in the country.[24] Seventy-two percent of those American citizens who live with an undocumented family member are children; put another way, of those 17 million people in mixed status families, more than two-thirds are American-citizen children who depend on one or more undocumented parent. When we look at the top ten U.S. states with mixed-immigration-status families, we see a high proportion in heavily Latino states (including, in order of the percentage of the state population who live in mixed-status families): California (12 percent), Texas (10 percent), Nevada (9 percent), Arizona (7 percent), New Jersey (7 percent), Illinois (6 percent), New York (6 percent), New Mexico (6 percent), Colorado (5 percent), and Washington (5 percent).[25] To turn Huntington's book title on its head, who are we, indeed? What kind of nation puts these children at risk of losing their parents at a moment's notice and without due-process protections afforded parents whose rights to custody of their children are terminated because they are jailed or imprisoned? In the spring and summer of 2019, the nation was transfixed and horrified by the Homeland Security Department's separation of children, including infants and toddlers, from their parents. The fact is, this kind of separation occurs daily for American-citizen children whose parents are deported or imprisoned in so-called "detention centers."

Will we choose the politics of fear over the politics of accountability, with its accompanying inclusion of migrants? The politics of accountability embraces four policy shifts that together constitute a program of reparations for Latinos. These policy prescriptions can be implemented via a combination of congressional and executive branch action. First, every undocumented Latino migrant in the country today should receive legal authorization to live and work here and a path to citizenship. While it is appropriate to screen out those proven to have committed a violent crime, realize that, in order to reverse the current travesty, the amnesty has to be broad and deep. Second, future Central American and Caribbean migrants who seek to live in the United States—that is, those from Guatemala, Honduras, El Salvador, Cuba, and the Dominican Republic—should have a lower threshold to be admitted as refugees. Given recent and ongoing American military involvement (both direct and covert), this measure is defensible as a form of direct, collective reparations for America's destructive role in these two regions. This second change would most impact the most vulnerable and discriminated-against migrants: the disproportionate number from Central America who are Indigenous; the disproportionate share from the Caribbean who are Black; unaccompanied minors; and those who fear persecution, no matter the source. Third, Puerto Rico should be immediately made a U.S. state, ending the 122 years of second-class citizenship as an American colony. Finally, a new subsecretariat division should be formed under the Department of Labor that has the power to enforce rules against the exploitation of immigrant workers, regardless of their citizenship status.

Although these measures focus on immigrant rights, because of the pervasiveness of mixed-immigration-status families and residential segregation of Latinos—poor and working-class Latinos who are U.S. citizens live in the same neighborhoods as immigrant Latinos—they will have a far-reaching impact on Latinos generally. This four-part program of comprehensive reparations focuses on those Latinos who are immigrants, who are children with immigrant parents, and those who live and/or work in closest proximity to immigrants. Those Latinos who are not immigrants—whether they are the "I didn't cross the border, the border crossed me" variety or simply because they find themselves to some extent removed from other Latinos (due to their longevity in the United States, where they live or work, or who their partners, friends, or neighbors are)—also are at a crossroads. Historically speaking, as part of the effective operation of white supremacy, Mexican Americans and Puerto Ricans experienced a far more privileged racial position than African Americans. In the main, they did not reject this advantage or seek to establish solidarity with Blacks (examples like Ed Roybal in Los Angeles and Henry González in Texas are the exceptions that prove the rule). By and large, until the 1970s, Latinos largely accepted their role as a buffer group assigned to police the White-over-Black boundary. They have likewise benefited from distancing themselves from the most dis-

advantaged Latinos, whether unauthorized migrants, low-wage workers, Afro-Latinos, and/or Indigenous Latinos. These privileged Latinos
must today decide whether to cast their lot with "honorary Whites" or
"the collective Black," as sociologist Eduardo Bonilla-Silva terms it.

To some extent, especially for Mexican American and Puerto Rican
Latinos, this changed with the success of the African American civil
rights movement and the rise of the Chicano and Boricua movements
of the 1970s. In that era, a sizable number of Latinos and Latino civil
rights organizations began to identify with Blacks under the "minority"
umbrella and in more radical formulations of solidarity, such as the
Rainbow Coalition in Chicago. In some ways, the transition reflected
the gradual realization that Latinos' aspiration to whiteness was nothing more than a hollow hope against entrenched racism. After all, the
slice of the Latino community that experienced whiteness, though not
negligible, was small. For most Latinos, their claim on whiteness was
a shield against discrimination rather than a ticket to White privilege.
Those with the most precarious claims on whiteness—like Mexican
Americans in Texas, Puerto Ricans in Florida, and American citizens in
Puerto Rico—sometimes held on the tightest to that shield (for instance
by choosing White as their census-race). Yet even they admit that others do not see them as "White," limiting greatly the value of claims to
whiteness in the twenty-first century.

It is precisely the fact that Latinos are *mestizos*—ancestrally mixed
Indigenous, African, and Spanish people—that has made the claim of
whiteness possible. Spanish colonial white supremacy, combined with the
regimes of *mestizaje* and *blanqueamiento*, produced Latin American soci-
eties with White, African, Indigenous, and racially mixed upon racially
mixed phenotypes. When Americans colonized northern Mexico, Central America, and the Spanish Caribbean, they denigrated as racially
inferior this "mongrelization," using it to justify conquest and exploitation. Among many Latinos, it produced a preference for White and
whiter-than-*mestizo* people, whether in dating and mating, on the job, or
in the selection of where to live. All Latinos, especially the beneficiaries

of anti-Indigenous and anti-African racism within the Latinx community, should today recognize these dynamics and take affirmative steps to counteract them. One result of growing consciousness of colorism and racism has been the resurgent counter-movements of pride and solidarity among Afro-Latinos and Indo-Latinos. Latino individuals but especially Latino collectives—including those organizations founded with a White and *mestizo* orientation such as LULAC, MALDEF, Latino-Justice PRLDEF (formerly known as the Puerto Rican Legal Defense and Education Fund), and UnidosUS (formerly National Council of La Raza)—should pledge support for the self-determination and self-recognition of Indo-Latinos and Afro-Latinos. Perhaps this will take the form of public education campaigns (such as that recently undertaken by the Mexican government) funded by those organizations that have generally served those Latinos in the *mestizo* ideal while ignoring those with observable African and Indigenous roots.

A few months before this book went to press, on November 12, 2019, hundreds of recipients, mostly Latinos, of Obama's 2012 Deferred Action for Childhood Arrivals (DACA) gathered in front of the U.S. Supreme Court building to make their voices heard. The court's nine justices, including the sole Latina member of the court, Justice Sonia Sotomayor, heard the case challenging Trump's decision to rescind DACA. Lawsuits filed by immigrant rights organizations, states and cities, and the University of California, among others, sought to prevent an order that would, overnight, convert 800,000 people from authorized to undocumented immigrants. How the Supreme Court decides this question in summer 2020 will determine the court's legitimacy and the future of Latino activism. On the former topic, congressional Democrats and candidates for the Democratic Party presidential nomination are already considering a plan to increase the number of justices on the Supreme Court, should the Roberts-led court rule against the DACA recipients. This would be the ultimate, irrefutable signal that the judiciary is as political and ideological as the executive and congressional branches of the federal government. Perhaps that is not a terrible thing, but it would be an earthquake in American law and society.

Beyond Washington's corridors of power, the demise of DACA would further radicalize a generation of Latinos and their allies who have organized and litigated to protect it even as they fight for broader protections for their parents. Racial projects can serve to promote racism or an anti-racist agenda. Clearly, the Trump administration's use of racist imagery and implementation of anti-immigrant policies—from the announcement of the Muslim travel ban the week he became president to his announcement nine months later rescinding DACA, are projects that promote an anti-Latino racial logic. But those who support the demonization of immigrants, in general, or Latinos, specifically ought to beware: race-based activism has a dialectical relationship with racial violence. Consider the cases of California, Nevada, and Arizona.

November 2019 marked the twenty-fifth anniversary of California voters' passage of Proposition 187 by a landslide. The law did not survive a constitutional challenge in federal court, but it would have cut off government services and resources to undocumented immigrants. It nonetheless produced a political tsunami, though opposite that hoped by its godfather, Republican governor Pete Wilson, whose career ended because of Prop. 187. Today California is "a sanctuary state" that does not allow local and state law enforcement personnel to cooperate with ICE, refuses more detention centers for immigrants, and leads the nation in the expansion of rights and benefits to undocumented immigrants.[26] Democrats in California control every single state-wide elected office and have super-majorities in both house of the legislature. Political scientists Matt Barreto and Gary Segura call it "the Prop. 187 Effect," and say it gave rise to a new generation of Latino politicians and activists.[27] Kevin de León, the charismatic former president pro tempore of the California state senate, credits Prop. 187 with motivating his career as a community organizer and politician. While de León lost his 2018 bid for Senate to incumbent Diane Feinstein, as this book went to press he appears headed to victory as a Los Angeles City Council member representing majority-Latino District 14.[28]

The next de León is Astrid Silva, a thirty-one-year-old Latina with DACA status. For five years prior to Trump's announcement, she had been able to live and work in Las Vegas, Nevada without fear of deportation. When the Supreme Court heard oral arguments in the DACA lawsuit, she was in the audience. Her November 2019 calendar included conversations with no fewer than five candidates for the Democratic presidential nomination (Joe Biden, Cory Booker, Pete Buttigieg, Kamala Harris, and Elizabeth Warren).[29] Whether or not DACA ends, Silva—and many people like her—will continue to be part of the fabric of American life. If the Democrats maintain control of the House of Representatives and take the White House in 2020, DACA recipients and many other undocumented immigrants will gain citizenship. If not, it is likely that many, if not most, will be deported over time; even in that case, however, their strong ties to American citizens will mean they return again or find ways to stay, whether in or out of the shadows.

Even Arizona, long a bastion of right-wing Republican power, is in the process of becoming purple thanks to Latinos who saw red when "Sheriff Joe" made prisoners wear pink. Joe Arpaio, the son of Italian immigrants, served as sheriff of Maricopa County (metropolitan Phoenix) from 1993 to 2016, when he lost his re-election bid. He brags about helping write the Trump playbook, telling a reporter in 2012 that he planned to turn every "illegal immigrant" he was forced to release from county jail into "the Willie Horton" George H.W. Bush had in 1988.[30] Arpaio was instrumental in fanning the flames of hysteria over Mexican immigration, working closely with Republican politicians to pass Senate Bill 1070—known as the "show me your papers bill"—and get it signed into law by Governor Jan Brewer in 2010. Although it was immediately challenged by the Obama Department of Justice on the grounds that immigration law was an area controlled by the federal government, some of the most egregious features of the law went into effect. The result was the widespread racial profiling of Latinos by law enforcement. Arpaio was convicted in 2017 of violating Latinos' civil rights, but Trump pardoned him before the judge could hand down a sentence.[31]

But Latinos will likely have the last laugh at Arpaio's expense. Trump won Arizona in 2016 by 92,000 votes, but since then, half a million new voters have registered in Arizona, many of them young Latinos. A decade after S.B. 1070, a grassroots Latino-led group, Living United for Change in Arizona (which goes by its Spanish acronym LUCHA, meaning fight or struggle), pushed forward a new $12 per hour minimum wage that went into effect in January 2020, galvanizing more voters.[32] Meanwhile, those Latinos who became politically active in opposition to S.B. 1070 today are state lawmakers, campaign managers, and the leaders of pro-immigrant, pro-Latino organizations in civic society. Arizona will never be the same. In Arizona, Nevada, and California, racist rhetoric and laws targeting Latinos were met with organizing, solidarity, and voter registration drives.

In a similar way, mass protests against an immigration bill seen as too punitive—protests that occurred in more than three hundred American cities in March of 2006—galvanized Latino consciousness. These spontaneous, grassroots, mobilizations spawned a more formally organized immigrants' rights movement that fought for passage of comprehensive immigration reform (which most recently was represented in the so-called Gang of Eight legislation in the U.S. Senate in 2013). The movement also produced a corps of young undocumented persons who "came out of the closet" to demand legal rights, eventually culminating in Obama's 2012 executive order providing undocumented persons brought to the United States as children the legal status to study and work in the country. Studies also have found that this protest activity led to a greater sense of racial identity as Latinos along with greater solidarity among Latinos that transcends national origin, nativity, and/or having foreign-born parents.[33]

It is possible this kind of Latino race consciousness will translate into even greater embrace of the other-race option by Latinos in the 2020 census. On the other hand, given the controversy over the citizenship question and reductions in funding for community education about the census by the Trump administration, it is possible that 2020 will see an undercount of Latinos and possibly an associated over-representation of White-race Latinos. Either way, the nonpartisan legitimacy of the decennial census will be diminished along with the notion of a constitutionally valid apportionment process for our representative democracy. Until and unless the Census Bureau figures out how to counteract the suppression of Latinos in mixed-immigration-status families and communities (brought on by the Trump administration's blocked effort in 2019 to ask those filling out the census questionnaire whether they were citizens) and count Latinos in a way that resonates with the lived reality of race, the census count will be subject to challenge, both legally and politically. The census will no longer stand as a reliable basis for political redistricting, the distribution of federal funds to cities and states, economic forecasts, or scholarly research.

For the 2020 census it is already too late. How then should Congress (which has typically played a strong role in oversight of the census) and whomever is elected president in November 2020 proceed? First, the new president should quickly appoint a director of the Census Bureau, which Trump has never done. Second, the executive branch should implement the 2018 recommendation to eliminate the so-called Hispanic ethnicity question as a companion to the race question. Instead, the 2030 census should incorporate a Latina/Latino/Latinx option among the choices for the race question. Since the bureau's rigorous pre-testing of possible formats showed no difference for two different versions that combined Latinos into the race question, it should select the one that also allows for specification of national origin in order to provide continuity with data collected between 1980 and 2020.[34] In order to maximize self-identification by Afro-Latinos and Indo-Latinos, the Census Bureau should in 2025 launch a public education campaign aimed at the full, accurate inclusion of Latinos in 2030. It should revolve around educating all people about Latinos' Indigenous and African roots under Spanish colonialism. The campaign's aim will be to emphasize to Latinos that, like everyone else, they may self-identify with two or more racial groupings on the census race question (i.e., Latino and Black; Latino and American Indian, etc.).[35]

Latinos have a distinctive history in the United States, one that has been powerfully shaped by the twin experiences of American colonialism in Latin America and racial subordination in this country, a thesis first articulated in the early 1970s under the banner of "internal colonialism." This theory posited the internal colony as a way of linking the racial oppression of Blacks, Chicanos, and Puerto Ricans to worldwide anti-colonial movements in Africa and elsewhere (sometimes call the Third World movement).[36] Yet the central preoccupation of the internal colonialism thesis of the 1970s was the utopic idea that U.S. racial minorities could and would fight their White oppressors in revolutionary, anti-colonial resistance. Instead, resistance to racial oppression split off into a radical movement and a more moderate one. The result was two-pronged, the adoption of modest legal reforms and a shift in American cultural values that included a stated commitment to racial equality. The two went hand-in-hand with the official suppression of outright white supremacy in politics and culture; but that white rage was merely hidden to fester and spread over decades. Behind those changes, white supremacy shape-shifted once again to neuter anti-discrimination laws and replace demands for equality with the rhetoric of colorblindness as a mask for racism. All the while, the anti-racist soldiers of the sixties and seventies became incorporated and invested in institutions (including state institutions) and organizations that promote the status quo and foster the attainment and maintenance of middle- and upper-middle-class lifestyles.

In some ways, the evolution of Latino identity from 1980 to 2020 tracks that path, with the unanticipated booster shot of the post-1965 growth in immigration, especially robust from Mexico. In the last three decades of the twentieth century, it was precisely that immigration wave that blossomed into an explosion in Spanish-language cultural production, from television networks to newspapers to radio stations. The rapid growth of the Latino population and its cultural voice—represented by the Spanish-language production but extending far beyond that— has itself produced an anti-Latino backlash that has moved from the Republican Party's right-wing fringe to its mainstream center. That, too, has fueled a renaissance of Latino activism and racial consciousness, in an ongoing cycle. Latinos as an American racial group are here to stay.

ACKNOWLEDGMENTS

I am grateful to zakia henderson-brown, my editor at The New Press, for her insight and patience. This project began in 2012 with Sarah Fan, who saw more promise in my short book proposal than it deserved. Over the succeeding five years, I took on increasingly heavy administrative duties at UCLA and had to move this project to the back burner. Despite a sabbatical and research leave in 2018, family matters took priority, and I feared this book was not to be. With Trump's election, the conversion of his racist rhetoric into policy and practice, and increasing national polarization on questions at the heart of this project, the book became increasingly urgent. January 2019 proved a turning point, and I thank the entire New Press team for moving so quickly to get this into the hands of readers.

Especially given its long gestation, I owe a debt to many friends and colleagues. Sherene H. Razack is at the top of the list; she is a generous listener whose brilliance cannot help but rub off on her friends and students. She provided encouragement and editing when I needed them most. Thank you from the bottom of my heart to the Razack-Brookwell family for feeding my soul and body these past four years. My colleagues in UCLA Law's Critical Race Studies Program provided encouragement, suggestions, and validation at several key points. Thank you to Aslı Ü. Bâli, Devon Carbado, Jerry López, Noah Zatz, Jennifer Chacón, Jasleen Kohli, Sherod Thaxton, Cheryl Harris, Asad Rahim,

Hiroshi Motomura, Sunita Patel, Jerry Kang, and Jyoti Nanda. Apart from specific feedback, I thank my colleagues and students for creating and maintaining CRS as an intellectual and political community for the past two decades.

For conversations about this book over the years, I thank Leisy Abrego, Kip Bobroff, Gena Carpio, Ernie Chávez, Nadine El-Enany, Joshua Guzmán, Berta Hernández-Truyol, Celia Lacayo, Chalane Lechuga, Nancy López, Roberto Mártinez, Rachel Moran, Daria Roithmayr, Manuela Romero, Casandra Salgado, and the late Mark Sawyer. Carroll Seron and Val Jenness listened closely and encouraged me at a critical moment in the writing process. I have benefited from sharing this project with audiences in varied disciplines, including the following: the Department of Criminology, Law and Society at UC Irvine; the Center for Race and Race Relations at the University of Florida School of Law; the Center for Racism, Social Justice and Health at UCLA's Fielding School of Public Health; the conference "Unspeakable: Racism, Antiracism and Colorblindness" at Arizona State University (2017); the Mexico City meeting of the Law and Society Association (2017); the Critical Race Studies in Education annual meeting (2018); and the annual meeting of the American Sociological Association (2019).

I am fortunate to have benefited from a truly gifted team of researchers and librarians without whom this book would not have been written. Thank you to everyone at the Hugh and Hazel Darling Law Library at UCLA (you are all darlings to me), especially Kevin Gerson, Gabe Juárez, Linda Karr O'Connor, Stephanie Anayah, Amy Atchison, Vicki Steiner, Shangching Huitzacua, Elise Meyers, Donna Gulnac, John Wilson, Sangeeta Paul, Lynn McClelland, Jenny Lentz, Scott Dewey, Kelly Leong, Cheryl Kelly Fischer, and the late June Kim. For assistance of various kinds I thank Elsa Duong and Tal Grietzer. Thank you to UCLA Law Deans Rachel Moran and Jennifer Mnookin for summer research support. I appreciate many brilliant research assistants, especially Emma Hulse and Sofia Pedroza, who worked with me in the final stages of this book, but also to a platoon of others over the past eight years: Viviana Arcia, Ethan Fallon, Navid Heyrani, Jassmin Poyaoan, Arifa Raza, Cesar Rivera, Paulette Rodríguez López, and Ashleigh Washington.

I am ever-grateful to my large extended family for nurturing me, believing in me, and continuing to attend my book talks! Thank you to my *tías* (Elida, Naomi, Norma, and Virginia); thank you to my *primas*—Angela, Juli, Kat, Kris, who put up with me and inspire me with all you do. To my brother Miguel, thank you for being a constant in my life and for the gift of your three sons. I thank my son Alejandro for being patient with me, for making me laugh, and for working hard these past few years to find his way. My parents, Eloyda and Antonio, are the very best. Words are not enough.

NOTES

Introduction

1. Andy Newman et al., "Alexandria Ocasio-Cortez Emerges as a Political Star," *New York Times*, June 27, 2018.

2. For the first quote, see Keka Araujo, "Rep. Ocasio-Cortez Explains Her Race and Ethnicity," Diversity Inc., February 15, 2019, https://diversityinc.com/alexandra-ocasio-cortez-black-ancestry-doesnt-mean-black. The second is from Shane Goldmacher, "Alexandria Ocasio-Cortez: Jewish Too?" *New York Times*, December 10, 2018.

3. "DCCC Chairman Luján's Floor Speech at Democratic National Convention." Press release, DCCC, July 27, 2016.

4. Dan McKay, "GOP Criticized for 'Complexion' Remark," *Albuquerque Journal*, December 20, 2019.

5. How to refer to Latinos is contentious. Terms include the gender-neutral and gender-nonconforming "Latinx," a term that in recent years has become popular among younger Latinos, Latino scholars, and in some popular media. Latinx arose, in part, because the words Latino/Latinos and Latina/Latinas, as words from the Spanish language, are gendered as male and female, respectively. I sometimes use Latinx in this book. Most of the time, however, I rely on the terms "Latino" or "Latinos" in a gender-inclusive way to refer to all Latinos (whether they identify as neither, both, or either male or female gender), without seeking to invoke Spanish-language grammatical rules of gender. In rare cases, in order to refer specifically to "Latina women" or "Latino men" in specific contexts where binary gender is relevant, I rely on the gender-specific terms Latina or Latino. At times, and particularly with reference to specific bureaucratic contexts or conclusions (which sometimes seep into the mainstream media), I use the terms

"Hispanic," "non-Hispanic White," and "non-Hispanic Black;" in such instances, the terms Hispanic and Latino are interchangeable. Throughout the book, quoted matter (contemporary and historical) uses various terminology different from my own preferences. Finally, the terms Latino and Hispanic, as this book will show, are rather recent formulations, such that when discussing the distant and recent history I sometimes use more historically apropos national origin terms such as Mexican American or Puerto Rican.

6. On identity performance, see Devon W. Carbado and Miti Gulati, *Acting White: Rethinking Race in Post-Racial America* (New York: Oxford University Press, 2013).

7. For key works on the American racial order, see Michael Omi and Howard Winant, *Racial Formation in the United States from the 1960s to the 1990s* (New York: Routledge and Kegan Paul, 1994); Eduardo Bonilla-Silva, *Racism without Racists: Color-Blind Racism and the Persistence of Racial Inequality in the United States*, 4th ed. (Lanham, MD: Rowman & Littlefield, 2017); Kimberlé Crenshaw, Neil Gotanda, and Gary Peller, *Critical Race Theory: The Key Writings That Formed the Movement* (New York: The New Press, 1996).

8. In the sense that racial categories are social and political constructs, it would be ideal to use quotation marks for all racial categories each time they appear in this book. While this would interfere in too cumbersome a way, imagine they are there throughout.

9. Jay S. Kaufman, "How Inconsistencies in Racial Classification Demystify the Race Construct in Public Health Statistics," *American Journal of Epidemiology* 134 (1999): 1079–84.

10. For studies of how definitions of who is White and who is not have changed, see Theodore Allen, *The Invention of the White Race* (New York: Verso, 1994); Karen Brodkin, *How Jews Became White Folks and What That Says about Race in America* (New Brunswick, NJ: Rutgers University Press, 1998); *How the United States Racializes Latinos: White Hegemony and Its Consequences*, edited by José A. Cobas, Jorge Duany, and Joe R. Feagin (Boulder, CO: Paradigm Publishers, 2009); Virginia Domínguez, *White by Definition: Racial Classification in Creole Louisiana* (New Brunswick, NJ: Rutgers University Press, 1997); Michelle Fine, Lois Weis, Linda C. Powell, L. Mun Wong, *Off White: Readings on Power, Privilege, and Society* (New York: Routledge, 2004); Neil Foley, *The White Scourge: Mexicans, Blacks, and Poor Whites in Texas Cotton Culture* (Berkeley, CA: University of California Press, 1997); Laura E. Gómez, *Manifest Destinies: The Making of the*

Mexican American Race (New York: New York University Press, 2018); Ian Haney López, *White by Law: The Legal Construction of Race* (New York: New York University Press, 2006); Cheryl Harris, "Whiteness as Property," *Harvard Law Review* 108, no. 8 (1993): 1707; Noel Ignatiev, *How the Irish Became White* (New York: Routledge, 1995); Matthew Jacobson, *Whiteness of a Different Color: European Immigrants and the Alchemy of Race* (Cambridge, MA: Harvard University Press, 1998); George Lipsitz, *The Possessive Investment in Whiteness: How White People Profit from Identity Politics* (Philadelphia, PA: Temple University Press, 2006); Neda Maghbouleh, *The Limits of Whiteness: Iranian Americans and the Everyday Politics of Race* (Stanford, CA: Stanford University Press, 2017); David R. Roediger, *The Wages of Whiteness: Race and the Making of the American Working Class* (New York: Verso, 1991); John Tehranian, "Performing Whiteness: Naturalization Litigation and the Construction of Racial Identity in America," *Yale Law Journal* 109, no. 4 (2000): 817.

11. Rubén G. Rumbaut, "Pigments of Our Imagination: On the Racialization and Racial Identities of 'Hispanics' and 'Latinos,'" in *How the United States Racializes Latinos: White Hegemony and Its Consequences*, edited by José A. Cobas, Jorge Duany, and Joe R. Feagin (Boulder, CO: Paradigm Publishers, 2009), 15–16.

12. My thinking about racial logics has been deeply influenced by Moon-Kie Jung, *Beneath the Surface of White Supremacy: Denaturalizing U.S. Racisms Past and Present* (Stanford, CA: Stanford University Press, 2015).

13. Today, two out of three American children attend schools where more than half of the student body shares their race. A.W. Geiger, "Many Minority Students Go to Schools Where at Least Half of Their Peers Are Their Race or Ethnicity," Pew Research Center, October 25, 2017, https://www.pewresearch.org/fact-tank/2017/10/25/many-minority-students-go-to-schools-where-at-least-half-of-their-peers-are-their-race-or-ethnicity [https://perma.cc/J3HC-P8LK].

14. In her landmark book, historian Peggy Pascoe notes that "in practice, miscegenation law acted as a kind of legal factory for the defining, producing, and reproducing of the racial categories of the state"; see Peggy Pascoe, *What Comes Naturally: Miscegenation Law and the Making of Race in America* (New York: Oxford University Press, 2009), 9. The facts in this paragraph come from Pascoe's chapter 5, "Seeing Like a Racial State," 131–159.

15. Pascoe, *What Comes Naturally*, 131–132; see also Leti Volpp, "American Mestizo: Filipinos and Antimiscegenation Laws in California," *University of California Davis Law Review* 33 (1999–2000): 795–835.

16. Pascoe, *What Comes Naturally*, 158–159.

17. Indeed, it was far from inevitable that Filipino Americans would come to be defined as Asian American rather than as Latino. Since the Philippines had experienced Spanish colonial rule followed by American colonial rule, they were similarly situated to Latin American nations. Yet within the United States, Filipinos have come to be Asian Americans, an important story of racialization in its own right. I discuss the Filipino story at various points when it intersects with that of Latinos. On Filipino racialization in the United States, see Anthony Christian Ocampo, *The Latinos of Asia: How Filipino Americans Break the Rules of Race* (Palo Alto, CA: Stanford University Press, 2017).

18. In a previous book, I coined the phrase "double colonization" to describe these dynamics. While most writers have concerned themselves with either Spanish colonization (more commonly) or American colonization (much less frequently), by looking at both together we can best understand how two different systems of white supremacy clashed, merged, and ultimately shaped the common sense of anti-Latino racism today. See Gómez, *Manifest Destinies*.

19. At the same time, to the extent the U.S. racial order has global relevance and impact, the purchase of "Latinos" may travel.

20. Also in 1980, the census first added the category "Asian/Pacific Islander" as an option under race. Dina G. Okamoto, *Redefining Race: Asian American Panethnicity and Shifting Ethnic Boundaries* (New York: Russell Sage Foundation, 2014), 47.

21. Luis Noe-Bustamante and Antonio Flores, "Facts on Latinos in the U.S.," *Pew Research Center* (2019). See also United States Census Bureau, "Fact Finder: Annual Estimates of the Resident Population by Sex, Age, Race, and Hispanic Origin for the United States and States: April 1, 2010 to July 1, 2018," July 8, 2019, https://perma.cc/J93C-ANWM.

22. Noe-Bustamante and Flores, "Facts on Latinos in the U.S." See also United States Census Bureau, "QuickFacts: United States," n.d., https://www.census.gov/quickfacts/fact/table/US/RHI725218; and U.S. Census Bureau, General Population Characteristics, United States Summary, PC80-1-B-1 (1980), 1–12, https://www2.census.gov/prod2/decennial/documents/1980/1980censusofpopu8011u_bw.pdf.

23. Antonio Flores, Mark Hugo López, and Jens Manuel Krogsta, "U.S. Hispanic Population Reached New High in 2018, but Growth Has Slowed," Pew Research Center, July 8, 2019, https://www.pewresearch.org/fact-tank/2019/07/08/u-s-hispanic-population-reached-new-high-in-2018-but-growth-has-slowed/ [https://perma.cc/NK4K-XBM9].

24. Lisa R. Pruitt, "Latina/os, Locality, and the Law in the Rural South," *Harvard Latino Law Review* 12, no. 1 (2009): 135–170.; see also, Amada Armenta, *Protect, Serve, and Deport: The Rise of Policing as Immigration Enforcement* (Berkeley, CA: University of California Press, 2017).

25. This number includes the federal government's estimated of the 62 percent of Latinos who say they are of Mexican ancestry as well as the additional 7 percent of Latinos who give their national origin as "other Hispanic" (rather than as, say, Mexican American or Puerto Rican, etc.). Research suggests that some Mexican Americans who are descended from early settlers of what was then the far northern portion of the Spanish colony of New Spain (later, Mexico), do not identify as "Mexican" origin but do identify as Latino/Hispanic and, within Latino, as "other Hispanic." These are Latinos (who are sixth or more generations born in the United States), who have zero family ties in Mexico, and who disproportionately reside in New Mexico. While some scholars do not classify this population as Mexican American, I do so for reasons elaborated in my 2007 (2018 edition) book; see Gómez, *Manifest Destinies*. In a nationally representative sample of Latinos, those who opted to call themselves "Spanish," rather than "Latino" or by a national origin term like Mexican American, represent a similar grouping compared to those longtime New Mexicans and likely include many of them. Of 327 Latinos surveyed who chose to call themselves only Latino (without a specific national origin), only 41 (less than 10 percent) identified a direct connection to Spain via a parent or a grandparent. Tanya Golash-Boza, "Dropping the Hyphen? Becoming Latino(a)-American," *Social Forces* 85, no. 1 (2006): 27–55, 53. A more recent study of Latino residents of Albuquerque who had at least three generations of ancestors born in New Mexico similarly found that, when asked a question that mimicked the census Latino inquiry, one-third of them identified as Mexican American while another two-thirds identified as "other Hispanic." See Casandra Danielle Salgado, "'The Border Crossed Us!': Mexican-Americans, Colonization, and Race" (PhD dissertation, University of California, Los Angeles, 2019). Virtually all Latinos in New Mexico have ancestral origins in what is today Mexico, whether when it was designated as New Spain by the Spanish or the independent Mexican nation after 1820. See, generally, Gómez, *Manifest Destinies*.

26. Data as of 2017. Noe-Bustamante and Flores, "Facts on Latinos in the U.S."

27. On the size and distribution of the Latino electorate, see "Mapping the Latino Electorate by State," Pew Research Center, January 19, 2016; see, generally, Matt A. Barreto and Gary M. Segura, *Latino America: How America's Most Dynamic Population Is Poised to Transform the Politics of the Nation* (New York: Public Affairs, 2014).

28. Antonio Flores and Mark Hugo López, "Key Facts about Latinos in the 2018 Midterm Elections," Pew Research Center, October 15, 2018, https://pewresearch.org/fact-tank/2018/10/15/key-facts-about-latinos-in -the-2018-midterms-elections.

29. The Cuban Americans are Ted Cruz (R-TX), Bob Menendez (D-NJ), Marco Rubio (R-FL). Catherine Cortez Masto (D-NV) is Mexican American. See David Welna, "How Ted Cruz's Father Shaped His Views on Immigration," NPR, June 20, 2013, 3:01 AM, https://www.npr .org/sections/itsallpolitics/2013/06/20/193585553/how-ted-cruzs-father -shaped-his-views-on-immigration [https://perma.cc/H5WE-QD62]; Burgess Everett, "Cortez Masto Seizes on 'Hispandering' Attack," *Politico*, September 23, 2016, 4:12 PM, https://www.politico.com/story/2016/09 /catherine-cortez-masto-joe-heck-hispandering-228592 [https://perma. cc/5298-E6HV]; Jeffrey Gettleman, "Robert Menendez, a Politician Even at 20," *New York Times*, December 10, 2005, https://www.nytimes.com/2005 /12/10/nyregion/robert-menendez-a-politician-even-at-20.html [https:// perma.cc/5M9E-QL7U]; Manuel Roig-Franzia, "Marco Rubio's Compelling Family Story Embellishes Facts, Documents Show," *Washington Post*, October 20, 2011, https://www.washingtonpost.com/politics/marco-rubios -compelling-family-story-embellishes-facts-documents-show/2011/10/20 /gIQAaVHD1L_story.html [https://perma.cc/7QLE-TTJS].

30. Kim Parker, Rich Morin, and Juliana Menasce Horowitz, "Looking to the Future, Public Sees an America in Decline on Many Fronts: 3. Views of Demographic Changes," Pew Research Center, March 21, 2019, https:// www.pewsocialtrends.org/2019/03/21/views-of-demographic-changes-in -america [https://perma.cc/Q7HW-W7QG]. See also Ryan Miller, "46% of Whites Worry Becoming a Majority-Minority Nation Will 'Weaken American Culture,' Survey Says," *USA Today*, March 21, 2019.

31. Todd J. Gillman, "Beto O'Rourke Ends Campaign Pause after El Paso Massacre, Vows Crusade Against Trump, Intolerance, and Gun Violence," *Dallas Morning News*, August 15, 2019.

32. Amelia Thomson-DeVeaux, "Most Latinos Now Say It's Gotten Worse for Them in the U.S.," FiveThirtyEight.com, August 8, 2019.

33. *Peña-Rodriguez v. Colorado*, 137 S.Ct. 855 (2017).

34. Raymond Rocco, *Transforming Citizenship: Democracy, Membership, and Belonging in Latino Communities* (East Lansing, MI: Michigan State University Press, 2014), 71.

35. Asian Americans experience the same phenomenon, but Blacks and Whites typically do not, not even when they are immigrants.

36. Jorge Duany, "Racializing Ethnicity in the Spanish-Speaking Caribbean: A Comparison of Haitians in the Dominican Republic and Dominicans in Puerto Rico," in *How the United States Racializes Latinos: White Hegemony and Its Consequences*, edited by José A. Cobas, Jorge Duany, and Joe R. Feagin (Boulder, CO: Paradigm Publishers, 2009), 214–227.

37. See Mary Waters, *Black Identities: West Indian Immigrant Dreams and American Realities* (Cambridge, MA: Harvard University Press, 2001).

38. Portes and Rumbaut, *Immigrant America*, 93.

39. Portes and Rumbaut, *Immigrant America*, 93.

40. I typically use "United States" or its abbreviation while avoiding reference to "America," consistent with the recognition that "America" formally encompasses all of the Americas—North America, Central America, and South America. In some instances, however, references to the United States as America is used for ease of communication.

41. Lisa Lowe, *The Intimacies of Four Continents* (Durham, NC: Duke University Press, 2015), 36.

42. Lowe, *The Intimacies of Four Continents*, 36.

43. María Joséfina Saldaña-Portillo, *Indian Given: Racial Geographies across Mexico and the United States* (Durham, NC: Duke University Press, 2016), 117.

1: We Are Here Because You Were There

1. Ambalavaner Sivanandan, "Catching History on the Wing," 50th Celebration Conference for the Institute of Race Relations, *IRR News*, November 6, 2008.

2. My claim is not that U.S. imperialism in other Latin American countries has been minimal or innocuous, but that it has been comparatively more extreme in these nine countries.

3. A total of 36,225,538 Latinos live in these four states, out of a total population of around 120,000,000. I calculated the number and the percentage of Latinos, by national origin group, in each state based on census data. United States Census Bureau, "Annual Estimates of the Resident Population by Sex, Age, Race, and Hispanic Origin for the United States and States: April 1, 2010 to July 1, 2018 [by state]," July 1, 2018.

4. Ian Morris, "Corporate Might" (Review of *Anarchy: The East Indian Company, Corporate Violence, and the Pillage of Empire* by William Dalrymple), *New York Times Book Review*, October 6, 2019, 15.

5. For an introduction to settler colonialism, see Sherene H. Razack, *Race, Space, and the Law: Unmapping a White Settler Society* (Toronto: Between the Lines, 2002). See also Sherene H. Razack, *Dying from Improvement: Inquests and Inquiries into Indigenous Deaths in Custody* (Toronto: University of Toronto Press, 2015) on settler colonialism in Canada; J. Kehaulani Kauanui, *Hawaiian Blood: Colonialism and the Politics of Sovereignty and Indigeneity* (Durham, NC: Duke University Press, 2008) on settler colonialism in Hawaii; Gómez, *Manifest Destinies* on settler colonialism in the Mexican Cession; Genevieve Carpio, *Collisions at the Crossroads: How Place and Mobility Make Race* (Berkeley, CA: University of California Press, 2019) on settler colonialism in southern California.

6. The states are, in alphabetical order, Arizona, California, Colorado, Kansas, Nevada, New Mexico, Oklahoma, Texas, Utah, and Wyoming.

7. See, generally, Juan R. Torruella, "Why Puerto Rico Does Not Need Further Experimentation with Its Future," *Harvard Law Review Forum* 131, no. 4 (2018): 65–104; Julian Go, *American Empire and the Politics of Meaning: Elite Political Cultures in the Philippines and Puerto Rico during U.S. Colonialism* (Durham, NC: Duke University Press, 2008); Sam Erman, *Almost Citizens: Puerto Rico, the U.S. Constitution, and Empire* (New York: Cambridge University Press, 2019).

8. Julian Go, *Patterns of Empire: The British and American Empires, 1688 to the Present* (Cambridge: Cambridge University Press, 2011), 143, table 4.2.

9. "Base Structure Report-Fiscal Year 2018 Baseline: A Summary of the Real Property Inventory Data," Department of Defense, https://www.acq.osd.mil/eie/Downloads/BSI/Base%20Structure%20Report%20FY18.pdf [https://perma.cc/4QBB-CRJK], pp. 62–63. For the number of military personnel, see "Military and Civilian Personnel by Service/Agency by State/Country," Defense Manpower Data Center, September 2019, downloaded from: https://www.dmdc.osd.mil/appj/dwp/dwp_reports.jsp (on file with author). These sites do not include the now defunct bombing range on the Puerto Rican island of Vieques, which the United States Navy turned over to the U.S. Department of the Interior in 2003 due to massive protest.

10. Gómez, *Manifest Destinies*, 7, 18, 194n23.

11. David Montejano, *Anglos and Mexicans in the Making of Texas, 1836–1986* (Austin, TX: University of Texas Press, 1987).

12. As quoted in Gómez, *Manifest Destinies*, 19.

13. As quoted in Gómez, *Manifest Destinies*, 19.

14. See Gómez, *Manifest Destinies*, 19–22.

15. Editorial from the *American Whig Review*, as quoted in Reginald Horsman, *Race and Manifest Destiny: The Origins of American Racial Anglo-Saxonism* (Berkeley, CA: University of California Press, 1981), 236–237.

16. For a detailed account, see Gómez, *Manifest Destinies.*

17. This cursory history necessarily glosses over the bloody resistance to U.S. forces in New Mexico and the American military's violent retribution, which included razing several Mexican villages and Indian Pueblos, killing thousands, and publicly executing dozens. For a detailed account of the U.S.-Mexico War and its impact on Mexican Americans, see Gómez, *Manifest Destinies*, 15–47.

18. Gómez, *Manifest Destinies*, 194n20. "The Mexican Cession" euphemistically downplays the violent, imperial aspects of the U.S. aggression against Mexico. For a lengthy discussion, see Gómez, *Manifest Destinies*, 15–47.

19. As quoted in Reginald Horsman, *Race and Manifest Destiny: The Origins of American Racial Anglo-Saxonism* (Cambridge, MA: Harvard University Press), 241.

20. Richard Griswold del Castillo, *The Treaty of Guadalupe Hidalgo: A Legacy of Conflict* (Norman, OK: University of Oklahoma), 44.

21. For a detailed discussion of New Mexico's statehood dynamics, see Gómez, *Manifest Destinies*, 58–84.

22. Jason M. Colby, *The Business of Empire: United Fruit, Race, and U.S. Expansion in Central America* (Ithaca, NY: Cornell University Press, 2011), 27.

23. Gilbert G. González and Raul Fernández, "Empire and the Origins of Twentieth-Century Migration from Mexico to the United States," *Pacific Historical Review* 71, no. 1 (2002): 19-57. On corporate colonialism, see Jason Colby's wonderful study of the United Fruit Company in Guatemala and Honduras, *The Business of Empire.*

24. George J. Sánchez, *Becoming Mexican American: Ethnicity, Culture, and Identity in Chicano Los Angeles* (New York: Oxford University Press, 1995); Mario Barrera, *Race and Class in the Southwest* (Notre Dame, IN: University of Notre Dame Press, 1979).

25. González and Fernández, "Empire and the Origins of Twentieth-Century Migration," 42–43.

26. See, generally, Kelly Lytle Hernández, *Migra! A History of the U.S. Border Patrol* (Berkeley and Los Angeles, CA: University of California Press, 2010).

27. Joan Moore and Harry Pachon, *Hispanics in the United States* (Englewood Cliffs, NJ: Prentice-Hall Inc., 1985), 7.

28. Zaragosa Vargas, *Crucible of Struggle: A History of Mexican Americans from Colonial Times to the Present* (New York: Oxford University Press, 2011), 275.

29. Steven W. Bender, *Mea Culpa: Lessons on Law and Regret from U.S. History* (New York: New York University Press, 2015), 40.

30. Vargas, *Crucible of Struggle*, 216.

31. Vargas, *Crucible of Struggle*, 215.

32. Tom I. Romero III, "Observations on History, Law, and the Rise of the New Jim Crow in State-level Immigration Law and Policy for Latinos," *American Quarterly* 66, no. 1 (2014): 153–160, 157.

33. Vargas, *Crucible of Struggle*, 224–225.

34. On the Japanese-Mexican Labor Association's 1,200-person strike, see Devon W. Carbado, "Yellow by Law: The Story of *Ozawa v. United States*," in *Race Law Stories*, edited by Rachel F. Moran and Devon W. Carbado (New York: Foundation Press, 2008). On the application of the alien land law to Mexicans, see Romero, *Observations on History, Law, and the New Jim Crow*, 157 (describing the case of *Morrison v. California*, decided by the U.S. Supreme Court in 1934).

35. Vargas, *Crucible of Struggle*, 219; see also Sánchez, *Becoming Mexican American*.

36. On the Bracero Program, see Foley, *The White Scourge*, 205–206.

37. Natalie Molina, *Fit to Be Citizens?: Public Health and Race in Los Angeles, 1879–1939* (Berkeley and Los Angeles, CA: University of California Press, 2006).

38. Mireya Loza, *Defiant Braceros: How Migrant Workers Fought for Racial, Sexual, and Political Freedom* (Durham, NC: University of North Carolina Press, 2016).

39. Foley, *The White Scourge*, 205.

40. David Fitzgerald, "Inside the Sending State: The Politics of Mexican Emigration Control," *The International Migration Review* 40, no. 2 (2006): 259–293.

41. Marcel Paret, "Legality and Exploitation: Immigration Enforcement and the U.S. Migrant Labor System," *Latino Studies* 12, no. 4 (2014): 503–526.

42. Paret, "Legality and Exploitation," 503–526.

43. Bender, *Mea Culpa*, 40.

44. Mérida M. Rua, *A Grounded Identidad: Making New Lives in Chicago's Puerto Rican Neighborhoods* (New York: Oxford University Press, 2012), 144.

45. Paret, "Legality and Exploitation," 514. On the historical evolution of the illegal alien, see Mae M. Ngai, *Impossible Subjects: Illegal Aliens and the Making of Modern America* (Princeton, NJ: Princeton University Press, 2004).

46. Portes and Rumbaut, *Immigrant America*, 23.

47. Paret, "Legality and Exploitation," 514.

48. Portes and Rumbaut, *Immigrant America*, 175 (2 million given amnesty); 379 (holding employers harmless).

49. Mónica Verea, "Immigration Trends after 20 Years of NAFTA," *Norteamérica: Revista Académica del CISAN-UNAM* 9, no. 2 (2014): 109–143, 123.

50. Portes and Rumbaut, *Immigrant America*, 374 (on public assistance ban). In 1998, during the Clinton administration, there were nearly 21,000 arrests and more than 13,000 prosecutions in federal court for immigration offenses. John Gramlich, "Far More Immigration Cases Are Being Prosecuted," Pew Research Center, September 27, 2019 (citing Bureau of Justice statistics from 1998–2018).

51. Nestor P. Rodríguez and Cecilia Menjívar, "Central American Immigrants and Racialization in a Post-Civil Rights Era," in *How the United States Racializes Latinos: White Hegemony and Its Consequences*, ed. Jose A. Cobas, Jorge Duany, and Joe R. Feagin (Boulder, CO: Paradigm Publishers, 2009), 195.

52. Rodríguez and Menjívar, 195.

53. Paret, "Legality and Exploitation," 514, 518.

54. The H-2A visa for temporary laborers from a foreign country was expanded under the 1990 Immigration Act and then grew dramatically by 2010. Alejandro Portes and Rubén G. Rumbaut, *Immigrant America: A Portrait*, 2nd ed. (Berkeley, CA: University of California Press, 2014), 371.

55. Under the Priority Enforcement Policy announced July 1, 2015, Obama directed federal officers to target immigrants who were recent arrivals to the country and/or who had records of violent crimes. Leisy Abrego, et al., "Making Immigrants into Criminals: Legal Processes of Criminalization in the Post-IIRIRA Era," *Journal on Migration and Human Security* 5, no. 3 (2017): 694–715, 709.

56. Gramlich, "Far More Immigration"; Portes and Rumbaut, *Immigrant America*, 32–34.

57. Portes and Rumbaut, *Immigrant America*, 176.

58. Portes and Rumbaut, *Immigrant America*, 176.

59. Colby, *The Business of Empire*, 24.

60. Colby, *The Business of Empire*, 25.

61. See generally, Larry Gara, *The Presidency of Franklin Pierce* (Lawrence, KA: University of Kansas Press, 1991).

62. Colby, *The Business of Empire*, 27.

63. T.J. Stiles, *The First Tycoon: The Epic Life of Cornelius Vanderbilt* (New York: Knopf, 2009), 268–327.

64. William H. Taft, "Some Recent Instances of National Altruism," *National Geographic* 18 (1907): 429–438.

65. Colby, *The Business of Empire*, 85.

66. Colby, *The Business of Empire*, 86.

67. John A. Booth and Thomas W. Walker, *Understanding Central America* (Boulder, CO: Westview Press, 1999).

68. María Cristina García, *Seeking Refuge: Central American Migration to Mexico, the United States and Canada* (Berkeley, CA: University of California Press), 14.

69. The United States formed the Latin American Ground School in the Panama Canal Zone in 1943 as a place to train Latin American troops in American military techniques. From 1949 to 1962, it was called the Caribbean School before being named the School of the Americas in 1963. For a comprehensive history, see Lesley Gill, *The School of the Americas: Military Training and Political Violence in the Americas* (Durham, NC: University of North Carolina Press, 2004), 72–74.

70. Gill, *School of the Americas*, 72–74, 233–234.

71. Booth and Walker, *Understanding Central America*, 75.

72. Booth and Walker, *Understanding Central America*, 77.

73. Booth and Walker, *Understanding Central America*, 79.

74. Saldaña-Portillo, *Indian Given*, 237.

75. William I. Robinson, *Transnational Conflicts: Central America, Social Change, and Globalization* (New York: Verso 2003), 73.

76. Cristina García, *Seeking Refuge*, 113.

77. Cristina García, *Seeking Refuge*, 113.

78. Karina O. Alvarado, Alicia Ivonne Estrada, and Ester E. Hernández, "Introduction," in *U.S. Central Americans: Reconstructing Memories, Struggles, and Communities of Resistance*, edited by Karina O. Alvarado, Alicia Ivonne Estrada, and Ester E. Hernández (Tucson, AZ: University of Arizona Press, 2017), 6.

79. Alvarado et al., "Introduction," in Alvarado, Estrada, and Hernández, *U.S. Central Americans*, 118.

80. Alvarado et al., "Introduction," in Alvarado, Estrada, and Hernández, *U.S. Central Americans*, 6.

81. The following books on American imperialism in Central America have influenced my analysis: Shannon Speed, *Incarcerated Stories: Indigenous Women Migrants and Violence in the Settler-Capitalist State* (Chapel Hill: University of North Carolina Press, 2019); Thomas D. Shoonover, *The United States in Central America, 1860–1911: Episodes of Social Imperialism and Imperial Rivalry in the World System* (Durham, NC: Duke University Press, 1991); Robinson, *Transnational Conflicts*; Cristina García, *Seeking Refuge*; Booth and Walker, *Understanding Central America*; Colby, *The Business of Empire*.

82. Alvarado et al., "Introduction," in Alvarado, Estrada, and Hernández, *U.S. Central Americans*, 17.

83. Alvarado et al., "Introduction," in Alvarado, Estrada, and Hernández, *U.S. Central Americans*, 17; Colby, *The Business of Empire*, 63.

84. Alvarado et al., "Introduction," in Alvarado, Estrada, and Hernández, *U.S. Central Americans*, 17; Colby, *The Business of Empire*, 87.

85. Go, *Patterns of Empire*, 55.

86. Colby, *The Business of Empire*, 155.

87. Alvarado et al., "Introduction," in Alvarado, Estrada, and Hernández, *U.S. Central Americans*, 19 (citing 2010 census data).

88. Gill, *School of the Americas*, 82.

89. Alvarado et al., "Introduction," in Alvarado, Estrada, and Hernández, *U.S. Central Americans*, 14, 18.

90. Go, *Patterns of Empire*, 196. Noriega died in 2017, after serving seventeen years of his sentence in a Miami prison.

91. Robinson, *Transnational Conflicts*, 123.

92. Robinson, *Transnational Conflicts*, 123.

93. Gill, *School of the Americas*, 78, 83.

94. Alvarado et al., "Introduction," in Alvarado, Estrada, and Hernández, *U.S. Central Americans*, 14.

95. Alvarado et al., "Introduction," in Alvarado, Estrada, and Hernández, *U.S. Central Americans*, 13.

96. Alvarado et al., "Introduction," in Alvarado, Estrada, and Hernández, *U.S. Central Americans*, 15.

97. Alvarado et al, "Introduction," in Alvarado, Estrada, and Hernández, *U.S. Central Americans*, 15 (citing information from a Freedom of Information Act request issued by several members of the House of Representatives).

98. Sarah Blanchard et al., "Shifting Trends in Central American Migration: A Demographic Examination of Increasing Honduran-U.S. Immigration and Deportation," *Latin Americanist* 55, no. 4 (2012): 61–85, 67.

99. For Honduran unaccompanied children apprehended by the Border Patrol, the number in fiscal year 2016 was 10,468, and in fiscal year 2019 was 20,398. For Honduran family units apprehended during the same two years, they numbered 22,226 and 188,416, respectively. See U.S. Border Patrol, "Southwest Border Apprehensions Fiscal Year 2019" (showing fiscal years 2016 to 2019).

100. D'Vera Cohn, et al., "Many Immigrants with Temporary Protected Status Face Uncertain Future," Pew Research Center, November 27, 2019, https//www.pewresearch.org/fact-tank/2019/11/27/immigrants-temporary-protected-status-in-us.

101. Guatemala also shares a small section of its northeastern border with Belize, a nation colonized by England.

102. For an analysis of how the Guatemalan state alternatingly practiced genocide and coercive assimilation of the Maya population, see Speed, *Incarcerated Stories*. See also Nestor P. Rodríguez and Cecilia Menjívar, "Central American Immigrants and Racialization in a Post-Civil Rights Era," in *How the United States Racializes Latinos: White Hegemony and Its Consequences*, edited by José A. Cobas, Jorge Duany, and Joe R. Feagin (Boulder, CO: Paradigm Publishers, 2009).

103. Colby, *The Business of Empire*, 45.

104. Colby, *The Business of Empire*, 30.

105. Colby, *The Business of Empire*, 119.

106. Colby, *The Business of Empire*, 136.

107. Speed, *Incarcerated Stories*, 37 (detailing Guatemala's long history of policies to coerce the Maya people to assimilate).

108. Colby, *The Business of Empire*, 143.

109. Colby, *The Business of Empire*, 166–170.

110. Alvarado et al., "Introduction," in Alvarado, Estrada, and Hernández, *U.S. Central Americans*, 9.

111. Colby, *The Business of Empire*, 204–205.

112. Speed, *Incarcerated Stories*, 38.

113. Speed, *Incarcerated Stories*, 38.

114. Alvarado et al., "Introduction," in Alvarado, Estrada, and Hernández, *U.S. Central Americans*, 9.

115. Alvarado et al., "Introduction," in Alvarado, Estrada, and Hernández, *U.S. Central Americans*, 11.

116. Stephan Macekura, "'For Fear of Persecution': Displaced Salvadorans and U.S. Refugee Policy in the 1980s," *Journal of Policy History* 23, no. 3 (2011): 357–382, 258.

117. María Cristina García, *Seeking Refuge*, 90.

118. Speed, *Incarcerated Stories*, 39. See also María Cristina García, *Seeking Refuge*.

119. Alvarado et al., "Introduction," in Alvarado, Estrada, and Hernández, *U.S. Central Americans*, 11–12.

120. In fiscal year 2019 alone, 188,416 Guatemalan family units were apprehended, eight times the number of families stopped at the border just four years earlier; U.S. Border Patrol, "Southwest Border Apprehensions Fiscal Year 2019."

121. "Recent Migration to the United States from Central America: Frequently Asked Questions," Washington, DC: Congressional Research Service, January 29, 2019, 14.

122. On November 1, 2019, President Trump announced that "refugees who are national or habitual residents of El Salvador, Guatemala, or Honduras" will be allocated 1,500 of 18,000 refugee spots; "Presidential Determination on Refugee Admissions for Fiscal Year 2020," Memorandum from the secretary of state, November 1, 2019.

123. María Cristina García, *Seeking Refuge*, 20 (noting that "the Fourteen Families controlled 60 percent of the farmland, the entire banking system, and most of the nation's industry").

124. Cristina García, *Seeking Refuge*, 20; see also Alvarado et al., "Introduction," in Alvarado, Estrada, and Hernández, *U.S. Central Americans*, 8; Colby, *The Business of Empire*, 193.

125. Rodríguez and Menjívar, "Central American Immigrants and

Racialization," 186; Alvarado et al., "Introduction," in Alvarado, Estrada, and Hernández, *U.S. Central Americans*, 7.

126. Mara Loveman, *National Colors: Racial Classification and the State in Latin America* (New York: Oxford University Press, 2014), 233, table 6.2A.

127. Booth and Walker, *Understanding Central America*, 37.

128. Booth and Walker, *Understanding Central America*, 37; Alvarado et al., "Introduction," in Alvarado, Estrada, and Hernández, *U.S. Central Americans*, 8; Gill, *School of the Americas*, 74.

129. María Cristina García, *Seeking Refuge*, 21.

130. Alvarado et al., "Introduction," in Alvarado, Estrada, and Hernández, *U.S. Central Americans*, 7.

131. Robinson, *Transnational Conflicts*, 89.

132. Booth and Walker, *Understanding Central America*, 114–115; see also Alvarado et al., "Introduction," in Alvarado, Estrada, and Hernández, *U.S. Central Americans*, 8; Gill, *The School of the Americas*, 83.

133. Alvarado et al., "Introduction," in Alvarado, Estrada, and Hernández, *U.S. Central Americans*, 7–8; Booth and Walker, *Understanding Central America*, 114.

134. Cristina García, *Seeking Refuge*, 21.

135. Booth and Walker, *Understanding Central America*, 115; see also Oscar Chacón, "Globalization, Obsolete and Inhumane Migratory Policies, and their Impact on Migrant Workers and their Families," *Journal of Poverty* 15, no. 4 (2011): 465–474, 467.

136. Alvarado et al., "Introduction," in Alvarado, Estrada, and Hernández, *U.S. Central Americans*, 8.

137. Macekura, "'For Fear of Persecution,'" 357–382, 358.

138. For fiscal year 2020, there were 12,021 Salvadoran unaccompanied children apprehended and 56,897 family units apprehended. "U.S. Border Patrol Southwest Border Apprehensions Fiscal Year 2019."

139. Alvarado et al., "Introduction," in Alvarado, Estrada, and Hernández, *U.S. Central Americans*, 9.

140. Gómez, *Manifest Destinies*, 77–80.

141. Gómez, *Manifest Destinies*, 78.

142. Gómez, *Manifest Destinies*, 78.

143. Go, *American Empire and the Politics of Meaning*, 1.

144. José A. Cobas, Jorge Duany, and Joe R. Feagin, "Racializing Latinos: Historical Background and Current Forms," in *How the United States*

Racializes Latinos: White Hegemony and Its Consequences, edited by José A. Cobas, Jorge Duany, and Joe R. Feagin (Boulder, CO: Paradigm Publishers, 2009), 6.

145. Go, *American Empire and the Politics of Meaning*, 6; Go, *Patterns of Empire*, 58. The United States ruled the Philippines until 1945, when it granted "independence" to the Filipino people with the following conditions: a 99-year lease for 23 military bases; the mandate that Filipino currency be pegged to the U.S. dollar; and the constitutional requirement that American corporations and citizens have access to raw materials and duty-free trade. See Go, *Patterns of Empire*, 122–123. Today, the United States has negotiated with the authoritarian regime of Rodrigo Duterte to re-establish five new military bases in the Philippines. Andrew Tilghman, "The U.S. military Is Moving into These 5 Bases in the Philippines," *Military Times*, March 21, 2016, https://www.militarytimes.com/news/your-military/2016/03/21/the-u-s-military-is-moving-into-these-5-bases-in-the-philippines [https://perma.cc/3HEV-C32L].

146. Go, *American Empire and the Politics of Meaning*, 56, 81.

147. Go, *American Empire and the Politics of Meaning*, 58.

148. Ofelia García, "Racializing the Language Practices of U.S. Latinos," in *How the United States Racializes Latinos: White Hegemony and Its Consequences*, edited by José A. Cobas, Jorge Duany, and Joe R. Feagin (Boulder, CO: Paradigm Publishers, 2009).

149. Whalen, "Colonialism, Citizenship, and the Making of the Puerto Rican Diaspora," in Whalen and Vázquez-Hernández, *The Puerto Rican Diaspora*, 13.

150. Ediberto Román, *Other American Colonies* (Durham, NC: Carolina Academic Press), 25.

151. See Juan R. Torruella, "Why Puerto Rico Does Not Need Further Experimentation With Its Future: A Reply to the Notion of Territorial Federalism," *Harvard Law Review Forum* 131, no. 4 (2018): 65–104.

152. José Ramón Sánchez, *Boricua Power: A Political History of Puerto Ricans in the United States* (New York: New York University Press, 2007), 54.

153. Ramón Sánchez, *Boricua Power*, 34.

154. Cobas, Jorge, and Feagin, "Racializing Latinos," in Cobas, Duany, and Feagin, *How the United States Racializes Latinos*, 23.

155. For all statistics in this paragraph, see Jorge Duany, *Blurred Borders: Transnational Migration between the Hispanic Caribbean and the United States* (Chapel Hill, NC: University of North Carolina Press, 2011), 88.

156. Duany, *Blurred Borders*, 88, table 4.1.

157. Duany, *Blurred Borders*, 88 (noting that the Puerto Rican Migrant Division looked at the Bracero Program as a model).

158. Duany, *Blurred Borders*, 84; one wonders what motivated those plantations to replace low-wage, native workers in one island colony with those from another, quite distant island colony, and my guess is it had to do with suppressing or averting organizing among workers, which is always more challenging across linguistic and cultural differences.

159. Duany, *Blurred Borders*, 88.

160. Duany, *Blurred Borders*, 89, figure 4.2.

161. Acosta-Belén and Santiago, *Puerto Ricans in the United States*, 128.

162. Acosta-Belén and Santiago, *Puerto Ricans in the United States*, 76–78.

163. Mérida M. Rúa, *A Grounded Identidad: Making New Lives in Chicago's Puerto Rican Neighborhoods* (New York: Oxford University Press, 2012), 38. As is often the case, the migrant offices in New York City, Chicago, Cleveland, and Camden, New Jersey were put to different, unintended uses by the Puerto Rican migrants who subverted them to cope with "the day-to-day problems and struggles . . . and the issues of racism and marginality to which they were exposed" on the mainland. Acosta-Belén and Santiago, *Puerto Ricans in the United States*, 162.

164. Whalen and Vázquez-Hernández, *The Puerto Rican Diaspora*, 153.

165. Whalen, "Colonialism, Citizenship, and the Making of the Puerto Rican Diaspora," in Whalen and Vázquez-Hernández, *The Puerto Rican Diaspora*, 37.

166. Duany, *Blurred Borders*, 83 (quoting American officials from 1898 to 1945).

167. Duany, *Blurred Borders*, 82–83.

168. For three recent discussions of these events, see Joseph Blocher and Mitu Gulati, "Puerto Rico and the Right of Accession," *Yale Journal of International Law* 43, no. 2 (2018): 229–272; Juan R. Torruella, "Why Puerto Rico Does Not Need Further Experimentation with Its Future: A Reply to the Notion of Territorial Federalism," *Harvard Law Review Forum* 131, no. 4 (2018): 65–104; Antonio Weiss and Brad Setser, "America's Forgotten Colony: Ending Puerto Rico's Perpetual Crisis," *Foreign Affairs* 98, no. 4 (2019): 158–169.

169. Robert May, *The Southern Dream of a Caribbean Empire* (Baton Rouge, LA: Louisiana State University Press, 1973).

170. Colby, *The Business of Empire*, 27.

171. Go, *Patterns of Empire*, 654–61.

172. Colby, *The Business of Empire*, 56.

173. Colby, *The Business of Empire*, 60.

174. Colby, *The Business of Empire*, 61.

175. Go, *Patterns of Empire*, 61.

176. Jana K. Lipman, *Guantánamo: A Working-Class History Between Empire and Revolution* (Berkeley, CA: University of California Press, 2009), 3.

177. Lipman, *Guantánamo*, 3.

178. Duany, *Blurred Borders*, 36 (based on 2009 data).

179. Duany, *Blurred Borders*, 37–38.

180. As I have discussed, the vast majority of Cuban Latinos came to the United States as political refugees fleeing the communist revolution; between 1959 and 1980, some 600,000 Cubans migrated to the United States. Another 163,666 migrated during the 1980s Mariel exodus, for example. Duany, *Blurred Borders*, 40–41.

181. Duany, *Blurred Borders*, 55.

182. Duany, *Blurred Borders*, 57.

183. Duany, *Blurred Borders*, 59.

184. Ginetta E.B. Candelario, *Black behind the Ears: Dominican Racial Identity from Museums to Beauty Shops* (Durham, NC: Duke University Press, 2007), 45.

185. Duany, "Racializing Ethnicity in the Spanish-Speaking Caribbean," in Cobas, Duany, and Feagin, *How the United States Racializes Latinos*, 215.

186. As quoted in Candelario, *Black behind the Ears*, 47.

187. Colby, *The Business of Empire*, 31.

188. Candelario, *Black behind the Ears*, 65; see also Duany, *Blurred Borders*, 55–56.

189. See Candelario, *Black behind the Ears*.

190. Candelario, *Black behind the Ears*.

191. Duany, "Racializing Ethnicity in the Spanish-Speaking Caribbean," in Cobas, Duany, and Feagin, *How the United States Racializes Latinos*, 215.

192. Colby, *The Business of Empire*, 179.

193. Saldaña-Portillo, *Indian Given*, 237.

194. Saldaña-Portillo, *Indian Given*, 237.

195. See William I. Robinson, *Transnational Conflicts: Central America, Social Change, and Globalization* (New York: Verso 2003).

196. Cristina García, *Seeking Refuge*, 33.

197. Kirk Semple and Brent McDonald, "Mexico Breaks Up a Migrant Caravan, Pleasing White House," *New York Times*, January 24, 2020. As this book went to press, the Ninth Circuit Court of Appeals has ordered the federal government to return to pre-Trump policies. The case will likely be appealed to the U.S. Supreme Court.

198. Nadine El-Enany, *(B)ordering Britain: Law, Race and Empire* (Manchester, England: Manchester University Press, 2020).

199. El-Enany, *(B)ordering Britain*.

200. Eunice Lee and Karen Musalo, "Seeking a Rational Approach to the Regional Refugee Crisis: Lessons from the Summer 2014 'Surge' of Central American Women and Children at the U.S.-Mexico Border," *Journal on Migration and Human Security* 5, no. 1 (2017): 137–179.

201. United Nations, https: //www.refugeesmigrants.un.org; María Cristina García, *Seeking Refuge*.

202. The U.S. definition specifies the more narrow grounds of "persecution or a well-founded fear of persecution on account of race, religion, nationality, membership in a particular social group, or political opinion." Department of Homeland Security, https://www.dhs.gov/immigration-statistics/refugees-asylees.

203. Sarah Sherman-Stokes, "Reparations for Central American Refugees," *Denver Law Review* 96, no. 3 (2018): 585–634, 628–629.

204. Sherman-Stokes, "Reparations for Central American Refugees," 585–634, 634.

2: Idealized *Mestizaje* and Anti-Black and Anti-Indian Racism

1. Candelario, *Black behind the Ears*, 118.

2. Translation: We are all Dominicans, We are all Indians.

3. Candelario points out that the Museo del Hombre Dominicano is the most popular museum in the Dominican Republic and that 94 percent of its visitors are schoolchildren and the general public. *Black behind the Ears*, 112.

4. Troy Floyd, *The Columbus Dynasty in the Caribbean, 1492–1526* (Albuquerque, NM: University of New Mexico Press, 1973).

5. Candelario, *Black behind the Ears*, 113–114.

6. Candelario, *Black behind the Ears*, 148.

7. Henry Louis Gates, Jr., "Dominicans in Denial," *The Root*, August 5, 2011.

8. Candelario, *Black behind the Ears*, 41, 45.

9. In 1845, U.S. secretary of state John C. Calhoun, a South Carolina slave owner who had previously been vice president under Presidents John Quincy Adams and Andrew Jackson, dispatched the emissary John Hogan to Santo Domingo. Hogan recommended using the Dominicans as a buffer against the Haitians. Candelario, *Black behind the Ears*, 46.

10. *The Oxford Encyclopedia of Latinos and Latinas in the United States* (New York: Oxford University Press, 2005).

11. Bernardo Vega, *Dominican Cultures: The Making of a Caribbean Society* (Princeton, NJ: Markus Wiener Publishers, 2007).

12. Vega, *Dominican Cultures*, 19.

13. Candelario, *Black behind the Ears*, 109.

14. Candelario, *Black behind the Ears*, 16–17 (reproducing a list from an early 1970s study that included six factors in phenotype for Dominicans: "skin color, hair color, eye color, hair texture, facial features, and other bodily features such as ears and buttocks").

15. Candelario, *Black behind the Ears*, 17.

16. Candelario, *Black behind the Ears*, 18.

17. Candelario, *Black behind the Ears*, 118.

18. Loveman, *National Colors*, 296.

19. This is my description, not Candelario's, of figure 9 from "Indigenous Peoples of Orinoco River region of Venezuela," Museo del Hombre Dominicano. Candelario, *Black behind the Ears*, 118.

20. Candelario, *Black behind the Ears*, 118–119.

21. Candelario, *Black behind the Ears*, 121.

22. Candelario, *Black behind the Ears*, 127–128.

23. Candelario, *Black behind the Ears*, 113–114 (figure 6, "Entrance to the Museo Hombre Dominicano"; all three statues pictured in a black and white photograph).

24. Candelario concludes that the Dominican child who visits the museum experiences it as "part of a larger discursively mediated racial project that elides blackness into indigeneity and subsumes women into 'Man'

even as it rhetorically affirms a cultural nationalism." *Black behind the Ears*, 128.

25. A research team interviewed Cáceres on June 27, 2013. Loveman, *National Colors*, 296.

26. Jorge Duany, *The Puerto Rican Nation on the Move: Identities on the Island and in the United States* (Chapel Hill, NC: University of North Carolina Press, 2000), 174 (attributing the anti-African sentiment to four centuries of African slavery).

27. See generally, Gómez, *Manifest Destinies*.

28. The estimates in this paragraph are from Lowe, *The Intimacies of Four Continents*, 36.

29. Marta Menchaca, *Recovering History, Constructing Race: The Indian, Black, and White Roots of Mexican Americans* (Austin, TX: University of Texas Press, 2001), 61.

30. Saldaña-Portillo, *Indian Given*, 117.

31. Ana María Alonso, *Thread of Blood: Colonialism, Revolution, and Gender on Mexico's Northern Frontier* (Tucson, AZ: University of Arizona Press, 1995), 53.

32. There is a large literature across many countries and regions on *blanqueamiento*. I have been especially influenced by the following works on the subject: Saldaña-Portillo, *Indian Given*; Richard Graham, *The Idea of Race in Latin America* (Austin, TX: University of Texas Press, 1990); Tanya María Katerí Hernández, *Racial Subordination in Latin America: The Role of the State, Customary Law, and the New Civil Rights Response* (New York: Cambridge University Press, 2013); Alonso, *Thread of Blood*; Menchaca, *Recovering History, Constructing Race*; Peter Wade, *Blackness and Race Mixture: The Dynamics of Racial Identity in Colombia* (Baltimore, MD: Johns Hopkins University Press, 1993); Ramón Gutiérrez, *When Jesus Came, the Corn Mothers Went Away: Marriage, Sexuality, and Power in New Mexico, 1500–1846* (Stanford, CA: Stanford University Press, 1991).

33. Hernández, *Racial Subordination in Latin America*, 20.

34. See, generally, Pascoe, *What Comes Naturally*.

35. Michelle A. McKinley, *Fractional Freedoms: Slavery, Intimacy, and Legal Mobilization in Colonial Lima, 1600–1700* (New York: Cambridge University Press, 2016), 11.

36. Hernández, 20.

37. Mark Q. Sawyer, *Racial Politics in Post-Revolutionary Cuba* (New

York: Cambridge University Press, 2006), 43; see also, Hernández, *Racial Subordination*; see generally, Colby, *The Business of Empire*. Chinese immigrants were also banned.

38. Hernández, *Racial Subordination in Latin America*, 34 (Chile), 29 (Cuba).

39. Information on the Argentinian census comes from Loveman, *National Colors*, 150; see also, Hernández, *Racial Subordination in Latin America*, 34.

40. Benjamin Madley, *An American Genocide: The United States and the California Indian Catastrophe* (New York, NY: Yale University Press, 2016), 23.

41. Madley, *An American Genocide*, 3.

42. Colby, *The Business of Empire*, 40.

43. Colby, *The Business of Empire*, 40; Speed defines *ladino* as "essentially the equivalent of *mestizo*, meaning 'mixed race.'" Speed, *Incarcerated Stories*, 37.

44. David Weber, *Foreigners in Their Native Land: Historical Roots of the Mexican Americans* (Albuquerque, NM: University of New Mexico Press, 2003 [1973]), 33–35.

45. Gutiérrez, *When Jesus Came, the Corn Mothers Went Away*, 103.

46. Gómez, *Manifest Destinies*, 47–80 (and citations therein).

47. Menchaca, *Recovering History, Constructing Race*, 58–63.

48. For example, as late as 1924, sixteen members of Virginia's legislature were one-sixteenth Indian, having been descendants of Pocahontas and John Rolfe. Not surprisingly, then, when Virginia passed the Racial Purity Law in that year, they wrote in an exception for Whites like themselves, with one-sixteenth or less Indian blood; they did not recognize a similar exception for those who were one-sixteenth or less Black. See generally, Kevin Noble Maillard, "The Pocahontas Exception: The Exemption of American Indian Ancestry from the Racial Purity Law," *Michigan Journal of Race & Law* 12, no. 107 (2007): 351–593; see also, Pascoe, *What Comes Naturally*, 158–159.

49. Harris, "Whiteness as Property."

50. See Gómez, *Manifest Destinies*, 61–67.

51. As quoted in Gómez, *Manifest Destinies*, 62.

52. The quotes from Davis appear in Gómez, 2018, 62–64, citing W.W.H. Davis, *El Gringo: New Mexico and Her People* (Lincoln, NB: University of Nebraska Press, 1982 [1857]).

53. Both *New York Times* quotes from Gómez, *Manifest Destinies*, 66–67.

54. Frederick Simpich, "The Yield of Texas," *National Geographic*, 87 (1945): 163–184 (defining "wetback"); Frederick Simpich, "Seeing Our Spanish Southwest," *National Geographic* 77 (1940): 711–756 (reference to Mexican blood); Frederick Simpich, "Down the Rio Grande," *National Geographic*, 76 (1939): 415–462 ("lazy Mexicans").

55. Frederick Simpich, "So Big Texas," *National Geographic* 53 (1928): 637–693.

56. Frederick Simpich, "Along Our Side of the Mexican Border," *National Geographic* 38 (1920): 61–80.

57. Frederick Simpich, "Skypaths through Latin America," *National Geographic* 59 (1931): 1–79.

58. Taft, "Some Recent Instances of National Altruism," 429–438.

59. William H. Taft, "Some Impressions of 150,000 Miles of Travel," *National Geographic* 57 (1930): 523–606.

60. Eric Lutz, "Trump's Vendetta against Puerto Rico Is Still Going Strong," *Vanity Fair*, December 18, 2019.

61. Taft, "Some Recent Instances of National Altruism," 429–438.

62. E. John Long, "Puerto Rico: Watchdog of the Caribbean," *National Geographic* 76 (1939): 697–738.

63. See Pedro A. Malavet, "The Flag Follows the Constitution . . . but Doesn't Quite Catch Up to It: The Story of *Downes v. Bidwell*," in *Race Law Stories*, edited by Rachel F. Moran and Devon W. Carbado (New York: Thomson Reuters/Foundation Press, 2008).

64. Loveman, *National Colors*; see also Jorge Duany, "Neither White nor Black: The Representation of Racial Identity Among Puerto Ricans on the Island and in the U.S. Mainland," in *Neither Enemies nor Friends: Latinos, Blacks, Afro-Latinos*, edited by Anani Dzidzienyo and Suzanne Oboler (New York: Palgrave McMillan, 2005), 172–188 (focusing on the decrease in the "colored" population on the island between 1899 to 1935, and coming to similar conclusions).

65. Duany, "Neither White nor Black," 179.

66. As quoted in Duany, "Neither White nor Black," 179.

67. Carlos Vargas-Ramos, "Some Social Differences on the Basis of Race among Puerto Ricans," Research Brief, Center for Puerto Rican Studies, Hunter College, CUNY, December 2016. See also Natasha S. Alford, "Why Some Black Puerto Ricans Choose 'White' on the Census," *New York Times*, February 9, 2020.

68. See, generally, Charles Ramírez Berg, *The Classical Mexican Cinema: The Poetics of the Exceptional Golden Age Films* (Austin, TX: University of Texas Press, 2015).

69. Colby, *The Business of Empire*, 153 (noting that Vasconcelos's "celebration of *mestizos* appealed to nationalists throughout Latin America, many of whom coupled their newfound racial pride with denunciation of Washington."). See also Christina A. Sue, *The Land of the Cosmic Race: Race Mixture, Racism, and Blackness in Mexico* (New York: Oxford University Press, 2013), 10.

70. Saldaña-Portillo, *Indian Given*, 203.

71. On the casta paintings, see Ilona Katzew, *Casta Painting: Images of Race in Eighteenth Century Mexico* (New Haven, CT: Yale University Press, 2004).

72. Colby, *The Business of Empire*, 153; Saldaña-Portillo, *Indian Given*, 203.

73. Loza, *Defiant Braceros*, 29.

74. Speed, *Incarcerated Stories*, 37.

75. Sue, *The Land of the Cosmic Race*, 16.

76. Edward Telles, *Pigmentocracies: Ethnicity, Race, and Color in Latin America* (Chapel Hill, NC: University of North Carolina Press, 2014).

77. Sue, *The Land of the Cosmic Race*, 17–18.

78. Sue, *The Land of the Cosmic Race*, 14.

79. Silvia's story is described in Sue, *The Land of the Cosmic Race*, 3–5.

80. Loveman, *National Colors*, 181.

81. Loveman, *National Colors*, 165.

82. Loveman, *National Colors*, 165.

83. Loveman, *National Colors*, 196.

84. Loveman, *National Colors*, 265–267.

85. Lisandro Pérez, "Racialization among Cubans and Cuban Americans," in *How the United States Racializes Latinos: White Hegemony and Its Consequences*, edited by José A. Cobas, Jorge Duany, and Joe R. Feagin (Boulder, CO: Paradigm Publishers, 2009), 137.

86. Pérez, "Racialization among Cubans and Cuban Americans," in Cobas, Duany, and Feagin, *How the United States Racializes Latinos*, 137.

87. Sawyer, *Racial Politics in Post-Revolutionary Cuba*, 45.

88. On anti-Black racism in Cuba, see Sawyer, *Racial Politics in Post-Revolutionary Cuba*, and Pérez, "Racialization among Cubans and Cuban

Americans," in Cobas, Duany, and Feagin, *How the United States Racializes Latinos*.

89. Pérez, "Racialization among Cubans and Cuban Americans," in Cobas, Duany, and Feagin, *How the United States Racializes Latinos*, 136, table 8.1.

90. See, Loveman, *National Colors*, 265–267.

91. The National Museum of Mexican Art, "The African Presence in México: From Yanga to the Present," exhibition catalog, 2006, https://perma.cc/H2T4-NH2P.

92. Sue, *The Land of the Cosmic Race*, 189, 192.

93. Overall, one in four children in the United States have a parent born in another country, with 57 percent having a parent born in Latin America (and with nearly 40 percent of that group having a Mexican-born parent). "Part of Us: A Data-Driven Look at Children of Immigrants," unpublished report by the Urban Institute, March 14, 2019.

94. This discussion is based on 2010 national data, since detailed 2020 census data will not be available until 2021. Some census data is generated in between the comprehensive decadal censuses (such as the American Community Survey of a 5 percent sample of American households, sometimes called the "long-form" census). I use that more recent data where available.

95. Technically, the census option is presented as "some other race." Pew Research Center, "Hispanic and Foreign-Born Populations in the U.S. Statistical Portraits," March 30, 2010, https://www.pewhispanic.org/2010/03/30/2008-statistical-information-on-hispanic-and-foreign-born-populations-in-united-states; see also, U.S. Census Bureau, "Population by Hispanic or Latino Origin and Race for the United States: 1980, 1990, 2000, 2010."

96. For Latinos' self-identified race on the 2010 census and 2018 samples, see United States Census Bureau, "Fact Finder: Annual Estimates of the Resident Population by Sex, Age, Race, and Hispanic Origin for the United States and States: April 1, 2010 to July 1, 2018: 2018 Population Estimates."

97. Rodríguez and Menjívar, "Central American Immigrants and Racialization," 188; see also Alicia Ivonne Estrada, "(Re)Claiming Public Space and Place: Maya Community Formation in Westlake/MacArthur Park," in *U.S. Central Americans: Reconstructing Memories, Struggles, and Communities of Resistance*, edited by Karina O. Alvarado, Alicia Ivonne Estrada, and Ester E. Hernández (Tucson, AZ: University of Arizona Press, 2017), 166 (emphasizing that Maya in the United States have many reasons to fear outing themselves as Indigenous).

98. For an opposing view, see Floridalma Boj López, "Weavings That Rupture: The Possibility of Contesting Settler Colonialism through Cultural Retention among the Maya Diaspora," in *U.S. Central Americans: Reconstructing Memories, Struggles, and Communities of Resistance*, edited by Karina O. Alvarado, Alicia Ivonne Estrada, and Ester E. Hernández, Tucson, AZ: University of Arizona Press), 189–90 ("This casual lumping together within the Latina/o umbrella obscures the important differences that indigeneity makes for indigenous migrants from Latin America and a long-standing genealogy of hemispheric analysis through indigenous worldviews and histories that disrupts how national boundaries define indigenous experiences."), 198.

99. Data from the 2017 American Community Survey, U.S. Census Bureau.

100. Data from the 2017 American Community Survey, U.S. Census Bureau.

101. Estrada, "(Re)Claiming Public Space and Place," in Alvarado, Estrada, and Hernández, *U.S. Central Americans*, 166–187, 284n18.

102. Loza, *Defiant Braceros*, 47.

103. Rodríguez and Menjívar, 187; see also, Boj López, "Weavings That Rupture," in Alvarado, Estrada, and Hernández, *U.S. Central Americans: Reconstructing Memories, Struggles, and Communities of Resistance*, 198; Maritza E. Cárdenas, "Performing Centralamericanismo: Isthmian Identities at the COFECA Independence Day Parade," in *U.S. Central Americans: Reconstructing Memories, Struggles, and Communities of Resistance*, edited by Karina O. Alvarado, Alicia Ivonne Estrada, and Ester E. Hernández (Tucson, AZ: University of Arizona Press), 131.

104. Data from the 2017 American Community Survey, U.S. Census Bureau.

105. See table 1.1 from Rumbaut, "Pigments of Our Imagination," in Cobas, Duany, and Feagin, *How the United States Racializes Latinos*, 28.

106. Rumbaut, "Pigments of Our Imagination," in Cobas, Duany, and Feagin, *How the United States Racializes Latinos*, 31, table 1.3.

107. United States Census Bureau, "Fact Finder, Annual Estimates of the Resident Population by Sex, Age, Race, and Hispanic Origin for the United States and States: April 1, 2010 to July 1, 2018: 2018 Population Estimates."

108. Remarking on similar results for a sample of young Latinos, sociologist Rubén Rumbaut attributes the increasing popularity of the White category as we move south to American racism. See Rumbaut, "Pigments

of Our Imagination," in Cobas, Duany, and Feagin, *How the United States Racializes Latinos*, 29.

109. Hephzibah V. Strmic-Paul, Brandon A. Jackson, and Steve Garner, "Race Counts: Racial and Ethnic Data on the U.S. Census and the Implications for Tracking Inequality," *Sociology of Race and Ethnicity* 4, no. 1 (2018): 1–13.

110. As quoted in Clara E. Rodríguez, "Counting Latinos in the U.S. Census," in Cobas, Duany, and Feagin, *How the United States Racializes Latinos*, 48.

111. Clara E. Rodríguez, *Changing Race: Latinos, the Census and the History of Ethnicity in the United States* (New York: New York University Press, 2000), 61–62 (mentioning factors such as phenotype, social class, language, phenotypic variation within the family, and neighborhood socialization that affect Latinos' racial identities).

112. Atiya Kai Stokes-Brown, *The Politics of Race in the Latino Community* (New York: Routledge, 2012), 25–26, 34–35.

113. Nicholas Vargas, "Latina/o Whitening?" *Du Bois Review* 12 (2015): 127–30; see also Nancy López, Edward Vargas, Melina Juárez, Lisa Cacari-Stone, and Sonia Bettez, "What's Your 'Street Race'? Leveraging Multidimensional Measures of Race and Intersectionality for Examining Physical and Mental Health Status Among Latinxs," *Sociology of Race and Ethnicity* 4, no. 1 (2018): 49–66.

114. See Reanne Frank, Ilana Redstone Akresh, and Bo Lu, "Latino Immigrants and the U.S. Racial Order: How and Where Do They Fit In?" *American Sociological Review* 75, no. 3 (2010): 378–401.

115. Rumbaut, "Pigments of Our Imagination" in Cobas, Duany, and Feagin, *How the United States Racializes Latinos*, 33 (table 1.4).

116. Nicolas De Genova and Ana Y. Ramos-Zayas, *Latino Crossings: Mexicans, Puerto Ricans, and the Politics of Race and Citizenship* (New York: Routledge, 2003), 209.

117. Julie A. Dowling, *Mexican Americans and the Question of Race* (Austin, TX: University of Texas Press, 2012), 133.

118. Dowling, *Mexican Americans*, 138.

119. Dowling, *Mexican Americans*, 33

120. Howard Bodenhorn and Christopher S. Rueback, "Colourism and African-American Wealth: Evidence from the Nineteenth-Century South," *Journal of Popular Economics* 20 (2007): 599–620.

121. Angela R. Dixon and Edward E. Telles, "Skin Color and Colorism: Global Research, Concepts, and Measurement," *Annual Review of Sociology* 43 (2017): 405–424. For studies showing that darker-skinned Latinos experience worse health outcomes, see John A. García et al., "Race as Lived Experience: The Impact of Multi-Dimensional Measures of Race/Ethnicity on the Self-Reported Health Status of Latinos," *Du Bois Review* 12, no. 2 (2015): 349–373; Gabriel R. Sánchez and Vickie D. Ybarra, "Lessons from Political Science: Health Status and Improving How We Study Race," in *Mapping "Race": Critical Approaches to Health Disparities Research*, edited by Laura E. Gómez and Nancy López (New Brunswick, NJ: Rutgers University Press, 2013), 104–116.

122. Beverly Araujo-Dawson, "Understanding the Complexities of Skin Color, Perceptions of Race, and Discrimination among Cubans, Dominicans, and Puerto Ricans," *Hispanic Journal of Behavioral Sciences* 37, no. 2 (2015): 243–256; see also M. Anne Visser, "Shedding Light on Economic Opportunity: Skin Tone and Job Quality During the Great Recession," *Journal of Ethnic and Migration Studies* 43, no. 9 (2017): 1562–1579.

123. Tanya Golash-Boza and William Darity, Jr., "Latino Racial Choices: The Effects of Skin Colour and Discrimination on Latinos' and Latinas' Race Self-Identification," *Ethnic and Racial Studies* 31, no. 5 (2008): 899–934.

124. Duany, "Neither White nor Black," 174.

125. Rúa, *A Grounded Identidad*, 48–49.

126. Michael Jones-Correa, *Governing American Cities: Inter-Ethnic Coalitions, Competition and Conflict* (New York: Russell Sage Foundation, 2001); see also Paula D. McClain and Niambi M. Carter, "Racial Distancing in a Southern City: Latino Immigrants' Views of Black Americans," *Journal of Politics* 68, no. 3 (2006): 571–584.

127. H. Alberts, "Changes in Ethnic Solidarity in Cuban Miami," *Geographical Review* 92, no. 2 (2005): 231–248.

128. Waters, *Black Identities*; but see also Vilna Bashi Treitler, *The Ethnic Project: Transforming Racial Fiction into Ethnic Factions* (Palo Alto, CA: Stanford University Press, 2013), ix.

129. Karletta M. White, "The Salience of Skin Tone: Effects on the Exercise of Police Enforcement Authority," *Ethnic and Racial Studies* 38, no. 6 (2015): 993–1010.

130. Duany, "Neither White nor Black," 174; see also Betina Cutaia Wilkinson and Emily Earle, "Taking a New Perspective to Latino Racial

Attitudes: Examining the Impact of Skin Tone on Latino Perceptions of Commonality with Whites and Blacks," *American Politics Research* 41, no. 5 (2012): 783–818 (finding that Puerto Ricans see their fate as linked with that of African Americans, in contrast to Cubans, who see their fate as tied to that of Whites).

131. See Nieva Grant, Laura Pulido, and Nathan J. Sessoms, "Beyond Conflict and Competition: How Color-Blind Ideology Affects African Americans' and Latinos' Understanding of Their Relationships," *Kalfou* 1, no. 1 (2014): 87–116; and McClain and Carter, "Racial Distancing in a Southern City."

132. Latinos in South Central had a per capita income of $4,461, compared to $7,111 for Latinos elsewhere in Los Angeles. Armando Navarro, "The South Central Los Angeles Eruption: A Latino Perspective," *Amerasia Journal* 19, no. 2 (1993): 69–85.

133. Navarro, "The South Central Los Angeles Eruption."

134. Peter A. Morrison and Ira S. Lowry, "A Riot of Color: The Demographic Setting of Civil Disturbance in Los Angeles," RAND Corporation, 1993; Joan Petersilia and Allan Abrahamse, "The Los Angeles Riots of Spring 1992," *Police Forum* 3, no. 4 (October 1993).

135. Navarro, "The South Central Los Angeles Eruption."

136. Navarro, "The South Central Los Angeles Eruption."

137. Aura Bogado, "'A Matter of Death and Death': Confronting Anti-Black Racism among Latinos," *Salon*, May 20, 2014.

138. Jazmín A. Muro and Lisa M. Martínez, "Is Love Color-Blind? Racial Blind Spots and Latinas' Romantic Relationships," *Sociology of Race and Ethnicity* 4, no. 4 (2018): 527–540.

139. Eduardo Bonilla-Silva, "From Bi-racial to Tri-racial: Towards a New System of Racial Stratification in the United States," *Ethnic and Racial Studies* 27, no. 6 (2004): 931–950; see also, Bonilla-Silva, *Racism without Racists*; Ed Morales, *Latinx: The New Force in American Politics and Culture* (New York: Verso, 2018), 265.

140. Morales, *Latinx*, 247.

141. Celeste Fraser Delgado and José Esteban Muñoz, *Everynight Life: Culture and Dance in Latin/o America* (Durham, NC: Duke University Press, 1997).

142. R.Z. Rivera, "Boricuas from the Hip Hop Zone," *Centro Journal* 5, no. 1 (1996): 209; see also Edna Acosta-Belén, "Haciendo Patria Desde La Metropoli: The Cultural Expressions of the Puerto Rican Diaspora," *Centro Journal* 21, 2 (2009): 48–83.

143. Acosta-Belén, "Haciendo Patria Desde La Metropoli."

144. Acosta-Belén, "Haciendo Patria Desde La Metropoli."

3: The Elusive Quest for Whiteness

1. As quoted in Brian D. Behnken, *Fighting Their Own Battles: Mexican Americans, African Americans, and the Struggle for Civil Rights in Texas* (Chapel Hill, NC: The University of North Carolina Press, 2011), 203. Mexican Americans, who sought legal status as intervenors in a desegregation lawsuit brought by Black parents, opposed the Houston Independent School District's determination that Mexican Americans were White and, thus, that placing African American and Mexican American children in the same schools constituted desegregation under *Brown v. Board of Education*.

2. Tom Dart, "'Racism from Cradle to Grave': Texas Cemetery Sued for 'Whites Only' Policy," *The Guardian*, May 6, 2016.

3. Foley, *The White Scourge*, 41.

4. A 1947 article estimated "conservatively that two-thirds of Texans killed [in World War II] were Mexican Americans." Mason Sutherland, "Carnival in San Antonio," *National Geographic* 92 (1947): 813–844, 827; see generally, *Mexican Americans and World War II*, edited by Maggie Rivas-Rodríguez (Austin, TX: University of Texas Press, 2005).

5. Bradford made similar statements to several reporters who interviewed him subsequent to his conversation with Barrera. Dart, "'Racism from Cradle to Grave.'"

6. Based on census data from 2000. https://en.wikipedia.org/wiki/Normanna,_Texas.

7. The G.I. Forum was represented by the Mexican American Legal Defense and Education Fund. MALDEF Press Release, July 25, 2016.

8. Maggie Rivas-Rodríguez, "Framing Racism: Newspaper Coverage of the Three Rivers Incident," in *Mexican Americans and World War II*, edited by Maggie Rivas-Rodríguez (Austin, TX: University of Texas Press, 2005), 217n27.

9. Rivas-Rodríguez, "Framing Racism," in Rivas-Rodríguez, *Mexican Americans and World War II*, 203–204; see also, Julie Leininger Pycior, *LBJ and Mexican Americans: The Paradox of Power* (Austin, TX: The University of Texas Press, 1997), 68.

10. Pycior, *LBJ and Mexican Americans*, 68.

11. Pycior, *LBJ and Mexican Americans*, 68.

12. Daniel C. Thompson, *A Black Elite: A Profile of Graduates of the United*

Negro College Fund Colleges (Westport, CT: Greenwood Press, 1986) (arguing HBCUs were instrumental in creating "the elite of elite" Blacks, whose parents and/or grandparents were educated at Black colleges); see also Michael A. Olivas, "Indian, Chicano, and Puerto Rican Colleges: Status and Issues," in *Racial and Ethnic Diversity in Higher Education*, edited by Laura I. Rendón, Caroline S. Turner, and Mildred García (Ginn Press, 2002) (non-African American minority groups do not have the networks of high-profile alumni that HBCUs do).

13. *Hernandez v. Texas*, 347 U.S. 475 (1954).

14. Treitler, *The Ethnic Project*, 15.

15. Gómez, *Manifest Destinies*, 88–89 (Las Vegas, New Mexico Territory); Albert Camarillo, *Chicanos in a Changing Society: From Mexican Pueblos to American Barrios in Santa Barbara and Southern California, 1848–1930* (Cambridge, MA: Harvard University Press, 1979), 187–191 (Santa Barbara, California).

16. Anthropologist Jennifer Nájera's ethnographic study of the town—which she never names, consistent with research protocols—is fascinating. Jennifer R. Nájera, *The Borderlands of Race: Mexican Segregation in a South Texas Town* (Austin, TX: University of Texas Press, 2015). In the southeastern New Mexico town of Roswell, where my parents and I were born, there was an overcrowded, underfunded Catholic church in the Mexican American barrio Chuihuahita, when a much larger, yellow brick Catholic church was built for Anglos on Main Street. My father says he's certain the Mexican Americans of Chuihuahita paid for that empty church.

17. Duany, *Blurred Borders*, 49.

18. Duany, *Blurred Borders*, 49.

19. Duany, *Blurred Borders*, 49.

20. Fernández, *Brown in the Windy City*, 10.

21. Fernández, *Brown in the Windy City*, 271n10.

22. Fernández, *Brown in the Windy City*, 3–5.

23. See, generally, María Krysan and Kyle Crowder, *Cycle of Segregation: Social Processes and Residential Stratification* (New York: Russell Sage Foundation, 2017).

24. Richard R. Valencia, *Chicano Students and the Courts: The Mexican American Legal Struggle for Educational Equality* (New York: New York University Press, 2008), 7.

25. Behnken, *Fighting Their Own Battles*, 196.

26. Valencia, *Chicano Students and the Courts*, 14–21.

27. Valencia, *Chicano Students and the Courts*, 14.

28. *Plessy v. Ferguson*, 163 U.S. 537 (1896).

29. Valencia, *Chicano Students and the Courts*, 16–17.

30. Valencia, *Chicano Students and the Courts*, 17.

31. Behnken, *Fighting Their Own Battles*, 5.

32. The Lemon Grove case is dramatized in the 1985 film *The Lemon Grove Incident* directed by Frank Christopher.

33. Valencia, *Chicano Students and the Courts*, 19.

34. They were Fred C. Noon and A.C. Brinkley, both based in San Diego. Valencia, *Chicano Students and the Courts*, 20.

35. Valencia, *Chicano Students and the Courts*, 20–21.

36. Derrick Bell, "*Brown v. Board of Education* and the Interest Convergence Dilemma," *Harvard Law Review* 93, no. 3 (1980): 518–533; see also Mary Dudziak, *Cold War Civil Rights: Race and the Image of American Democracy* (Princeton, NJ: Princeton University Press, 2011).

37. The most comprehensive source on the Méndez case is Chris Arriola, "Knocking on the School House Door: *Mendez v. Westminster*, Equal Protection, Public Education, and Mexican Americans in the 1940s," *La Raza Law Journal* 8 (1995): 166–207.

38. As quoted in Valencia, *Chicano Students and the Courts*, 27.

39. Valencia, *Chicano Students and the Courts*, 49.

40. Valencia, *Chicano Students and the Courts*, 50.

41. Valencia, *Chicano Students and the Courts*, 51.

42. Valencia, *Chicano Students and the Courts*, 56–58.

43. Valencia, *Chicano Students and the Courts*, 59–60.

44. F. Supp. 599 (S.D.Tex. 1970).

45. Behnken, *Fighting Their Own Battles*, 197. At roughly the same time, a federal judge in Denver reached a similar conclusion—also involving "desegregating" schools by combining African American and Mexican American children. See *Keyes v. School District No. 1*, 413 U.S. 189 (1973) and the voluminous scholarly literature on the case.

46. Sonia Song-Ha Lee, *Building a Latino Civil Rights Movement: Puerto Ricans, African Americans, and the Pursuit of Racial Justice in New York City* (Chapel Hill, NC: The University of North Carolina Press, 2014).

47. Song-Ha Lee, *Building a Latino Civil Rights Movement*, 3.

48. Song-Ha Lee, *Building a Latino Civil Rights Movement*, 173–174.

49. My knowledge of the Houston school desegregation case and parent mobilization is based on accounts in Behnken, *Fighting Their Own Battles* and Valencia, *Chicano Students and the Courts*. I am indebted to the first-hand account of Dr. Augustina Reyes, who was a young teacher in Houston's Huelga Schools. Reyes, "Houston School Boycott, 1970," October 23, 2012 (PowerPoint presentation on file with author).

50. Thomas E. Hachey, "American Profiles on Capitol Hill," *The Wisconsin Magazine of History* 57, no. 2 (1973–1974): 141–153.

51. Behnken, *Fighting Their Own Battles*, 204–205.

52. Behnken, *Fighting Their Own Battles*, 203.

53. Reyes, "Houston School Boycott."

54. *Tasby v. Estes*, 342 F. Supp. 945 (1971).

55. Nearly two-thirds of public school children in the United States attend schools where more than half the student body shares their race or ethnicity. A.W. Geiger, "Many Minority Students Go to Schools Where at Least Half of Their Peers Are Their Race or Ethnicity," Pew Research Center, October 25, 2017, https://www.pewresearch.org/fact-tank/2017/10/25/many-minority-students-go-to-schools-where-at-least-half-of-their-peers-are-their-race-or-ethnicity [https://perma.cc/J3HC-P8LK].

56. Reyes, "Houston School Boycott."

57. See *Meyer v. Nebraska* 262 U.S. 390 (1923).

58. The joke appears on his 2000 album *You're in America Now, Speak Spanish*.

59. Steven W. Bender, *Comprende? The Significance of Spanish in English-Only Times* (Berkeley, CA: Floricanto Press, 2008).

60. Nicholas Kulish, "John Tanton, 85, Catalyst in Anti-Immigration Drive, Dies," *New York Times*, July 21, 2019.

61. Gómez, *Manifest Destinies*, 174.

62. See, generally, Daniel Ho Sang, *Racial Propositions: Ballot Initiatives and the Making of Postwar California* (Berkeley, CA: University of California Press, 2010).

63. Manuel Pastor, *State of Resistance: What California's Dizzying Descent and Remarkable Resurgence Mean for America's Future* (New York: The New Press), 85.

64. Portes and Rumbaut, *Immigrant America*, 201.

65. Portes and Rumbaut, *Immigrant America*, 40–45.

66. Interview with author in 1985. Laura E. Gómez, "What's in a Name? The Politics of 'Hispanic' Identity," B.A. honors thesis, Harvard University, 1986, 97–98.

67. García, "Racializing the Language Practices of U.S. Latinos," in Cobas, Duany, and Feagin, *How the United States Racializes Latinos*, 103.

68. Portes and Rumbaut, *Immigrant America*, 237.

69. Gómez, *Manifest Destinies*, 174.

70. As quoted in Montejano, *Anglos and Mexicans*, 127.

71. Monica Muñoz Martínez, *The Injustice Never Leaves You: Anti-Mexican Violence in Texas* (Cambridge, MA: Harvard University Press, 2018), 11.

72. William D. Carrigan and Clive Webb, "Repression and Resistance: The Lynching of Persons of Mexican Origin in the United States, 1848–1928," in *How the United States Racializes Latinos: White Hegemony and Its Consequences*, edited by José A. Cobas, Jorge Duany, and Joe R. Feagin (Boulder, CO: Paradigm Publishers, 2009), 72.

73. Carrigan and Webb, "Repression and Resistance," in Cobas, Duany, and Feagin, *How the United States Racializes Latinos*, 70. Martínez reports 232 Texas lynchings. Martínez, *The Injustice Never Leaves You*, 6.

74. Martínez, *The Injustice Never Leaves You*, 7.

75. Rosa Flores, "Their Ancestors Were Slain a Century Ago along the U.S.-Mexico Border," CNN.com, July 20, 2019.

76. Flores, "Their Ancestors Were Slain."

77. David A. Díaz, "Texas Recognizes Thousands of South Texas Mexican Americans Murdered by Texas Rangers in 1915," *Edinburg Politics*, October 12, 2017.

78. David A. Díaz, "Texas Recognizes Thousands."

79. Gómez, *Manifest Destinies*, 176; Edward J. Escobar, *Race, Police, and the Making of a Political Identity: Mexican Americans and the Los Angeles Police Department, 1900–1945* (Berkeley, CA: University of California Press, 1999).

80. Michael A. Olivas, ed., *"Colored Men" and "Hombres Aquí": Hernandez v. Texas and the Emergence of Mexican-American Lawyering* (Houston, TX: Arte Público Press, 2006), 201.

81. David Montejano, "The Beating of Private Aguirre," in *Mexican Americans and World War II*, edited by Maggie Rivas-Rodríguez (Austin, TX: University of Texas Press, 2005), 41–66, 53.

82. Montejano, "The Beating of Private Aguirre," 41–66, 57.

83. Montejano, "The Beating of Private Aguirre," 56.

84. Mexican Americans received seventeen Congressional Medals of Honor, more than any other ethnic group. Of the 600,000 soldiers drafted in South Texas, Mexican Americans were 500,000 of them; Mexican Americans were 50–75 percent of the casualties from Texas during World War II. Pycior, *LBJ and Mexican Americans*, 53.

85. Vargas, *Crucible of Struggle*, 274–75. On Chávez, see the documentary film *El Senador*, directed by Paige Martínez.

86. López, *White by Law*.

87. Michelle Alexander, *The New Jim Crow: Mass Incarceration in the Age of Colorblindness* (New York: The New Press, 2010), 28.

88. Rima Vesely-Flad, "Policing Dark Bodies in Polluted Spaces: Stop and Frisk in New York City, 1993–2013," in *Racial Purity and Dangerous Bodies: Moral Pollution, Black Lives, and the Struggle for Justice* (Minneapolis, MN: Fortress Press, 2017).

89. Sunita Patel, "Jumping Hurdles to Sue Police," *Minnesota Law Review*, forthcoming 2020.

90. Aziz Z. Huq, "The Consequences of Disparate Policing: Evaluating Stop and Frisk as a Modality of Urban Policing," *Minnesota Law Review* 101 (2017): 2397.

91. Patel, "Jumping Hurdles to Sue Police."

92. *Floyd v. City of New York*, 813 F. Supp. 2d 457 (S.D.N.Y. 2011).

93. Patel, "Jumping Hurdles to Sue Police."

94. Shane Goldmacher, "Michael Bloomberg Pushed 'Stop-and-Frisk' Policy, Now He's Apologizing," *New York Times*, November 17, 2019.

95. Ian Haney López and Michael A. Olivas, "Jim Crow, Mexican Americans and the Anti-Subordination Constitution: *Hernandez v. Texas*," in *Race Law Stories*, edited by Rachel F. Moran and Devon W. Carbado (New York: Thomson Reuters/Foundation Press, 2008).

96. The legislation was signed into law by Warren on June 14, 1947. Valencia, *Chicano Students and the Courts*, 36–37.

97. *Hernandez v. Texas*, 347 U.S. 475, 482 (1954).

98. *Hernandez v. Texas*, 347 U.S. 475, 478 (1954).

99. Haney López and Olivas, "Jim Crow, Mexican Americans and the Anti-Subordination Constitution," in Moran and Carbado, *Race Law Stories*.

100. Pycior, *LBJ and Mexican Americans*, 31.

101. Pycior, *LBJ and Mexican Americans*, 23–24.

102. Pycior, *LBJ and Mexican Americans*, 34, 39.

103. Even today, I am taken aback when Whites (or occasionally others) find it impolite to refer to me as Mexican, or even food as Mexican—instead preferring euphemisms such as Spanish.

104. Foley, *The White Scourge*, 209.

105. Saldaña-Portillo, *Indian Given*, 193.

106. Foley, *The White Scourge*, 206–207.

107. Saldaña-Portillo, *Indian Given*, 288.

108. Saldaña-Portillo, *Indian Given*, 288–289; Behnken, *Fighting Their Own Battles*, 101.

109. Valencia, *Chicano Students and the Courts*, 60.

110. Historian Brian D. Behnken's study of Mexican Americans and African Americans' civil rights battles in Texas does a wonderful job laying out the complexities of Sánchez's positions and how they evolved over time. Behnken, *Fighting Their Own Battles*.

111. Saldaña-Portillo, *Indian Given*, 192–193.

112. Ernesto Chávez, *"!Mi Raza Primero!"—Nationalism, Identity, and Insurgency in the Chicano Movement in Los Angeles, 1966–1978* (Berkeley, CA: University of California Press, 2002).

113. Ian Haney López, *Racism on Trial: The Chicano Fight for Justice* (Cambridge, MA: Harvard University Press, 2004).

114. He went on to serve thirty years in Congress.

115. Vargas, *Crucible of Struggle*, 280.

116. Chávez, *"!Mi Raza Primero!"* 19.

117. "Red Sign-up Ordered by City Council," *Los Angeles Times*, September 14, 1950; "Council Hears Parker's Recording on 'Wild Tribes,'" *Los Angeles Times*, February 3, 1960; "City FEPC Again Loses in 7-to-7 Tie Vote," *Los Angeles Times*, January 8, 1958; Chávez, *"!Mi Raza Primero!"* 20 (reporting that the Mexican Chamber of Commerce called out the accusation as racially stereotypical).

118. Ramón Sánchez, *Boricua Power*, 129.

119. Ramón Sánchez, *Boricua Power*, 130.

120. Ramón Sánchez, *Boricua Power*, 150.

121. Fernández, *Brown in the Windy City*, 17.

122. See, Rua, *A Grounded Identidad*; Teresa Córdova, "Harold Washington and the Rise of Latino Electoral Politics in Chicago, 1982–1987," in *Chicano Politics and Society in the Late Twentieth Century* edited by David Montejano (Austin, TX: University of Texas Press, 1999).

123. See, generally, Rua, *A Grounded Identidad*.

124. Xóchitl Bada and Gilberto Cárdenas, "Blacks, Latinos, and the Immigration Debate: Conflict and Cooperation in Two Global Cities," in Cobas, Duany, and Feagin, *How the United States Racializes Latinos*, 176.

125. Gilda Ochoa, *Becoming Neighbors in a Mexican American Community: Power, Conflict, and Solidarity* (Austin, TX: University of Texas Press, 2004), 36.

126. As quoted in Gustavo Arellano, "Prop. 187 Forced a Generation to Put Fear Aside and Fight. It Transformed California, and Me," *Los Angeles Times*, October 29, 2019.

4: To Count, We Must Be Counted

1. Michael S. Rosenwald, "A Busboy Held Bobby Kennedy after He Was Shot. The Photo Haunted Him Until His Own Death This Week," *Los Angeles Times*, October 5, 2018 (quoting a StoryCorps interview with Romero).

2. Gustavo Arrellano, *Taco USA: How Mexican Food Conquered America* (New York: Scribner, 2012), 242.

3. Seven interstate freeways, all built in the 1950s and 1960s, wind through East L.A. Eric Avila, *The Folklore of the Freeway: Race and Revolt* (Minneapolis, MN: University of Minnesota Press, 2014), 136.

4. On Dolores Huerta's inspirational life, see 2017's *Dolores*, directed by Peter Bratt.

5. Pycior, *LBJ and Mexican Americans*.

6. Associated Press, "Juan Romero, Teenager Who Aided a Dying Robert Kennedy, Is Dead at 68," *New York Times*, October 4, 2018.

7. This description is drawn from Gustavo Arrellano's account. Arrellano, *Taco USA*, see generally, 236–242.

8. Arrellano, *Taco USA*, 9.

9. On the Viva Kennedy Clubs and national politics, see Pycior, *LBJ and Mexican Americans*, 116–17; Rodolfo Acuña, *Occupied America: The Chicano's Struggle Toward Liberation* (San Francisco, CA: Canfield Press, 1972), 223.

10. Pycior, *LBJ and Mexican Americans*, 120.

11. Pycior, *LBJ and Mexican Americans*, 67.

12. Pycior, *LBJ and Mexican Americans*, 94.

13. Pycior, *LBJ and Mexican Americans*, 162.

14. *Katzenbach v. Morgan*, 384 U.S. 641 (1966). See also Ramón Sánchez, *Boricua Power*, 201; Juan Cartagena, "Latinos and Section 5 of the Voting Rights Act: Beyond Black and White," *National Black Law Journal* 18, no. 2 (2004): 201–223; Katherine Culliton-González, "Time to Revive Puerto Rican Voting Rights," *Berkeley La Raza Law Journal* 19 (2008): 27–70.

15. Claudia Meléndez Salinas, "Joaquín Ávila, Civil Rights Champion, Visits Salinas," *Monterey County Herald*, August 19, 2015, https://www.montereyherald.com/2015/08/19/joaquin-avila-civil-rights-champion-visits-salinas [https://perma.cc/9Y6K-JW3P]. On Joaquín Ávila's career, see Sam Roberts, "Joaquín Ávila, Advocate of Hispanic Voting Rights, Dies at 69," *New York Times*, March 15, 2018, https://www.nytimes.com/2018/03/15/obituaries/joaquin-avila-advocate-of-hispanic-voting-rights-dies-at-69.html [https://perma.cc/6BJ3-8EF6].

16. Mindy Romero, "How Latino Voters and Legislators Are Changing California Politics," *Los Angeles Times*, September 27, 2016. On the California Voting Rights Act, see Joanna E. Cuevas Ingram, "The Color of Change: Voting Rights in the 21st Century and the California Voting Rights Act," *Harvard Latino Law Review* 15 (2012): 183–232 (describing California's voting rights law as "unique"); Perry Grossman, "The Case of State Attorney General Enforcement of the Voting Rights Act Against Local Governments," *University of Michigan Journal of Law Reform* 50, no. 3 (2017): 565–627 (noting that California is one of the few states to have enacted voting rights legislation modeled on the VRA); David C. Powell, "The California Voting Rights Act and Local Governments," *California Journal of Politics and Policy* 10, no. 2 (2018): 1–7 (discussing amendments to the California voting rights law).

17. Vargas, *Crucible of Struggle*, 310.

18. Vargas, *Crucible of Struggle*, 310–311.

19. Vargas, *Crucible of Struggle*, 361.

20. Paret, "Legality and Exploitation," 503–526.

21. Sánchez, *Boricua Power*.

22. Interview with author in 1985. Gómez, "What's in a Name? The Politics of 'Hispanic' Identity," 83.

23. https://www.unidosus.org/about-us/who-we-are/a-look-at-unidosus.

24. Interview with author in 1985. Gómez, "What's in a Name? The Politics of 'Hispanic' Identity," 77.

25. Interview with author in 1985. Gómez, "What's in a Name? The Politics of 'Hispanic' Identity," 107, 72–73.

26. Solís is currently one of five supervisors of Los Angeles County, an elected position she has held since 2014.

27. Gómez, "What's in a Name? The Politics of 'Hispanic' Identity," 248–250.

28. National Research Council, "Modernizing the U.S. Census" (Washington, DC: The National Academies Press, 1995), 239, Appendix C.

29. Thurgood Marshall, "Reflections on the Bicentennial of the United States Constitution," *Harvard Law Review* 101, no. 1 (1987): 1–5, 2.

30. Eric Foner, "Blacks and the U.S. Constitution: 1789–1989," *New Left Review* 183 (1990): 63–74, 66.

31. Foner, "Blacks and the U.S. Constitution," 66.

32. Strmic-Paul, Jackson, and Garner, "Race Counts," 1.

33. Strmic-Paul, Jackson, and Garner, "Race Counts," 1.

34. Patricia Cline Cohen, *A Calculating People: The Spread of Numeracy in Early America* (New York: Routledge, 1999), 212.

35. Cohen, *A Calculating People*, 162, 185.

36. On the 1840 census, see Cohen, *A Calculating People*, 177–199.

37. Strmic-Paul, Jackson, and Garner, "Race Counts," 223.

38. This history draws on table 7.1 in National Research Council, "Modernizing the U.S. Census," 145–146.

39. Cohen, *A Calculating People*, 212.

40. National Research Council, "Modernizing the U.S. Census," 145, table 7.1.

41. *Scott v. Sandford*, 60 U.S. 393 (1857). For a discussion of the linkage between this Supreme Court opinion and the U.S. occupation of Mexico, see Gómez, *Manifest Destinies*, 138–146.

42. *Plessy v. Ferguson*, 163 U.S. 537 (1896).

43. See Cheryl I. Harris, "The Story of *Plessy v. Ferguson*: The Death and Resurrection of Legal Formalism," in *Constitutional Law Stories*, edited by Michael C. Dorf (New York: Foundation Press, 2004).

44. Bill Ong Hing, *Making and Remaking Asian America Through Immigration Policy 1850–1990* (Stanford, CA: Stanford University Press, 1993), 30–32, 62.

45. Hing, *Making and Remaking Asian America*, 33.

46. The definitive study of laws prescribing marriage across races is Pascoe, *What Comes Naturally*; see also Rachel F. Moran, *Interracial Intimacy: The Regulation of Race and Romance* (Chicago, IL: University of Chicago Press, 2001).

47. Pascoe, *What Comes Naturally*, 20.

48. Gómez, *Manifest Destinies*, 152.

49. Gómez, *Manifest Destinies*, 232n155.

50. Pascoe, *What Comes Naturally*, 142. At the time, sixteen Virginia legislators had some Indian ancestry, though less than one-sixteenth blood quantum; they were supposedly descendants of the union between Pocahontas and John Rolfe, by which Virginia's first families acquired great tracts of land. Kevin Noble Maillard, "The Pocahontas Exception: The Exemption of American Indian Ancestry from Racial Purity Law," *Michigan Journal of Race & Law* 12, no. 107 (2007): 151–193.

51. Laura E. Gómez, "Opposite One-Drop Rules: Mexican Americans, African Americans, and the Need to Reconceive Turn-of-the-Twentieth-Century Race Relations," in *How the United States Racializes Latinos: White Hegemony and Its Consequences*, edited by José A. Cobas, Jorge Duany, and Joe R. Feagin (Boulder, CO: Paradigm Publishers, 2009).

52. National Research Council, "Modernizing the U.S. Census," 127.

53. National Research Council, "Modernizing the U.S. Census," 127.

54. Portes and Rumbaut, *Immigrant America*, 21.

55. Rules prohibit the sharing of census information for 75 years from the date of collection. In a violation in 1942 census officials supplied confidential names and addresses of Japanese and Japanese Americans to the War Department in order to incarcerate them under order of the president. Strmic-Paul, Jackson, and Garner, "Race Counts," 5. When the Census Bureau recommended the addition of a "Middle Eastern and North African" racial option for 2020, opponents said they feared a repeat of the abuse of confidential census information to identify and persecute those

who selected that option. Khaled A. Beydoun, "Boxed In: Reclassification of Arab Americans on the U.S. Census as Progress or Peril?" *Loyola University Chicago Law Journal* 47 (2016): 693–759. See also William Seltzer and Margo Anderson, "After Pearl Harbor: The Proper Role of Population Data Systems in Times of War," unpublished paper, annual meeting of the Population Association of America, Los Angeles, CA, March 25, 2000, https://margoanderson.org/govstat/newpaa.pdf.

56. Foley, *The White Scourge*, 210.

57. Strmic-Paul, Jackson, and Garner, "Race Counts," 3.

58. Laura E. Gómez, "Taking the Social Construction of Race Seriously in Health Disparities Research," in *Mapping "Race": Critical Approaches to Health Disparities Research*, edited by Laura E. Gómez and Nancy López (New Brunswick, NJ: Rutgers University Press, 2013), 5.

59. C. Matthew Snipp, "Racial Measurement in the American Census: Past Practices and Implications for the Future," *Annual Review of Sociology* 23 (2003): 570–571.

60. Moran, *Interracial Intimacy*, 160.

61. Moran, *Interracial Intimacy*, 160.

62. Snipp, "Racial Measurement in the American Census," 570.

63. Snipp, "Racial Measurement in the American Census," 569.

64. Wendy D. Roth and Biorn Ivemark, "Genetic Options: The Impact of Genetic Ancestry Testing on Consumers' Racial and Ethnic Identities," *American Journal of Sociology* 124 (2018): 1.

65. Strmic-Paul, Jackson, and Garner, "Race Counts," 3.

66. Moran, *Interracial Intimacy*, 164.

67. Moran, *Interracial Intimacy*, 173.

68. Pycior, *LBJ and Mexican Americans*, 200.

69. Pycior, *LBJ and Mexican Americans*, 129–130.

70. *Confederacion de la Raza Unida v. Brown*, 345 F. Supp. 909 (N.D. Cal. 1972). See also, U.S. Commission on Civil Rights, *Counting the Forgotten: The 1970 Census Count of Persons of Spanish Speaking Background in the United States* (Washington, DC: U.S. Commission on Civil Rights, 1974).

71. Mark Hugo López, Ana González-Barrera, and Jens Manuel Krogstad, "More Latinos Have Serious Concerns about Their Place in America under Trump," Pew Research Center, October 25, 2018.

72. Gómez, *Manifest Destinies*, 159.

73. On accent discrimination, see Mari J. Matsuda, "Voices of America: Accent, Anti-discrimination Law, and a Jurisprudence for the Last Reconstruction," *Yale Law Journal* 100, no. 5 (1991): 1329–1410.

74. Laura E. Gómez, "The Birth of the 'Hispanic' Generation: Attitudes of Mexican-American Political Elites toward the Hispanic Label," *Latin American Perspectives* 19 (1992): 45–58; see also, Gómez, *Manifest Destinies*; Gómez, "What's in a Name? The Politics of 'Hispanic' Identity."

75. G. Cristina Mora, *Making Hispanics: How Activists, Bureaucrats and Media Constructed a New American* (Chicago, IL: University of Chicago Press, 2014).

76. One of the first Mexican American professionals hired by the census, Leobardo Estrada, told me he was directed by census director Vincent Barabba—a political appointee who had done marketing for Nixon's 1968 campaign—to inform the advisory committee. Interview by author with UCLA professor, December 2017. Estrada would go on to become a UCLA professor and who was himself later nominated to lead the Census Bureau. In the end, Clinton pulled the nomination due to pressure from conservative senators.

77. Cristina Mora, *Making Hispanics*, 93, 101.

78. Interview with author in 1985. Gómez, "What's in a Name? The Politics of 'Hispanic' Identity," 56.

79. Arlene Dávila, *Latinos, Inc.: The Marketing and Making of a People* (Berkeley, CA: University of California Press, 2001), 40.

80. Fraga et al. report that Latinos, like other people of color, are "often undermobilized" and taken for granted by candidates and political parties. Luis R. Fraga et al., *Latinos in the New Millennium: An Almanac of Opinion, Behavior and Policy Preferences* (New York: Cambridge University Press, 2012), 257.

81. Dávila, *Latinos, Inc.*, 23 (quoting an advertising company's media kit). On the domination of Cuban Americans in advertisings, see *Latinos, Inc.*, 23, 29–32, 45.

82. Gómez, "What's in a Name? The Politics of 'Hispanic' Identity," 52.

83. Gómez, "What's in a Name? The Politics of 'Hispanic' Identity," 16.

84. Dávila, *Latinos, Inc.*, 63.

85. Dávila, *Latinos, Inc.*, 219.

86. Dávila, *Latinos, Inc.*, 110.

87. Dávila, *Latinos, Inc.*, 115.

88. Lucas Shaw, "How the Hollywood Marketing Machine Tailors Campaigns for Hispanics," *The Wrap*, July 16, 2014.

89. Box Office Mojo, *Coco*, https://www.boxofficemojo.com/releasegroup /gr2402243077/?landingModalImageUrl=https%3A%2F%2Fm.media -amazon.com%2Fimages%2FG%2F01%2FIMDbPro%2Fimages %2Fhome%2FwelcomeToBomojov2._CB1571421611_.png [https://perma. cc/MC7G-JSVK].

90. On the Indigenous roots of Día de los Muertos, see Hugo G. Nutini, *Todos Santos in Rural Tlaxcala: A Syncretic, Expressive, and Symbolic Analysis of the Cult of the Dead* (Princeton: Princeton University Press, 1988). For a sharp critique of *Coco*, see Eren Cervantes-Altamirano, "Understanding Mexican Nationalism and Mestizaje Through the Film Coco," LatinoRebels.com, November 28, 2017 [https://www.latinorebels.com/2017/11/28 /understanding-mexican-nationalism-and-mestizaje-through-the-film -coco/].

91. Nicholas A. Jones and Jungmiwha Bullock, "The Two or More Race Population: 2010," September 2012, U.S. Census Bureau, C2010BR-13, 20.

92. Kelly Mathews et al., "2015 National Census Test Race and Ethnicity Analysis Report," February 28, 2017, 4. https://www.census.gov/prod /cen2010/briefs/c2010br-02.pdf.

93. Mathews et al., "2015 National Census Test Race and Ethnicity Analysis Report." ("If no major questionnaire changes are implemented, SOR may be the second-largest "race" group in 2020.")

94. Strmic-Paul, Jackson, and Garner, "Race Counts," 4.

95. Significant numbers of "Arab Americans" also select "some other race," but Arab Americans as a whole make up 4 million people compared to 59 million Latinos. Strmic-Paul, Jackson, and Garner, "Race Counts," 4–5 (noting that estimates of this population range from a low of 1.9 million, from the census, to 3.7 million from the Arab American Institute).

96. Ben Casselman, "The Census Is Still Trying to Find the Best Way to Track Race in America," fivethirtyeight.com, November 26, 2014.

97. Casselman, "The Census," 3 (noting that the census has used this approach to designing and improving questions for the past half-century).

98. Mathews et al., "2015 National Census Test Race and Ethnicity Analysis Report."

99. One reason for opposing the 2020 proposed elimination of the His-

panic ethnicity question and addition of Latino as a race category was that it would obscure the ability to identify which Latinos, by national origin, are identifying as Black or Indian, thereby compounding the erasure of these groups. See Nancy López, "Killing Two Birds with One Stone? Why We Need Two Separate Questions on Race and Ethnicity in 2020 Census and Beyond," *Latino Studies Journal* 11 (2013): 428–438. But if the 2015 tests are predictive—and if the "combined question plus" is used (option 3) in the future, say 2030, the problem López identifies might be less significant. That is, those Latinos who identify racially as Black or Indian still would do so but also would indicate their Latino national origin.

100. It is notable that Trump never has appointed a director of the Census Bureau, so the recommendation went from census officials directly to the cabinet secretary.

101. Wilbur Ross, "Memorandum to Under Secretary for Economic Affairs Karen Dunn Kelly re: Reinstatement of a Citizenship Question on the 2020 Decennial Census Questionnaire," March 26, 2018, https://perma.cc/X29A-Y8VX.

102. The lawsuits are California v. Ross, New York v. U.S. Department of Commerce, City of San Jose v. Ross, La Union del Pueblo Entero v. Ross, New York Immigration Coalition v. U.S. Department of Commerce, and Epic v. Commerce.

103. *Department of Commerce v. New York*, 139 S.Ct. 2551 (2019).

104. Amy Howe, "Argument Analysis: Divided Court Seems Ready to Uphold Citizenship Question on 2020 Census," *SCOTUS blog*, April 23, 2019, https://www.scotusblog.com/2019/04/argument-analysis-divided-court-seems-ready-to-uphold-citizenship-question-on-2020-census.

105. Suzanne Gamboa, "After Stephen Miller's White Nationalist Views Outed, Latinos Ask, 'Where's the GOP Outrage?'" NBC.com, December 7, 2019, https://www.nbcnews.com/news/latino/after-stephen-miller-s-white-nationalist-views-outed-latinos-ask-n1096071.

106. Ari Berman, "The Man Behind Trump's Voter Fraud Obsession," *New York Times*, June 13, 2017, https://www.nytimes.com/2017/06/13/magazine/the-man-behind-trumps-voter-fraud-obsession.html.

107. Raul A. Reyes, "How the GOP's Shady Plan to Help Erect White Republicans Works," CNN, May 31, 2019, https://www.cnn.com/2019/05/30/opinions/republicans-gerrymandering-census-hispanics-reyes/index.html [https://perma.cc/67ZV-H72Y].

108. There is controversy about how much support from Latino voters Trump received in 2016. Many exit polls put the number at 30 percent, but political scientist and Latino Decisions, Inc. principal Matt Barreto put the number at 10 points lower. Barreto argues the exit polling data is flawed with respect to Latino voters—especially those who lean to the left—because these polls are "random," meaning that they under-survey Latinos and African Americans, who disproportionately reside in segregated neighborhoods. His data over-sampled Latinos who live in heavily-Latino precincts and he used bilingual surveyors, thereby picking up voters who would be passed over in general exit polls. For a survey of the polling data for 2016, see Harry Enlen, "Trump Probably Did Better with Latino Voters than Romney Did," FiveThirtyEight.com, November 18, 2016.

109. Michael Wines, "Hard Drives Reveal New Details on Census Question," *New York Times*, May 31, 2019, https://infoweb.newsbank.com/apps /news/document-view?p=AWNB&t=language%3AEnglish%21English &sort=YMD_date%3AD&maxresults=20&f=advanced&val-base -0=census&fld-base-0=alltext&bln-base-1=and&val-base-1=2020%20 citizen&fld-base-1=alltext&fld-nav-0=YMD_date&val-nav-0=past%20 365%20days&docref=news/173C3EE0E5B7FD98 [https://perma. cc/687V-Y4J6].

110. For example, one analysis purported to utilize Hofeller's research on the impact of basing apportionment on the number of citizens, versus the number of persons (including, of course, noncitizens and children). It showed hypothetically that this would result in gains of two GOP congressional seats in Texas because the smaller numbers of citizens in heavily Latino districts would be much lower, causing those districts to be combined with others and thus a net gain of majority-White, Republican leaning districts in Texas. Amelia Thomson DeVeaux. "How a Supreme Court Ruling Could Supercharge Republicans," FiveThirtyEight.com, June 20, 2019.

111. Rachel M. Cohen, "Letting Noncitizens Vote in the Trump Era," *The Nation*, November 1, 2018, https://www.thenation.com/article/archive /noncitizen-voting-trump.

112. Thom File, "Characteristics of Voters in the Presidential Election of 2016: Population Characteristics," United States Census Bureau, September 2018, https: //perma.cc/J44Q-8XZ8.

Conclusion

1. Samuel P. Huntington, *Who Are We? The Challenges to America's National Identity* (New York: Simon and Schuster, 2004).

2. F.A. Mouton, "P.W. Botha—Reformer or 'Groot Krokodil'?" *African Historical Review* 28, no. 1 (1996): 189–201, 194n21.

3. Samuel P. Huntington, "The Clash of Civilizations?" *Foreign Affairs* 72, no. 3 (1993): 22–49.

4. Patrick J. Buchanan, *The Death of the West: How Dying Populations and Immigrant Invasions Imperil Our Country and Civilization* (New York: St. Martin's Press, 2001); Patrick J. Buchanan, *State of Emergency: The Third World Invasion and Conquest of America* (New York: Thomas Dunne Books/St. Martin's Griffin, 2006).

5. Buchanan, *State of Emergency*, 128.

6. See https://en.wikipedia.org/wiki/Pat_Buchanan (and sources therein).

7. On Buchanan's antisemitism and brand of "dark populism," see Richard Bernstein, "Politics: Patrick J. Buchanan; "The Roots of a Populist Who Would Be President," *New York Times*, March 24, 1996.

8. On the incident generally, see Ibram X. Kendi, "The Day 'Shithole' Entered the Presidential Lexicon," *The Atlantic*, January 13, 2019.

9. On Trump's MS-13 claims in his 2019 state of the union address, see Ali Winston and Ali Watkins, "What Trump Left Out about MS-13's Rise in New York," *New York Times*, February 6, 2019. For an insightful analyses of how ICE deportations in the 1990s created the MS-13 gang in El Salvador, see José Miguel Cruz, "Central American Maras: From Youth Street Gangs to Transnational Protection Rackets," *Global Crime* 11, no. 4 (2010): 379–398; Sonja Wolf, "Mara Salvatrucha: the Most Dangerous Street Gang in the Americas?" *Latin American Politics and Society* 54, no. 1 (2012): 65–101.

10. It was eventually determined that 3,000 people died because of the hurricane. Vann R. Newkirk II, "A Year after Hurricane Maria," *The Atlantic*, August 28, 2018.

11. Puerto Ricans protested in July 2019, leading to Rosselló's resignation and the ouster of his handpicked successor. Protestors denounced Rosselló's minimizing of deaths from Hurricane María, FBI probes into corruption in his administration, and leaked messaging app chats with ten friends and top aides that included jokes about people who died in the

aftermath of the hurricane and disparaging remarks about gay people (such as Ricky Martin).

12. Pilar Melendez, "Trump Reignites Personal Feud with San Juan Mayor," TheDailyBeast.com, August 28, 2019.

13. The statistics on hate crimes in this paragraph are from the FBI report for 2018, issued in early November 2019. See Adeel Hassan, "Hate-Crime Violence Hits a 16-Year High, FBI Reports," *New York Times*, November 12, 2019.

14. Brian Levin and Lisa Nakashima, "Report to the Nation: Illustrated Almanac," unpublished paper, Center for the Study of Hate and Extremism, California State University, San Bernardino.

15. Hassan, "Hate-Crime Violence Hits a 16-Year High."

16. It is not known how many of the victims who were Mexican nationals were immigrants living in the United States—and, therefore, Latinos under my definition—or Mexicans visiting El Paso to shop that day.

17. Vivian Ho, "'People Are Afraid to Be 'Hispanic': Trump Visits an Angry, Grieving El Paso," *The Guardian*, August 7, 2019.

18. Erin Ailworth, "El Paso Prosecutors to Seek Death Penalty for Walmart Shooter," *Wall Street Journal*, September 12, 2019.

19. Michael Omi and Howard Winant, *Racial Transformation in the United States from the 1960s to the 1990s* (New York: Routledge, 1994 [1986]), 140.

20. Consider that two out of three children who attend public schools do so mostly with peers of their own race. A.W. Geiger, "Many Minority Students Go to Schools Where at Least Half of Their Peers Are Their Race or Ethnicity," Pew Research Center, October 25, 2017, https://www.pewresearch.org/fact-tank/2017/10/25/many-minority-students-go-to-schools-where-at-least-half-of-their-peers-are-their-race-or-ethnicity [https://perma.cc/J3HC-P8LK]. In California's Los Angeles and Orange counties, one in five Latino children attend a school that is 95 percent or more Latino. Kyle Stokes, "The California Schools Where the Kids Are All the Same Race, All in One Map," *KPCC*, December 3, 2017, https://www.scpr.org/news/2017/12/03/78190/the-california-schools-where-the-kids-are-all-the [https://perma.cc/4VSR-57DF].

21. These are figures from 2017 a decade after the all-time high of unauthorized immigration. An estimated 6.5 million Latinos are unauthorized immigrants, 4.9 million from Mexico (a decrease of two million since

2007) and 1.9 million from Central American countries (an increase of 400,000 since 2007). Another 1.5 million migrated from countries in Asia. In the decade after 2007, the five U.S. states that registered an increase in unauthorized migrants were, in order of magnitude of the increase, Massachusetts, Maryland, Louisiana, North Dakota, and South Dakota. Jens Manuel Krogstad et al., "Five Facts about Illegal Immigration in the U.S.," Pew Research Center, June 12, 2019.

22. In 2007, there were 12.2 undocumented persons living in the United States, 8.4 million of them Mexican. A decade later, the share of the population that is undocumented has decreased to 3 percent. Krogstad et al., "Five Facts about Illegal Immigration."

23. See, generally, Jennifer M. Chacón, "Producing Liminal Legality," *Denver University Law Review* 92, no. 4 (2016): 709–769.

24. Silva Mathema, "Keeping Families Together: Why All Americans Should Care about What Happens to Unauthorized Immigrants," Center for American Progress, March 16, 2017.

25. Mathema, "Keeping Families Together."

26. The California Court of Appeals ruled, as this book went to press, that the sanctuary state law was legal, rebuffing a claim by the city of Huntington Beach in Orange County. *City of Huntington Beach v. Becerra*, No. G057013, 2020 WL 113677 (Cal. Ct. App. Jan. 10, 2020). The case is likely to go to the Supreme Court. California in 2019 became the first U.S. state to extend health benefits to undocumented adults age nineteen to twenty-six (estimated to be 138,000 persons). "California Will Give Health Coverage to the Undocumented," *San Francisco Chronicle*, July 11, 2019, https://sfchronicle .com/politics/article/California-will-give-health-coverage-to-13964206.php.

27. Barreto and Segura, *Latino America*, 176.

28. Arellano, "Prop. 187 Forced a Generation to Put Fear Aside and Fight."

29. Michelle L. Price, "DACA Dreamer Astrid Silva Can't Vote but 2020 Democrats Want Her Support," *Fortune*, November 19, 2019.

30. Joe Hagan, "The Long, Lawless Ride of Sheriff Joe," *Rolling Stone*, August 16, 2012.

31. Bill Chappell, "Federal Judge Will Not Void Guilty Ruling on Arpaio, Despite Trump's Pardon," NPR.org, October 20, 2017.

32. Alejandra Gómez and Tomás Robles, Jr., "How to Turn Anger and Fear into Political Power," *New York Times*, December 21, 2019.

33. Chris Zepeda-Millan and Sophia J. Wallace, "Racialization in Times of Contention," *Politics, Groups and Identities* 1, no. 4 (2013): 510–527, 522.

34. For an argument in favor of this and a summary of prior literature, see Christopher Lewis, "Latinos and the Principles of Racial Demography," *Du Bois Review* 16 (2019): 1–19. For a powerful statement of opposition, see Nancy López, "Killing Two Birds with One Stone?: Why We Need Two Separate Questions on Race and Ethnicity in 2020 and Beyond," *Latino Studies* 11 (2013): 428–438.

35. It is true that self-identification with two or more racial groups would not allow us to distinguish people who are biracial (understood as having one parent each from two different racial groups) from those who identify as Afro-Latino or Indo-Latino by virtue of longer-standing ancestors (for example, both parents could be *mestizos* who have some combination of Spanish, Indian, and African ancestry). But, in reality, we do not currently have such information for non-Latinos who, since 2000, have been able to self-identify with two or more racial groups.

36. For a review essay on the origins of the concept of "internal colony," see Ramón A. Gutiérrez, "Internal Colonialism: An American Theory of Race," *Du Bois Review* 1, no. 2 (2004): 281–295. Gutiérrez traces the term to Latin American economists writing in the early 1960s about uneven development. Gutiérrez, "Internal Colonialism," 285–286. It gained currency in the United States in 1972 with the publication of sociologist Robert Blauner's influential book *Racial Oppression in America* and the work of his PhD students in sociology at the University of California, Berkeley, in the 1970s. See Tomás Almaguer, "Toward the Study of Chicano Colonialism," *Aztlán* 2 (1971): 7–21 and "Historical Notes on Chicano Oppression: The Dialectics of Race and Class Domination in North America," *Aztlán* 5 (1974): 27–56.

INDEX

ABOUT THE AUTHOR

Laura E. Gómez is a professor of law, sociology, and Chicana/Chicano and Central American studies at UCLA. She is the author of *Manifest Destinies*, *Mapping "Race,"* and *Misconceiving Mothers*. She lives in Los Angeles.

PUBLISHING IN THE PUBLIC INTEREST

Thank you for reading this book published by The New Press. The New Press is a nonprofit, public interest publisher. New Press books and authors play a crucial role in sparking conversations about the key political and social issues of our day.

We hope you enjoyed this book and that you will stay in touch with The New Press. Here are a few ways to stay up to date with our books, events, and the issues we cover:

- Sign up at www.thenewpress.com/subscribe to receive updates on New Press authors and issues and to be notified about local events
- Like us on Facebook: www.facebook.com/newpressbooks
- Follow us on Twitter: www.twitter.com/thenewpress

Please consider buying New Press books for yourself; for friends and family; or to donate to schools, libraries, community centers, prison libraries, and other organizations involved with the issues our authors write about.

The New Press is a 501(c)(3) nonprofit organization. You can also support our work with a tax-deductible gift by visiting www.thenewpress.com/donate.